D1321219

LIVERPOOL
JOHN MOORES UNIVERSITY
I.M. MARSH LRC
Tel: 0151 231 5216

WITHDRAWN

LIVERPOOL JMU LIBRARY

3 1111 01074 4231

Racism and Anti-Racism in Football

Also by Jon Garland

THE FUTURE OF FOOTBALL: Challenges for the Twenty-First Century
(*co-editor with D. Malcolm and Michael Rowe*)

Also by Michael Rowe

THE FUTURE OF FOOTBALL: Challenges for the Twenty-First Century
(*co-editor with Jon Garland and D. Malcolm*)

THE RACIALISATION OF DISORDER IN TWENTIETH CENTURY BRITAIN

Racism and Anti-Racism in Football

Jon Garland
Research Fellow
University of Leicester

and

Michael Rowe
Lecturer in Policing
University of Leicester

© Jon Garland and Michael Rowe 2001

All rights reserved. No reproduction, copy or transmission of this publication may be made without written permission.

No paragraph of this publication may be reproduced, copied or transmitted save with written permission or in accordance with the provisions of the Copyright, Designs and Patents Act 1988, or under the terms of any licence permitting limited copying issued by the Copyright Licensing Agency, 90 Tottenham Court Road, London W1P 0LP.

Any person who does any unauthorised act in relation to this publication may be liable to criminal prosecution and civil claims for damages.

The authors have asserted their rights to be identified as the authors of this work in accordance with the Copyright, Designs and Patents Act 1988.

First published 2001 by
PALGRAVE
Houndmills, Basingstoke, Hampshire RG21 6XS and
175 Fifth Avenue, New York, N. Y. 10010
Companies and representatives throughout the world

PALGRAVE is the new global academic imprint of
St. Martin's Press LLC Scholarly and Reference Division and
Palgrave Publishers Ltd (formerly Macmillan Press Ltd).

ISBN 0–333–73079–8 hardback
ISBN 0–333–96422–5 paperback

This book is printed on paper suitable for recycling and made from fully managed and sustained forest sources.

A catalogue record for this book is available from the British Library.

Library of Congress Cataloging-in-Publication Data
Garland, Jon, 1967–
    Racism and anti-racism in football / Jon Garland and Michael Rowe.
        p. cm.
    Includes bibliographical references and index.
    ISBN 0–333–73079–8
    1. Soccer—social aspects—Great Britain. 2. Discrimination in sports—Great Britain. 3. Athletes, Black—Great Britain—Social conditions. 4. Race discrimination—Great Britain. I. Rowe, Michael, 1967– II. Title.
    GV943.9.S64 G37 2001
    306.4'83—dc21

2001021213

10 9 8 7 6 5 4 3 2 1
10 09 08 07 06 05 04 03 02 01

Printed and bound in Great Britain by
Antony Rowe Ltd, Chippenham, Wiltshire

Contents

List of Tables

Acknowledgements

There are numerous people and organisations that the authors would like to thank for their help in the preparation of this book, although unfortunately not all can be personally acknowledged since many of those we have spoken to were guaranteed anonymity. Therefore, what follows is by no means an exhaustive list of all of those who have aided and abetted us with the research for this work: Neil Watson at Leyton Orient; Dave Turton and Cyrille Regis at West Bromwich Albion; Brian Lomax and the Anti-Racism Committee at Northampton Town; Yasin Patel and the CARE team at Charlton Athletic; Ben Tegg and Piara Powar at Kick It Out; Ged Grebby of Show Racism the Red Card; Ray Gerlach at Hounslow Borough Council; Football Unites, Racism Divides; Leeds Fans United Against Racism and Fascism; Foxes Against Racism; the Football Supporters' Association; Richie Moran; the Leicester Asian Sports Initiative; the Metropolitan Police; Brendon Batson of the Professional Footballers' Association; Leicestershire Constabulary; the Football Trust; and various fans, players, coaches and officials at the following clubs: Arsenal; Tottenham Hotspur; Millwall; Brighton and Hove Albion; Bristol Rovers; Wolverhampton Wanderers; Aston Villa; Birmingham City; Celtic; Southend United; Everton; Leicester City; Derby County; Manchester City; Nottingham Forest; Leeds United; Norwich City; Luton Town; Highfield Rangers and many others who helped with aspects of the research.

Much gratitude also to Dominic Malcolm, Adrian Beck, Ken Livingstone and Ivan Waddington for their helpful comments on the drafts of the book; John Benyon and Martin Gill for their advice and assistance, and Mark Carver for conducting some of the early research. Thanks also to Alison Cousens and Keris Howard for many excellent late-night football debates, and also to our parents for passing on the passion for football.

JON GARLAND
MICHAEL ROWE

To **Karen** – *thanks for all your love and support, Jon*

To **Anna** – *who supported me when she could have been supporting Spurs, thanks, Mike*

1

Introduction: Contextualising Racism in British Football

Introduction

> Racism came in the form of letters, chanting from the crowds,
> banana throwing, monkey chanting, songs, and not just one or two
> but thousands singing racial abuse, chants, that kind of stuff, and
> letters through the post. I remember one time I got picked to play
> for England for the first time, and I got a letter saying that if I actu-
> ally stepped onto Wembley park I would get a bullet through the
> knees, and there was a bullet in the letter as well, wrapped up in
> cotton wool.
>
> (Cyrille Regis, ex-West Bromwich Albion
> and England striker, 1998)

Overt forms of racism in football, like those described in the quote
above, have been the focus of sustained challenges during the last
decade. Indeed, combating racism within football was a key development within the sport in the 1990s. Since the inception of the
Commission for Racial Equality's 'Let's Kick Racism Out of Football'
campaign at the start of the 1993/94 football season, the issue of
racism has had a high profile within the game. There have been a
number of conferences and seminars on the topic, as well as numerous articles in the press and on television and radio, which have
highlighted the problem and attempted to assess its levels and effects.
In 1998, the government-appointed Football Task Force published the
results of its examination of racism in the game (Football Task Force,
1998), a report that contained almost 30 recommendations for action.

The development of anti-racist programmes has been but one
feature of football in the last ten years, during which time the sport

I.M. MARSH LIBRARY LIVERPOOL L17 6BD
TEL. 0151 231 5216/5299

has undergone profound changes. Following the publication of the Taylor Report into the 1989 Hillsborough disaster (Taylor, 1989), which, among other things, recommended that clubs introduce all-seater stadia and place an increased emphasis on the comfort and safety of spectators, the football industry has enjoyed something of a renaissance. Attendances have increased throughout the four professional divisions, and media interest has rarely been so high. Since the formation of the FA Premier League for the 1992/93 season, the game, at least at the top level, has become big business, with some clubs such as Arsenal, Chelsea and Newcastle United having an annual turnover of over £40m, with Manchester United's exceeding £80m (Boon, Phillips and Hann, 2000). In 2000 considerable media coverage was aroused when the share value of Manchester United exceeded £1bn. Although no other club comes near it has become increasingly apparent that top-level football in Britain now offers very substantial rewards indeed.

The transformation of football fan 'cultures' has been especially evidenced during this period (see, for example, Armstrong, 1998; Brown, 1998), with a change in the demographic make-up of football crowds characterised by an increase in the numbers of female football fans (Sir Norman Chester Centre for Football Research, 2000).[1] This rise has been coupled with a reduction in the perceptions of the problems of football-related disorder, especially inside grounds (Garland and Rowe, 1999). Although some of the violence may have been displaced to locations away from grounds, the perception that the 'English disease' has been cured caused the French Director of Security at the 1998 World Cup to claim that: 'The English may have invented the poison of hooliganism, but they have also invented the remedy for this poison' (*Le Monde*, 1997).

Football in the 1990s was also characterised by a growth in 'fan democracy', with some clubs, such as AFC Bournemouth and Northampton Town witnessing the advent of supporters' trusts that have had a significant input into the running of their clubs (Lomax, 2000). Other bodies, such as the Football Supporters' Association (FSA), independent fan groups and fanzines also enjoyed a degree of influence both nationally and within certain clubs. Loose coalitions of several disparate fan groups also existed for limited periods with, in the case of supporters at Brighton and Hove Albion for example, a degree of success in changing the way their club is run. The campaign at Brighton involved the local fanzines, independent supporters' association and official supporters' club in a joint effort to oust unpopular directors whose policies appeared to be placing the club in a precarious position. During this campaign the idea of a 'Fans United' day was mooted, something which came to fruition in February 1997 when thousands of fans from dozens of different clubs converged on Brighton's Goldstone Ground to show sympathy and solidarity with their plight (North and Hodson, 1997). This new 'fan power', although by no means influential at all clubs, still nevertheless demonstrated a new, more proactive role for fans within the game.

In other aspects, fan cultures had also become more 'light-hearted', with the inflatables craze of the late 1980s (when fans brought inflatable objects to matches) heralding a more 'style conscious postfandom' where pop music exerts a strong influence on fan cultures (Redhead, 1997). Also evident was a growth in the use of 'fancy dress' costumes and other paraphernalia, and the appearance of jazz and samba bands in some crowds. Support for the England team during Euro '96 was characterised by widespread face-painting and communal singing of the pop song *Three Lions*. Whether influenced by 'rave culture' (Redhead, 1991) or other factors, by the end of the 1990s the contrast between fan cultures then, and in the more violent mid-1980s, has been widely noted.

Yet, despite these (and other) positive changes, manifestations of racism have still been present at all levels of the game. From grassroots through to the Premiership, racist abuse, intimidation, discrimination and harassment have been evidenced from supporters, players, coaches, managers and administrators, despite the plethora of anti-racist campaigns that have appeared throughout the 1990s. Although there have been several investigations into the extent of racism within the game (see, for instance, McArdle and Lewis, 1997; Garland and Rowe, 1999), there has been little academic analysis of the efficacy of football's anti-racist strategies. It is one of the aims of this book to attempt to fill this gap by providing a theoretical framework through which football's responses to the *racisms* evidenced can be assessed.

The book will attempt to place this anti-racism in context by analysing a number of interrelated factors. These will include the history of the involvement of black players in the game and the racism encountered; the policing of racism, including legislative and technological factors; and issues of national identity and the cultures of football, whether evidenced in fan behaviour, the institutional culture of football, or in the media's reporting of the English national team.

However, in order to place this analysis into context a discussion of the different forms of racism currently evident within the game will be undertaken, including those occurring at professional and non-league levels. Additionally, an historical perspective is offered in Chapter 2. In the course of this book a large number of racist incidents are outlined during the analysis of anti-racism, the policing of racism and during the discussion of nationality and identity in Chapter 5. Much of this material comes from literary sources, observation and also interviews undertaken for this book by the authors. These interviews were conducted in the period 1996–2000 with players, administrators, coaches, community officers, anti-racist campaigners, managers and fans, and form a substantive part of the evidence of racism within football, and the efforts taken to counter it, that are included in this work.[2]

Contemporary manifestations of racism within football

Racism within football is a complex phenomenon that manifests itself inconsistently throughout the game. Therefore, although the Football Task Force (1998) claimed a decline in the levels of racism in British football, such assertions need to be qualified by the fact that this may not be the case at many clubs or at all levels of the game. For example, 24 per cent of fans of Premiership clubs surveyed in 1999 (Sir Norman Chester Centre for Football Research, 2000) reported witnessing racist comments aimed at players, and 6 per cent heard racist abuse directed at spectators. The complexities of the manifestations of this racism also need to be considered, as both black and white players such as the Arsenal duo of Emanuel Petit and Thierry Henry have been victims of racist abuse (Cross, 2000). As Back, Crabbe and Solomos (1998: 84) state:

> Racist abuse in grounds occurs in an intermittent fashion, racist epithets and slogans are invoked in specific contexts and serve particular functions such that a series of fixtures may pass without any racist activity whilst a fixture with a heightened atmosphere or the appropriate circumstances can produce an explosion of racist activity.

Such a heightened atmosphere was present at an FA Cup tie in November 1997 between Hereford United and Brighton and Hove Albion, the club who had stayed in the Football League the previous season at Hereford's expense. As he warmed-up before the match, black Brighton striker Andy Ansah was the object of racist abuse:

> This fella had made his way to the front, calling me black bastard, nigger, telling me to fuck off back home and things like that. I carried on warming-up and I came back again and he stood there and started to do the finger across the throat, as if to say he was going to slice my throat, he was going to cut me across the throat. (*London Programme*, 1998)

The racist sentiments described here are not dissimilar to those described so vividly by Cyrille Regis at the beginning of this chapter, even though there is almost twenty years between the two events. Mass racist chanting was also documented at a Premier League match between Leicester City and Leeds United during the 1997/98 season, when hundreds of Leeds fans chanted 'You're just a town full of Pakis' at the home supporters. The overtly racist nature of this 'chant' caused widespread offence (Pryke, 1998), yet although similar abuse emanated from segments of the visiting supporters later in the game, no arrests were made under Section 3 of the 1991 Football (Offences) Act, a section designed to combat exactly the type of mass racist chanting evident on this occasion.

Of course, one of the obvious effects of unchecked overt racism like this was to create an environment where at most clubs the high-profile success of black players on the playing field failed to attract more than a handful of minority ethnic spectators in the stands. As Holland (1995) showed, one of the main reasons for this non-attendance was fear of racist attack or abuse, as a black professional player outlined when interviewed for this book:

> Like my brother loves football, he is a West Ham fan and I think he has only been to West Ham twice and that is because he has been told that it is not really for blacks, and blacks don't want to go there. He doesn't want to feel out of place.[3]

The inconsistent nature of manifestations of racism within football grounds is perhaps most commonly demonstrated by those fans who racially abuse the black players who play for their opponents, yet cheer those who play for their own side. This phenomenon was tellingly reported by black ex-professional Richie Moran, who told of his experiences on the terraces at Portsmouth:

One of the most memorable of those [occasions of racism] was when, after remonstrating with fans who were abusing black striker John Fashanu on his Wimbledon debut, I was informed by these people that: 'It's OK mate, you're one of our niggers'. (Moran, 2000: 191)

Another black fan reported to the authors:

You get a guy saying 'Come on you black bastard, fight for your team', and then you get somebody saying 'It's all right mate, they're not talking about you, no offence meant, we're talking about them black bastards on the pitch'.[4]

These incidents illustrate that the 'acceptance' of black players and spectators by certain white fans can be contingent upon them demonstrating allegiance to the 'right' club or team, a point graphically illustrated by the experience of a black England fan, discussed in Chapter 5, who found his English identity 'accepted' by white fans before the match against Scotland during Euro '96 when the 'common enemy' was seen as being Scottish supporters. On this occasion, the fan's ethnicity was accepted as English as the boundaries of inclusion were redrawn for this particular, highly-charged fixture: on other occasions, the same supporters would have subjected him to racist abuse (Back, Crabbe and Solomos, 1998). This phenomenon highlights the usefulness of the racialisation approach (discussed below), which emphasises the contradictory and incoherent nature of the racisms present within the footballing environment.

As mentioned above, the issue of racism within the professional game has received much attention in the last decade. However, the racism experienced at non-league levels has had comparatively little publicity in the media and less academic study, and yet has often been cruder, more frequent and more violent than that witnessed at professional level. One black ex-amateur player told of his experiences when playing for Highfield Rangers, a predominantly African Caribbean team based in Leicester:

we used to travel to a lot of mining villages and the abuse that they were coming out with was terrible. I used to hate going to places like that. It was little villages who had rarely seen black people and the abuse was awful.[5]

One of the most brutal attacks to gain publicity in recent years was directed at members of Bari FC, a predominantly Asian team from East London. In a match late in November 1998 against local opponents Romside, and after suffering racist taunts in the first half, the team suffered physical assault in the second resulting in hospitalisation for some players (Kick It Out, 1998). This incident was by no means in isolation, with other racist attacks being reported on other black and Asian amateur teams in many areas of England, including Newcastle Tigers in the north-east, Leeds Road TRA in West Yorkshire, and other incidents involving youth sides in Birmingham and Manchester (Football Unites Racism Divides, 1999).

Despite the evidence of this racism at grassroots level, the reaction of county football associations has been criticised by a number of bodies, including the Football Task Force, for being reluctant to punish racist clubs or players in their localities (Football Task Force, 1998) (some of the anti-racist work of other agencies involved in football at the grassroots level is discussed in Chapter 3). This criticism also highlights the issue of institutional racism within such bodies as county FAs, as well as in football more generally. The wider debate surrounding institutional racism became heightened following the publication of the Macpherson Report of the inquiry into the racist murder of black teenager Stephen Lawrence in 1993 (Macpherson, 1999), which offered a new, broader definition of institutional racism which included the notion of 'unwitting racism' (this point is examined in more detail in Chapter 3). Whether unwitting or not, the authors encountered racism and prejudice from a number of football administrators interviewed for this book. As one prominent club official stated:

> If they [Asians] change their attitudes like what we would have to do if we went abroad they'd stand a better chance, but in my eyes they don't want to do that. Like even in junior and Sunday football, they have their own clubs now. We don't have white only clubs. If they could integrate more the situation would change.[6]

The language used here is telling. Apparently unintentionally, the interviewee betrayed his personal opinion that Asians are 'foreigners' who are 'abroad' when living in England, thus revealing his own racialised barriers which obviously exclude Asian communities from being English or British, seeing them instead as being foreign 'others'. Not only this, but the interviewee also blamed the lack of willingness to integrate with, and be more like, white people as the key factor causing the problems experienced by these communities. This was a view reflected by others interviewed by the authors, discussed further in Chapter 3 below.

'Race', racism and anti-racism

Although the advent of anti-racist schemes has been a key feature of British football over the last decade or so, there has been little debate within the game about what is meant by anti-racism or indeed what is expected from anti-racist schemes. While the 'Let's Kick Racism Out of Football' campaign has provided advice and help for many initiatives (see Chapter 3) its role has never been to provide coordination of, or indeed 'blueprints' for, *all* of the diverse range of schemes that have appeared. Thus some of these schemes have appeared to lack a degree of conceptual clarity regarding their aims and objectives, and what it is that they understand by anti-racism and how this can be applied to affect the policies and practices of the organisations involved within football.

Indeed, almost all of those involved within the football industry who were interviewed for this book agreed that anti-racism was, in itself, a good idea, although what it was that they understood by anti-racism was rarely adequately explained. In some ways this is symptomatic of anti-racist projects in other spheres over a number of years, whereby a similar lack of a precise definition of anti-racism has been noted by a number of commentators (see, for example, Wrench and Solomos, 1993; Miles, 1994; Rattansi, 1994). The goals of such initiatives were also unclear: for example, were the local-authority anti-racist projects of the 1980s and 1990s concerned with creating a situation whereby equality of opportunity was the common aim, or were these programmes more interventionist in nature, being concerned about a redistribution of resources? Gilroy (1999: 243) highlighted this malaise, and went as far as to argue that the idea of anti-racism appeared to him to be merely a 'limited project defined simply, even simplistically, by the desire to do away with racism'.

The difficulties outlined above are evident in coterminous debates surrounding whether it is helpful or harmful to utilise popular conceptions of ideas of 'race' when analysing the processes of discrimination and the methods used to combat it. Miles (1984; 1993), for example, argues against the use of the 'race idea' in such contexts as it necessarily implies and reinforces notions that 'races' exist and are a biological reality. For Miles, 'races' are essentially ideological constructs with no ontological validity, and therefore employing the concept is damaging, even in the context of discussing more positive issues such as the development of anti-racism. Basing discussions around ideas of 'race' – it is argued – merely reinforces dominant 'common-sense' ideas about races, with all the inherent discriminatory and stereotypical baggage that that carries. This reflects Miles's argument, also made by others, including Fanon (1967), Solomos (1993) and Small (1994), that 'races' as such have no scientific basis and therefore it is more instructive to move the debate away from notions of race relations and instead to focus more on the processes of racism and discrimination. The utilisation of theoretical frameworks that employ notions of race merely reinforces the *racialisation* of relations between different groups.

Law (1996) suggests that relations between groups are not necessarily damaged, or divisions increased, by the use of terms such as 'race'. Instead, the idea of 'race' can be used as a method by which discriminatory and racist policies and practices can be challenged, something which Law (*ibid.*: 5) terms 'strategic essentialism'. For Law, as the 'race idea' exists in political and popular discourse it can be used strategically within the context of developing anti-racist strategies as long as it is understood to have 'no necessary political belonging' (*ibid.*: 6). By this, Law means that dilemmas involved with analysing racism and anti-racism within a framework that includes debates about 'races' are resolved as long as it is understood that such ideas do not *in themselves* imply exclusion or discrimination, although this should not prevent those involved in such debates being wary and critical of ideas of race.

This standpoint is explored and developed by Rowe (1998: 40–1), whose 'racialisation problematic':

> offers a framework which acknowledges the reality of social circumstances which have enabled ideas about 'race' to proliferate. In doing so, however – and this is a crucial point – a critical stance towards the concept of 'race' itself is adopted. This is reflected in the emphasis central to this framework ... which is on the ideas and stereotypes that have developed about 'race' in the particular context of a former imperial society.

Thus through this perspective the focus of debate is shifted away from 'race' and 'race relations' and onto the nature and processes of hetereogeneous *racisms*, and how these racisms differ due to temporal and spatial (and other) factors. This is not to dismiss the influence of macro-level societal features which impact in the local context and may influence complex racialised phenomena (Billig, 1978: Rattansi, 1992). This perspective also acknowledges Gilroy's 'coat of paint' theory of racism (Gilroy, 1999) which criticises those who see racism as being on the 'outside' of political and social life. For Gilroy, it is essential to acknowledge the permeation of racialised ideas into the centre of British institutions, and to see their presence as being in the mainstream, rather than at the edges, of society. Miles (1989: 76) concurs, suggesting that 'the racialisation of human beings entails the racialisation of the processes in which they participate and the structures and institutions that result'. As Small (1994: 34) suggests:

> When we examine the process of 'racialisation' we find that our beliefs about 'races' and 'race relations' have more to do with the attitudes, actions, motivations and interests of powerful groups in society; and less to do with the characteristics, attitudes and actions of those who are defined as belonging to inferior 'races'.

It is argued in this book that it is the multi-directional, inconsistent and unpredictable nature of racism within football that must be recognised by those who are seeking to understand and challenge it. Thus anti-racist ideas and policies should be influenced by an understanding of the dynamics of the racialisation process, something that it is argued later has been lacking from many of football's anti-racist strategies. Some of these projects have appeared to see racism as a static or fixed phenomenon, and often have linked such ideas solely with far-right neo-fascist groups. We are not arguing that such views are without benefit in certain contexts, as on occasion groups such as the British National Party have tried to influence and recruit football fans, and thus the party's ideas and philosophies have needed to be challenged by football-based anti-racist activists. What we are suggesting is that racist behaviour and discourse in football, like those in society at large, are contradictory, irrational and changeable and therefore simplistic notions of racism can be damaging to anti-racist agendas.

It is from within this racialisation framework that the problematic issues of ethnicity, racism, nationality and identity are discussed in this book. What now follows is a brief outline of the book's structure, beginning in Chapter 2 with the history of black players within the

British game and the racism experienced, and in which the complex relationship between football, national identity and ideas of 'race' is also explored. In this chapter parallels are drawn between the deployment of stereotypes within the game that are used to discriminate against black players (often, particularly prior to the 1990s, described by some in football as 'flair players' who lacked 'bottle' and only performed well in warm weather) and those values championed as being essentially British (for example grit, stoicism and bravery). These 'British' values are traced back to the sporting ideologies first developed during the late nineteenth century, when the British Empire was at its peak and sport was used as a method of instilling discipline and moral and physical improvement into the local populations. The growth and codification of football during this era is also acknowledged, as is its role in instilling moral, religious and cultural values not just in 'colonised' populations, but in the British populace as well.

Although it is a common-sense assumption that black players did not figure in the British game until the 1960s and 1970s, the chapter notes that the first black professionals can be traced back to the late Victorian era. The fact that the feats of these pioneers like Arthur Wharton and Walter Tull have been largely ignored or forgotten is compared with the marginalisation by mainstream society of the broader historical contribution of Britain's black population to British society. Interestingly, Vasili (1998) notes that class factors, as well as racism, may have played a role in the forgetting of Wharton's achievements as his status as a professional playing for a northern club made him the antithesis of the 'gentleman player' ideal so cherished at the time by the sporting élite.

The chapter proceeds by tracing the careers of other notable early black professionals against a background of prejudice and discrimination. It highlights the ambiguities of 'affectionate' racialised nicknames and the inherent problems with 'positive' racist stereotypes. The chapter concludes by highlighting the achievements of black professionals in the latter part of the twentieth century, focusing on those like Viv Anderson and Cyrille Regis who broke into the England national team, and Justin Fashanu the first black 'million pound player'. The rise of the far-right National Front in Britain in the 1970s and the overt racism that many black players faced is also assessed.

Following the charting of the history of minority ethnic players in British football, Chapter 3 then outlines the efforts that have been made to combat racism within football in the last two decades. As mentioned above, football has been the seat of a significant number of high-profile anti-racist initiatives, perhaps more so than in other more 'traditional' loci of anti-racism, such as local authorities. As a starting point the chapter outlines some of the reasons that such initiatives have developed in the relatively recent past, including, for example, the observation made by Back (1998) and others that there appeared to be a dichotomy between those who watched football, and those who actually lived in the environs of football stadia. For a significant number of clubs situated in inner-city areas, only a tiny percentage of the local minority ethnic populations watched their local team, even though these communities had a high-level of participation in the playing of the sport (Bains with Patel, 1996). This realisation characterised some of the new anti-racist programmes, and marked a significant progression from the previously widely-held view held within the football 'world' that minority ethnic groups, and Asian communities in particular, were not interested in watching the game.

This chapter proceeds by examining a number of these new anti-racist projects within football, starting with one of the most significant, the 'Let's Kick Racism Out of Football' campaign, instigated at the start of the 1993/94 football season by, among others, the Commission for Racial Equality and the Professional Footballers' Association. The evolution of this campaign and its success in persuading clubs of the existence of the problem of racism is charted, as is its efficacy in providing a framework for clubs and other agencies to develop their own schemes and agendas.

Some of the regional programmes that followed the initiation of 'Let's Kick Racism' are then discussed, including innovative campaigns such as 'Show Racism the Red Card' and 'Football Unites Racism Divides'. Following this, some of the more important club-based initiatives are analysed, such as those at Northampton Town, Leyton Orient, West Bromwich Albion, Glasgow Celtic and the multi-agency arts and sports scheme at Charlton Athletic. Fans' schemes are also assessed, with particular focus being paid to the 'Leeds Fans United Against Racism and Fascism' campaign. The chapter concludes by suggesting that a number of the problems associated with anti-racism within football are to do with a lack of a conceptual clarity of racism. It is argued that even some of the best anti-racist initiatives are still prone to identifying racism as being a fixed, coherent idea associated with a minority of far-right extremists (Malik, 1996), rather than viewing it as an inconsistent and contradictory phenomenon that has a variety of forms and guises.

Following on from the analysis of football's anti-racist projects, Chapter 4 seeks to assess the ways in which racism within the game has been policed. This chapter discusses the measures that have been developed that seek only to restrict or curb racist abuse, violence or harassment, but are not educative initiatives as such. These legislative, policing and technological steps do not seek to educate fans about the 'evils of racism', but simply aim to prohibit and/or punish manifestations of racist behaviour within the given environment of a football ground.

In order to ascertain how racism within football can be effectively policed the chapter starts by analysing the influence of far-right fascist groups on fan behaviour. This has been especially evident among those who follow England at home and abroad, and the chapter outlines the issues around which such groups have tried to recruit supporters. It also lists a number of incidents of racism and hooliganism with which such groups have been associated, including, for example, the disorder in Dublin in 1995 which led to the abandonment of the Ireland versus England fixture. The chapter also suggests that although these incidents show a level of activity of these groups their influence among football fans has often been exaggerated, to the extent that much of the literature on the far-right (such as Fielding's seminal 1981 study) does not even mention the targeting of football fans.

Following this analysis, the chapter then turns to an assessment of the efficacy of a number of interventions against supporters engaging in racist behaviour, including closed-circuit television (CCTV), the use of private policing personnel, and legislative measures. It is argued that although CCTV is beneficial in the context of policing hooliganism, its use to combat racist chanting and abuse is open to question. Similarly, a number of issues relating to the recruitment, training and selection of private stewards may mean that they are unlikely to intervene in instances of racist chanting and harassment. Such personnel may be reluctant to intervene and apply the relevant legislation, which, the chapter argues, was, in the case of the Football (Offences) Act of 1991, flawed until its amendment in 1999. The chapter concludes by questioning the acceptance of notions of 'zero tolerance' in the context of policing racism.

The role of national identity creation and exclusion within football is then explored in Chapter 5. The existence of 'Britishness' and a

'British' identity has been challenged in the last ten years or so by two separate macro-political developments. The first of these, the votes for a measure of devolution by the people of Scotland and Wales in the late 1990s, has seen the inauguration of national political institutions in both of those nations that can exercise a degree of power autonomously from Westminster. Although the level of support for devolution in Wales appeared to be markedly less than that in Scotland, it was still significant enough for the notion of an English 'backlash' against this assertion of Celtic nationhood to be mooted in mainstream political debate.[7]

The second of these processes is the continuing development of closer European political and economic integration, exemplified by the drive towards a single European currency. Part of this development has been the creation of a 'borderless European Union' following the signing of the Maastricht Treaty in 1991 which allows the free movement of labour from one country to another. In the case of football, this has had a dramatic impact through the imposition of the 'Bosman ruling' by the European Court of Justice in Luxembourg in 1995 which decided in favour of Belgian player Jean-Marc Bosman's claim of 'restraint of trade' when his club, RFC Liege, would not allow him a free transfer when he became out of contract. This ruling effectively meant that players from the European Economic Area could freely move to a nation within the Area at the end of their contract, without any transfer fee having to be exchanged. The process of the 'Europeanisation' of British football therefore began, something which saw the influence of continental European Union players grow to such an extent that Chelsea's team in the club's fixture at Southampton in December 1999 contained not a single British player.

With this process of 'Europeanisation' as background, Chapter 5 attempts to analyse the methods by which English, Scottish and Welsh identities have been constructed through football in the light of these developments. The chapter does not seek to discover a definitive notion of what constitutes these separate identities, as it utilises Cohen's (1995) notion that identities are not fixed but rather are constantly reformulated and reconstituted. Therefore, the chapter rejects any notion of fixed and general national characteristics in favour of assessing the processes by which identities can become forged and also stereotyped through the prevalent cultures within football.

Therefore 'Englishness' is discussed through an analysis of the ideas of Englishness as exhibited by fans both at home and abroad. Many of the dominant cultural images of tournaments such as Euro '96 and France '98 suggest that often, notions of Englishness are exclusive of minority ethnic groups. Much of this imagery is influenced by memories of wartime success and an 'invented' history of greatness that reassures the population of a nation experiencing declining global influence (Carrington, 1998). The mythologising of the English World Cup success in 1966 is central to this reassurance and sense of national pride.

The English influence in global football politics, including FIFA, is also assessed. In particular the 'traditional' English playing values of commitment, stamina and bravery are studied in the context of the challenge posed by the influx of overseas coaches and players into the domestic game following the Bosman ruling. The 'Continental thoroughness' with which one 1930s English journalist noted that continental Europeans had learnt the game 'under British tuition, mark you' (Rose, quoted in Beck, 1999: 11) was now a significant influence on the domestic game. It is argued that English notions of primacy and the mentality of 'We taught them the game' are, in some respects, still evident in the thinking of those involved in English football.

In the case of the 'submerged nations' (Moorhouse, 1991) of Scotland and Wales, the constructing of national identities is somewhat different from the case of England. For Scotland, for example, the behaviour of their supporters, the 'Tartan Army', abroad is seen to play an 'ambassadorial role' for the nation (Finn and Giulianotti, 1998). This behaviour has been shaped by the desire of fans to create a distinct identity that is separate and diametrically opposed to the popular stereotype of the xenophobic and badly-behaved 'English hooligan', and thus they have made efforts to be exuberant, friendly and well-behaved. However, the chapter argues that much of this national identity is defined through a collective feeling of anti-Englishness that has been criticised by some sections of the Scottish media as being outmoded and contradictory to the supposedly internationalist outlook of the Tartan Army. Also, it is contended that this identity, by basing itself so centrally on a stereotypical notion of an English 'hooligan' may become anachronistic as English fan cultures themselves become less aggressive, violent and xenophobic, and more 'carnivalesque'.

Arguably, the key sporting difference between the English and Scottish nations and Wales is the centrality and importance of football in the construction of national identity and pride. Whilst for the former two nations football is the dominant sport, for Wales rugby is the dominant code (Holt, 1986). The popularity of football in the north of Wales is contradicted by the dominance of rugby in the south, meaning that Wales has never adopted football as the national sport in the same way as Scotland has, for example. The League of Wales's formation in 1992, something that came about in an effort to display the inherent strength and independence of Welsh football in the face of pressure from FIFA, in effect caused division as some clubs opted to stay within the English league structure. This, it is suggested, is an example of the weaker sense of a separate Welsh national identity that was reflected in the lukewarm vote for devolution in Wales in 1997.

The chapter concludes that the kind of national identities shaped and championed by those within the football industries in England, Scotland and Wales are still influenced by outdated notions that are inherently exclusive and fail to reflect the multicultural and diverse nature of the populations within these countries. This is a point developed in Chapter 6, which assesses the disparities and commonalities between newspaper coverage of Euro '96 and France '98. In particular, the chapter looks at the prevailing Eurosceptic political climate so prevalent during the time of Euro '96, a championship which occurred during the last year of an 18-year spell of Conservative party governance. During this tournament, the tabloids' xenophobic coverage of England's opponents and the easy use of national stereotypes was described as 'jingoistic gutter journalism' by the National Heritage Select Committee (1996: 1), and the chapter argues that this type of reportage reflected contemporary feelings of hostility towards the European Union evident within government circles. For the *Daily Mirror's* 'soccer war' against Germany read the government's 'beef wars' against the same nation.

The chapter continues by arguing that although some parallels can be drawn between the newspapers' coverage of Euro '96 and France '98 (continual reference to England's World Cup win of 1966, for example), generally the xenophobic insult so evident during the former tournament were lacking in the latter. Instead, the tabloids and broadsheets focused upon outbreaks of hooliganism among England fans by creating their own 'moral panics' (Cohen, 1981) through sensationalist reporting of these incidents. This is not to say that aggressive nationalism was absent from the tabloids, as the reports surrounding England's fixture against Argentina revealed. The use of military metaphors was also prevalent during this time. The chapter concludes by suggesting that the attitudes of aggression, parochialism and overt nationalism evidenced among England's supporters was a reflection of those demonstrated in much of the coverage of Britain's relations with its European neighbours.

2
Football, 'Race' and the Forging of British Identity

Introduction

During the period in which this book was being prepared, British society marked a significant anniversary: the 50th anniversary of the arrival of the *SS Empire Windrush*, whose passengers from Jamaica constituted the first of the postwar migrants to Britain from the Caribbean. After a period of years in which a series of anniversaries of Second World War battles were observed by ceremonies and considerable media coverage it might be regarded as significant that the fiftieth year in which reasonably large-scale black communities had become established passed relatively unobserved. Perhaps the continuing marginalisation of minority ethnic communities in many spheres should have provided indication that this anniversary would be largely sidelined. Many of the black footballers who have come to be household names since the 1970s came to be in this country as a consequence of the labour shortages which encouraged their parents or grandparents to come to Britain in the years after the Second World War. In this sense, the position of black and Asian people in contemporary football cannot be fully understood without consideration of the wider history of racism and colonialism in Britain. Just as broader changes in political and economic relations within the European Union have led to considerable migration of footballers around the continent, so too did colonialism, and its collapse, influence patterns of migration that brought minority ethnic players to the game in Britain. The increase in the number of black players during the 1970s was largely an unintended consequence of postwar recruiting campaigns that sought nurses, London Underground staff and other workers from former British colonies of the Caribbean. This much is

18

of little surprise, reflecting as it does the development of a multicultural Britain in which black and Asian people have made a significant impact in many aspects of society, although the relative absence of Asians from professional football remains to be explained. One theme of this chapter is to explore the postwar experiences of black footballers in Britain and examine the racism they often had to overcome in order to succeed.

Although it is to be regretted that more notice was not taken of the 50th anniversary of the arrival of *Windrush*, it should be remembered that this milestone needs to be carefully understood. It did not mark five decades of a black presence in Britain, but rather the period in which *large numbers* of black people settled in the 'mother country'. While there were grounds for celebration and reflection, it must be recognised that black and Asian people have been present for very much longer than fifty years and that those who suggest that multicultural Britain is of relatively recent origin ignore the centuries in which different ethnic groups have been present in these islands. Fryer (1984) points out that the inclusion of black soldiers within the Roman army which occupied southern parts of the country for three and a half centuries from about AD 200 meant that there were Africans living in Britain before the Anglo-Saxons arrived. An indirect consequence of the slave trade was that a reasonably sizeable population of black servants was established in London by the sixteenth century. Although the number of minority ethnic people living in Britain before the twentieth century was relatively small – Fryer (1984: 68) estimates a population of 15 000 at the end of the eighteenth century – it is important to note that, in some cases, they were at the heart of political and cultural élites and of some influence or renown.

Recent developments such as closer European integration, globalisation and Scottish and Welsh devolution have led to reflections on the nature of English identity in which right-wing groups have at times sought to establish an exclusive notion of Englishness built around an ethnically-white rural idyll. The historical fallacy which underpins such nostalgic romanticism was neatly illustrated by the comedian Lenny Henry who reflected on a National Front proposal to pay ethnic minorities to 'return home' by observing 'great, £500 – and I only come from Birmingham'. In such a climate it is important to stress that the development of a multiethnic and multicultural British society has been underway for five centuries and not just five decades. Consistent with this exhortation to adopt a longer historical perspective is another theme of this chapter, which is to consider the role that black footballers have played since the origins of the modern game in the nineteenth century.

Football has proved significant to the history of racialised ideas in British society in a wide range of ways. In recent decades it has provided an arena in which the conspicuous success of black players has been heralded by many as a valuable talisman that provides role models for young people and helps to overcome prejudice. That black footballers are heroes to millions is held to be a powerful testament to the potential of multiethnic Britain. This wider social function of the game may be considered relatively progressive, although it might be that role models premised around notions of black sporting prowess also serve to perpetuate negative stereotypes of academic failure, for example (Cashmore, 1982).

Claims that the game embodied qualities desirable in society more generally were evident within both the formation and codification of the modern game and the role that it played in colonial expansion. The early development of modern football, and perhaps most notably the long-standing division between those who sought to preserve the amateur status of players and those who preferred to embrace professionalism, revealed much about notions of masculinity, class relations and English identity during an era in which the Empire reached its apogee. In many respects the long-running divisions between those who sought to preserve the amateur status of the game, largely – but not entirely – those associated with southern-based clubs and of an élite public school background, and those who advocated professionalisation, who tended to represent northern industrial teams, was really about what constituted the ideal-type sportsman. Those who sought to preserve amateurism tended to adopt a 'sport for sport's sake' stance that emphasised the physical and moral improvement that could accrue from playing football, and held that the introduction of commercial values into the sport, in the form of professional players, represented the debasement of this ideal. Mason (1980: 72) sums up this position in the following terms:

> to accept professionalism would mean accepting that what up until then had been a voluntary leisure activity run by the participants for the participants would become a business. It would then be run like any other business and that would mean maximising profits by playing to win, if not at all costs, then with not too much attention to sporting scruples.

In addition, Mason (1980) records, concern was expressed that professionalisation would lead to funds increasingly accruing to a small élite of clubs that would come to enjoy an unfair advantage over others and be able to retain the best players on a financial, rather than sporting, basis. Recent years have seen discussion of the establishment of a European Super League and multinational media conglomerates have sought partnerships with globally-recognised clubs such as Arsenal and Manchester United, debate of which seems to suggest that concern about the deleterious effects of commerce on sport have remained fairly constant for more than 100 years.

Advocates of professionalism relied on a variety of arguments, some of which were more or less pragmatic – how can payment of players be effectively prevented? – others of which implicitly challenged the élitism that sought to retain the game for those with enough wealth to indulge in football without worrying about making a living. Mason (1980: 74) notes that the FA finally made professionalism legal in 1885, but introduced strict limits on the scope of clubs and players to participate in the transfer market, and prevented professionals from sitting on Association committees, thus seeking to ensure that the 'gentleman amateurs' retained positions of authority within the game.

The role that football played within the colonial system, both directly as a tool for inculcating educational and cultural values among 'native' peoples and indirectly as the game came to be exported around the world, also reveals much about the values of the day, which continue to be of some relevance in the contemporary period. These aspects of the history of football are considered first in this chapter, and related to wider processes of racialisation and the formation of English identity. Following that discussion the history of black players from the nineteenth to the late twentieth century will be examined, and the various reactions to them assessed.

The Empire, football and moral and physical improvement

While the problem of racism in football has only been identified in recent decades, and black players have only been present in any number for forty years or so, associations between the game and the formation of 'race' and nation are of a much longer provenance. The structures and rules of the game which continue to shape contemporary football – globalisation and corporate sponsors notwithstanding – were formed during a period in British history that was dominated by

LIVERPOOL JOHN MOORES UNIVERSITY
LEARNING & INFORMATION SERVICES

notions of 'race' and Empire (Rich, 1990). The high point of British imperialism coincided with the emergence of football as an organised leisure activity for both players and spectators – a pursuit that was widely regarded as complementary to the pursuit of Empire. Given their co-terminous development it is perhaps not surprising that, even from its earliest modern form, 'race' has been central to British football. It is this association that is outlined in this section.

Although varieties of football have been played in Britain for hundreds of years, many features of the contemporary game stem from the last decades of the nineteenth century. The nature of the sport prior to this period genuinely merited the title 'the peoples' game', involving as it did something between two dozen and hundreds of players taking part in matches that might cover enormous distances, and endure for several hours or even days, with rules that remained largely undefined (Dunning and Sheard, 1979; Brailsford, 1991). The relatively well-known 'games' such as that played around Ashbourne in Derbyshire where the people of the town took part in a 'match' that seems to have been little more than a mass-brawl, if a relatively good-natured one, might have been played for many generations but it was not until the mid-nineteenth century that the game came to be codified and institutionalised. In 1848 the élite players of the universities and public schools met at Cambridge University and agreed to a set of rules which forbade handling the ball or hacking opponents, changes regarded as key to the further success of the game (Mason, 1980). Dunning and Sheard (1979) demonstrate that the development of football within the public schools from the mid-eighteenth to the mid-nineteenth centuries occurred in the face of opposition from the educational authorities. Football was only one issue around which masters and pupils clashed during this period, and indeed Dunning and Sheard (1979: 52) record a series of rebellions some of which were only quelled by the intervention of local militia and the reading of the Riot Act. That football continued to survive, and became embedded by the 1860s, in the public schools of England reflected the ascendancy of the new bourgeoisie whose sons championed the game, at the expense of the landed gentry with whom the masters and headmasters were more closely identified.

The last decades of the nineteenth century also saw the formation of many football clubs, often based around the workplace, church or street. Many of these clubs were casually organised and very short-lived, but others benefited from the investment of considerable resources and continue to exist to the present day (Dunning and

Sheard, 1979; Mason, 1980; Holt, 1989). In many respects the development of football in this period was contingent upon the investment and commitment of key individuals, whether as players, administrators or investors, and the socioeconomic developments – such as reductions to the working week – meant that large numbers of people had the leisure time and the necessary resources to support the sport. The combination of both factors in the same period meant that (Brailsford, 1991: 115):

> The late Victorian sporting world was ready for football. Its eventual shape and style were almost predetermined by the new expectations of those it would entertain, either as players or spectators. Football was already a time-limited game, fitted by the schools into their afternoon session. It would be played by teams of equal numbers and would have its set rules to ensure fair play. It would enlist local enthusiasm and local support, interested in victory, but only if the victory was won through keen competition.

As well as witnessing changes to the rules of the game and manner in which it was played, this period also saw the establishment of institutional structures that continue to dominate the game. It was in 1863 that the Football Association was established, with its northern rival, the Football League, being founded in 1883. The first meeting of the International Board of the FA was held in 1886, although it is indicative that the 'internationalism' only extended as far as discussing relations between the 'home' nations of Wales, Scotland, Ireland and England.

One of the reasons why the increasing organisation of the game proved so important to raising the overall profile of football was that it coincided with broader socioeconomic and cultural changes, which also had a profound effect on the fortunes of the game. Butler (1991: 3) argued that:

> The advantage of organised team games was recognised, and football, easily and naturally, found a new role. The game was no longer just a child of the streets. It had now been adopted by the ruling and professional classes of England with their genius for organisation. It had crossed a hugely significant bridge with perfect timing, because the old habit of playing in the streets was being broken by improved law and order and because the leisure time of the working classes was being smothered by industrialisation.

Others have charted the socioeconomic background to the development of football in its contemporary form, accounts that cannot be
repeated in full here. In contrast to the above extract many of these
accounts indicate that the organised game in its modern form was not
simply 'adopted' from the folk game but was largely invented by the
'ruling and professional classes' (Dunning, 1979; Korr, 1978; Mason,
1980; Wagg, 1984). What is particularly relevant to discussion of the
relationship between football, national identity and ideas of 'race' is
that it was in this period that the potential role that the game might
play in instilling moral, religious and cultural values came to be
stressed. In many respects the association of such benefits with football came as a direct result of the public school and university roots of
the game.

By the mid-nineteenth century the headmasters of certain of the
main public schools came to value team games as one way to propagate an educational experience that would equip pupils mentally,
physically and morally with the values they would need to rely upon
in the outside world. Mangan (1996) argues that the nineteenth
century was characterised by an increasing fascination with militarism
and a widely held belief that war provided for the greatest expression
of national achievement and individual fulfillment. In such a context
the primary role for the public schools was to convert the sons of the
upper middle classes into subalterns imbued with the values held to
be central to Britain's military aspirations. One of the key ways in
which this was to be achieved was by using sport as a means of teaching boys the importance of team spirit, collective effort and the strict
adherence to individual roles. In this way 'continuous speculation
about the relationship between patriotism and the playing field'
(Mangan, 1996: 15) was rife during the very period when broader
socioeconomic changes ensured that the organised game was also
spreading in towns and cities across England. A clear association was
established between sport and British military and imperial ambition.

Kirk-Greene (1987) argues that in the absence of any more rigorous
selection criteria, sporting prowess was identified as a vital prerequisite for young men to secure a place in the administration of the
Empire. Even into the contemporary post-Second World War period,
Kirk-Greene (1987: 83) suggests, the recruitment of civil servants in
Britain has placed great emphasis on attracting candidates held to be
of 'good character':

And just how did a young man in search of a career in imperial service acquire his seemingly indispensable qualification of 'having character'? ... by playing games of course, by having made, and best of all having led, the school eleven or the college fifteen. Unquestioningly participation in organized games was part of the public school lore and ethos, and captaincy became tantamount to a quasi-guarantee of instant authority and all-round approbation.

Once it was established that sport was an excellent vehicle by which important moral and physical values could be imparted to middle-class boys who would go on to occupy key positions in the Empire, it was perhaps a relatively short conceptual leap to harness recreational games in order to 'civilise' lower orders, both domestically and in the colonies themselves. As hinted at in the introduction to this chapter, the role that black players found in football in Britain, and players from other European countries have enjoyed in more recent times reflect broader processes of migration and international trade, and it is clear that the growth of football as a more-or-less global game has been in part due to the Victorian imperial system.

The complexity of the British Empire is reflected in the manner in which different sports predominated in different geo-political territories. Perkins (1989) argues that discussion of 'the Empire' as though it were a unitary coherent system fails to reflect the extent of Britain's hegemonic position as a superpower during the nineteenth century. Instead, Perkins argues (1989: 148):

> [We ought to regard] ... the Empire not as a monolith but as part of a continuum in the exercise of British power and influence, from the most directly ruled Crown Colony through shades of increasing self-government up to Dominion status, and out beyond the red-tinted areas to places never under the Union Jack where British merchants, bankers, railway and mining engineers, ranchers, oil prospectors, missionaries, schoolmasters, sailors and navvies, and sojourners and settlers of every kind lived and worked.

As this network of British administrators, business people, engineers, prospectors, soldiers, and civil servants traversed much of the globe, they tended to take with them the various sports in which they had been schooled. So, the public school and Oxbridge-educated colonial élites, who were predominantly based in the directly-ruled Colonies or Dominions, tended to gather together to recreate the cricket matches they regarded as character-forming. In other parts of

Britain's realm as a superpower, where the middle class or the industrial bourgeoisie were engaged in engineering projects, banking and a myriad of commercial activity, football tended to predominate. While the upper-class expatriates who dominated the formal Empire preferred to indulge in 'gentlemanly' sports in which the amateur spirit was enshrined, those of other social backgrounds who were preeminent in the informal Empire that was predicated on trade and commerce favoured football. In this way (Perkins, 1989: 149):

> The English brothers Charnock introduced soccer to Russia amongst their cotton workers at Zuyevo. A Mr Nicholson of Thomas Cook's in Vienna joined Lord Rothschild's gardeners in the First Vienna Football Club, and Jimmy Hogan coached the Austrian *Wunderteam* and later the Hungarian national soccer team. In Argentina members of the British colony at Buenos Aires competed for Sir Thomas Lipton's soccer trophy. In Brazil Charles Miller, of English parentage and Southampton United, organized soccer matches among the British gas engineers, railway men and bank clerks of São Paulo. In Japan an English teacher named Johns demonstrates soccer at Kogakuryo School in 1874 . . .

The role of football in particular and sport in general within the Empire was complex, in some respects it was incidental to military endeavour or trading priorities, and was regarded as largely recreational. Mason (1986) records how the game was spread by the legions of salesmen, engineers, bankers and clerical workers who travelled the world in pursuit of business opportunities. He suggests that it was in this manner that the game was introduced to Bilbao, Romania, St Petersburg, Genoa, São Paulo, Moscow and Montevideo. Mason (1986: 69) draws particular attention to the development of the game following the arrival of some 30 000 British nationals in Buenos Aires:

> Settlement was accompanied by schools such as that founded by Alexander Watson Hutton. This Scotsman included football in his curriculum, and it was not long before a dozen clubs had been established in the Argentinean capital, mostly with British membership. By 1893, Hutton was President of the Argentinean FA and the English High School was an early winner of the championship. After 1900, though, the game was increasingly in Argentinean hands.

Beyond the realm of recreation, though, sport was, at times, utilised by military and civilian authorities as a means of social engineering: both among British nationals and local populations. Unlike the examples mentioned above, where the spread of the game was largely incidental to other activities, on other occasions football was encouraged for more instrumental reasons. Clayton (1987: 115) records that military officers held sport to be of great importance in maintaining good relations among soldiers:

> At its simplest, games were a chance to 'let off steam', important in the closed societies of fit young men; tensions that arose in crowded barrackrooms were thereby released. Games were also an opportunity for the very mild saturnalia that a well-disciplined unit occasionally permitted (Christmas rituals in which officers waited on soldiers at table were another example). The captain of the team was not always the senior-ranking player; a soldier could beat an officer in a race or take a ball off him in a tackle, all very satisfying.

Football matches were sometimes used as a kind of public relations exercise, designed to improve the image of the military among local populations. In the late colonial period, Clayton (1987) records, both British and French authorities encouraged soldiers to play football matches against local civilian sides in order to increase the acceptability of the military. Sport had played a similar role during the Boer War of 1899–1902, and Clayton (1987: 117) suggests that the conflict:

> established football on a popular basis among the coloured [sic] population of the Western Cape. Teams still playing today bear names clearly showing their British county regimental origins: the Sussex Rovers, Devonshire Rovers, Argyll Spurs, and Wiltshire Rovers. British battalions recruited local mule-drivers, ox-drivers, scouts and other minor auxiliaries. These learned football while serving along with the British infantrymen; on a few occasions British battalions even included coloured [sic] players of promise.

By the end of the nineteenth century, football had not only become codified and established, it had been identified as a repository of national virtue, which could be drawn upon in order to inculcate the essential and improving qualities of the British character among the lower classes domestically and the inferior natives within the Empire. The pseudo-scientific racism developed by European élites maintained

I.M. MARSH LIBRARY LIVERPOOL L17 6BD
TEL. 0151 231 5216/5299

that the colonial masters were culturally, morally and physically superior to the subject peoples of Africa and Asia – football, and other sports, were held to embody this privileged status. The emergence of first-class black footballers – admittedly in very small numbers initially – in the decades surrounding the turn of the century appeared to directly challenge this self-confidence.

The first black professionals, 1880s–1914

Just as the lengthy history of black people in Britain is largely overlooked, so too consideration of the specific history of black footballers is usually curtailed to a discussion of events that have unfolded in the last few decades. A recent study of *The First Black Footballer* (Vasili, 1998) explores some of the reasons for this historical amnesia, as well as providing a fascinating account of the sporting life and times of its subject – Arthur Wharton. The extent to which the athletic and footballing feats that Wharton achieved in the late nineteenth and early twentieth centuries have been forgotten is demonstrated by the fact that his achievements were unknown even to his descendants until Vasili's research became known to them. In his introduction to the book, the former Manchester United player Tony Whelan acknowledged that he had wrongly considered Clyde Best to be the first black professional in Britain and had been unaware of Wharton's career (Whelan, 1998). Vasili argues that this 'absence of memory' partly arose from a desire to deny Wharton's achievements that were so clearly contrary to the principles of nineteenth-century pseudo-scientific racism. However, racism is only part of the explanation, since other minority ethnic sportsmen, notably the Indian cricketer K.S. Ranjitsinhji, have come to occupy a place in the sporting history books. Malcolm (1997) demonstrates the interrelation between 'race' and class in the context of cricket by contrasting the relatively elevated position of high-status Indian cricketers, many of whom were products of the public-school Oxbridge system, with the experience of Caribbean migrant cricketers in the Lancashire Leagues who were expected to perform groundkeeping and other menial tasks. As in football, the 'West Indian' cricketers playing professionally for northern teams were afforded lower status than the gentleman amateurs, in this instance of Indian background, playing in the south. In order to understand Wharton's exclusion, class as well as 'race' must be taken into account, Vasili argues. Despite Wharton's contemporary reputation as a 'gentleman athlete', his involvement in football as a professional player for a northern club meant that he was the antithesis of the ideal sporting type that was mentioned earlier in discussion of the debate about professionalism in football. Given that Wharton's achievements remain relatively unknown, it is worthwhile outlining some milestones from his extraordinary sporting career. Vasili (1998: 1) records that the first mention of Wharton in the press was an 1884 report of a cricket match in which he had scored an inglorious duck – despite this setback, within a year he was established as the regular first-team goalkeeper for the Darlington Cricket and Football Club. His ability and unusual style of play – he became renowned for punching the ball away from the goal and swinging from the cross-bar in order to catch the ball between his knees (Ahmed, 1997) – led to local media interest, and in the seasons that followed Wharton was selected to play in several regional representative sides and made a number of appearances against the Corinthians – the team that continue to enjoy a reputation for embodying the 'true' amateur and sporting spirit of the game. One of Wharton's appearances for Preston North End against the Corinthians was in the Festival of Football held to celebrate Queen Victoria's Golden Jubilee in 1887 and attended by the Prince of Wales (Jenkins, 1990).

In 1886 Wharton's athletic career reached its apogee when he ran the 100 yards in ten seconds in both the heats and the final of the Amateur Athletic Association meeting, a feat that has come to be recognised as the first world record for the event (Vasili, 1998: 16). While his initial cricketing endeavour may have attracted attention only for the paucity of the results, Wharton's rapid rise to prominence on the athletics track and football field was truly remarkable and quickly led to national fame. Jenkins (1990: 23) records that:

> The rapid rise of Arthur Wharton, from unknown student in Darlington to record-breaking amateur athlete, Birchfield Harriers and goalkeeper with one of British football's élite clubs, had been accomplished in the nine months from July 1886 to March 1887.

For the next ten years, Wharton seems to have become one of the most visible and, at times, controversial of Britain's sporting personalities.

In the late 1880s demands were made in the press that Wharton ought to be selected to play for England, pleas that Vasili (1998: 74) argues were wholly consistent with his tremendous form during that period. That Wharton was not selected may be attributed to the parochialism of the FA, who continued to favour the 'ideal-type' player from southern clubs, and the fact that the award of an England cap was regarded as an honour bestowed for recent strong club performances with little or no intention of establishing settled teams of complementary players. One consequence of this was that the FA selectors enjoyed considerable powers of patronage, which meant that selectors could – and Vasili (1998: 76) argues certainly did – indulge their racist prejudices by refusing to allow players of colour to represent the English nation. Vasili (1998: 8) records how the FA was bent on establishing itself as a fully paid-up section of the establishment during this period and so:

> identified with the prevailing racialised conception of what 'England' was, what it was about and what it stood for: an Anglo-Saxon nation of teutonic origin propelled – 'burdened' – by its natural pre-eminence to lead the world towards ever greater levels of civilisation. As a consequence, having a brown-skinned goalie for the representative team was just not on, to use a contemporary idiom.

In addition to facing racism from members of football's governing body Wharton was abused on occasion by supporters at matches – provocation which sometimes provoked a violent response (Jenkins, 1990: 25) – and by journalists in print. Jenkins (1990: 25) records that Wharton was often hostile towards newspaper reporters on account of the barely-concealed colour prejudice that was often reflected in stories about him. On his arrival to play for Stalybridge Rovers in 1896, a local newspaper adapted a hunting metaphor in commenting that the club have 'bagged a real nigger as goalkeeper in Wharton, who is none other than the Darkie who used to guard the North End citadel' (Vasili, 1998: 87). On another occasion a journalist questioned the unusual style of Wharton's game by suggesting that it revealed his inferior intellectual ability – 'is the darkie's pate too thick for it to dawn upon him that between the sticks is no place for a skylark?' (Vasili, 1998: 69). In respectively portraying Wharton as a hunted animal and deriding his mental ability, the press drew upon familiar stereotypes of the late Victorian period that served to rationalise and justify colonial expansion. The 'half-devil and half-child' that Kipling had identified as the subject of the civilising mission of the British empire was understood by the tenets of scientific racism to be more simian than human (Rich, 1990).

Notwithstanding the use of such crude racist stereotypes, it appears that Wharton was more commonly known to the public by the super-ficially-affectionate nickname 'Darkie'. Although the tag often served to obscure Wharton's national origins with a 'catch-all' epithet – Jenkins (1990) records that he was usually held to have hailed from the Caribbean even though he was born and raised in the Gold Coast – it is interesting to note that it tended to be used in a manner osten-sibly devoid of prejudice or ill-will. As will be discussed again later in this chapter, a common feature of mainstream white society's response to black players has been to treat them as somehow 'exotic', providers of an interesting extra dimension, quite literally bringing a bit of colour to the game. As in so many other ways, Wharton seems to have been a pioneer in this respect, too, and while the ultimately negative connotations of epithets such as 'Darkie' must be acknowl-edged it is important to recognise the apparently positive and affectionate title by which he was occasionally known. As many writers have argued (Cole, 1996a; Miles, 1989; Rex, 1986; Small, 1994), in the absence of any biological or genetic basis for the concept it must be realised that 'race' is a socially-constructed phenomenon, capable of being formed and reformed in the context of broader social, economic, cultural and political developments. Not only is the nature and content of 'race' and racism contingent upon dimensions of time and space, but they are frequently complex, multifaceted and contra-dictory. Given this, deploying an affectionate nickname or ascribing particular sporting prowess to certain groups – actions and attitudes which in themselves might not appear especially pernicious – conceal racialised underpinnings whose consequences are negative in the final instance. Cashmore's (1982) example, mentioned earlier in this chapter, of the ultimately negative consequences of the stereotype that has held black schoolchildren to be gifted at sport, serves as an apposite example of the positive–negative dichotomy to be found in some manifestations of racism. A further illustration is provided by Cole (1996b: 13) who refers to the intellectual power and group soli-darity attributed to Jews in Nazi Germany, qualities that might be considered 'positive' on one level but which contributed to the most appalling consequences.

The arena of sport, like some fields of popular entertainment, has long provided some opportunity for black people in Britain to tran-scend 'racialised barriers' (Small, 1994). Wharton's attempts to leap (literally and metaphorically) over such boundaries were successful to a large extent, but the epithet 'Darkie', however innocuously it was deployed by many of those who employed it, served to underline Wharton's essential and unchanging otherness and 'inferiority' just as surely as those FA selectors who would not countenance a black goalkeeper representing England.

Another pioneering black footballer was Walter Daniel Tull, who in 1908 was resident of a Bethnal Green children's home following the death of his Barbadian father and English mother. Within a few short years Tull's footballing prowess saw him sign for Tottenham Hotspur – playing in their debut appearance in the first division – where his initial impact led to eulogies in the press which predicted a glorious future for the young player (Askwith, 1998). Whatever else may have transpired, Tull's career did not maintain its early potential at Spurs and – perhaps in part as a consequence of racial abuse he was subject to from a crowd at Bristol in 1910 – he spent much of the following season or so in the reserves before transferring to Northampton Town. The Cobblers – under the management of Herbert Chapman who would go on to considerable success with Huddersfield Town and Arsenal – paid a substantial fee for Tull and secured him against competition from other clubs including Leicester Fosse and Clapton Orient (Vasili, 1996: 59). At Northampton, Tull made 110 first-team appearances in the few seasons he was with the club, scoring nine goals.

The outbreak of the First World War led to Tull's achievement of another significant milestone, and his demise on the battlefields of Normandy. On joining the 17th (1st Football) Battalion of the Middlesex Regiment in December 1914, Tull not only became a manifestation of the link between football and the military ethos, he began a process that saw him become the first black officer in the British army. After being invalided back to Britain in 1916, Tull was sent to the officer cadet training school at Gailes in Scotland, the first black person so to do and against military regulations that prohibited black men serving as officers (Vasili, 1996: 64). Eventually Tull returned to France as a second lieutenant, was mentioned in dispatches for his bravery and died in the second battle of the Somme in 1918 (Vasili, 1996: 65). In the summer of 1999 the Walter Tull Memorial and Garden of Rest was opened at Northampton Town's ground in recognition of the contribution Tull made to his sport and his country and as testament to anti-racist struggle.

Like Wharton, Tull's success was achieved in the context of a society in which the racial inferiority of black people was 'proved' by science and moral philosophy and widely reproduced in popular culture.

Around the time that Tull was playing, racist violence occurred on a large scale in Cardiff, Liverpool, London, Newcastle and elsewhere that led to a number of deaths and the wholesale terrorism of black communities living in these cities (Ramdin, 1987; Rowe, 1998). Trades-union disputes with employers, for example in the shipping industry, revealed considerable animosity to the employment of black workers (Little, 1947), and political discussion relating to the future of the Commonwealth included consideration of how best to organise racial segregation in South Africa (Rich, 1990: 54–66).

In this light it is perhaps not surprising that Tull's rapid rise to success in the game was quickly forgotten – especially at a time when so many young men were killed – but what demands explanation is how he achieved so much in the first instance. First, it seems clear that Tull must have possessed considerable personal qualities to have reached the positions he did. Second, it must be recognised that even in a society seeped in racism, as Britain was in the early decades of the twentieth century, it was not wholly ubiquitous, and there was a fairly widespread, if marginal, liberal tradition that proclaimed the equality of all peoples (Rich, 1990). Third, as mentioned in discussion of Wharton, the achievements of a black person on a sports field were in many respects consistent with prevailing racist discourse. As Vasili (1996: 60) points out:

> winning through sport for black Britons like Tull could be seen as, ultimately, a Pyrrhic victory. Their achievements were defined in such a way as to confirm the scientific taxonomies of 'race': it was their 'animalism', a sub-human characteristic, that allowed them their physical prowess, possession of which necessarily excluded ownership of civilised, cultured traits such as a highly evolved intellect or refined sensitivities.

The early black professionals achieved their success against many odds and it seems in the face of considerable prejudice. Their recent rediscovery and restoration to the annals of the game are important to ongoing anti-racist efforts, emphasising as they do the long-term contribution that black people have made to the game. As has been argued, however, black athleticism was largely consistent with the tenets of scientific racism current at the time.

Consolidation, 1918–60

A number of black players played professionally during the period immediately after the First World War. An Egyptian, Tewfik Abdullah, was signed by Derby County in 1920 and Jack Leslie, an Anglo-African, made 382 appearances for Plymouth Argyle in the 1920s and 1930s. Leslie's experience in relation to the England side suggests that the racism that had excluded Wharton decades previously, continued to figure among the game's senior administrators who were still responsible for picking the national side. Leslie was selected for the squad but never picked for the team, the player was convinced that this was because the selectors only became aware of his colour following his initial selection (Vasili, 1998: 76). The Welsh national team were ahead of the English in this respect, playing Northampton Town's John Parris in 1938, making him the first black player to appear in a home international side (Sir Norman Chester Centre, undated). Another black player appearing at the highest level in club football was Roy Brown, who appeared alongside Stanley Matthews in the famous Stoke City side of the late 1930s. A decade or so later the Jamaican player Lindy Delaphena won the first division championship with Portsmouth, before joining Middlesbrough in 1950.

These sketchy details apart, information on the experiences of these players is difficult to obtain and so the extent of racist abuse they may have faced remains impossible to determine. However, the experience of one of the most famous players of the interwar period suggests that racism was a feature of football grounds during this era. Bill Dean's achievements at Everton in the 1920s and 1930s remain the stuff of legend, most notably the record of 60 goals he scored in season 1928/29. Dean continues to be better known by his nickname, 'Dixie': a moniker bestowed on account of his physical appearance. Dean's biographer described the player's reaction to the (Walsh, 1977: 40):

> title which he at first resented, always insisting on 'Bill' when friends and acquaintances addressed him. The reason perhaps was that he felt 'Dixie' had connotations with colour, the problems associated with the southern states of America, and therefore contained the inference that he was of that origin, or half caste.
>
> Dean was blessed with a mop of jet black curly hair, an obvious characteristic of coloured people, and this may have led to the association of the nickname. Tranmere supporters [who had instigated the sobriquet] had no intention of giving offence to their idol, the

name stuck and as Dean progressed to entertain and delight his admirers, 'Dixie' seemed an appropriate title, which as people got used to it, bore no relation to anything other than a superstar footballer. Not that the name could be offensive in any way, but in those days a great deal of ignorance and prejudice was prevalent on such matters, and people were generally more sensitive about them.

In some respects, of course, this discussion is reminiscent of Wharton and Tull's experience of being known as 'Darkie'. What is different, though, is that Dean – as his biographer rather gingerly implies – was not black, and so his apparent objection to the nickname is ambiguous: is he rejecting a racist epithet or dismayed to be mistaken for a black person? This ambivalence is further fuelled by Dean's reaction to racist abuse shouted at him following a game in the late 1920s (Walsh, 1977: 101):

> Dean was one of the last players to leave the field and as he passed the overhanging body of spectators one suddenly shouted in his ear, 'we'll get you, you black bastard!' Dean was extremely sensitive to such insults and reacted immediately. To an approaching policeman who had overheard this remark Dean said 'it's all right officer, I'll look after this', and he thereupon promptly punched the offender, knocking him flying into the crowd. Cheers followed from the onlookers, but the policeman rushed towards Dean, only to shake him by the hand and comment rather enthusiastically, 'That was a beauty, but I never saw it, officially or otherwise!' The twinkle in the officer's eye was a delight to Dean.

Once again it is impossible to establish the motive behind Dean's direct reaction to racist abuse. It is perhaps interesting to contrast the response of the police officer in this instance with the aftermath of Eric Cantona's 1995 assault on a Crystal Palace fan who, as the player left the pitch after being sent-off, allegedly shouted 'you dirty French bastard! Fuck off back to France'. Cantona executed what the press described as a 'kung fu' kick on the supporter, an action that led to his being banned from playing for the remainder of the season and a two-week prison sentence for common assault, which was transmuted to community service on appeal (see Fleming and Tomlinson, 1996, for a fuller account of the Cantona affair).

An episode that illustrates the convergence of football, 'race' and politics during this period was the 1948 tour made by the Nigerian national team to Britain. This was the first of a series of tours by Commonwealth footballers: teams from the Gold Coast, Trinidad, Uganda and the Caribbean visited during the 1950s. Vasili (1995: 55) describes how these series:

> were seen by the football establishment here and in the empire as sporting and political inductions. Those who played were treated and feted beyond what was necessary for purely diplomatic propriety. Those who accompanied them as managers and trainers were aware of their carefully prescribed roles. These were no ordinary footballers. Their brief was to watch, listen and learn – not only about the way football was played in Britain but, more importantly, about how superior the British political and economic system was to the alternatives on offer to Africans.

The selection of players to represent Nigeria was a keenly contested political process, with competing interests seeking to ensure that footballers associated with them were included in the team. There was also concern that the entourage presented an image to the British public that reinforced the high standards of civilisation in Nigeria and in so doing provided clear evidence of the success of the colonialists who ran the country.

The Nigerian side's first game was against Marine, in Liverpool – which the visitors won 5–2 – followed by a draw with a South Liverpool side. A series of games in London saw the Nigerians lose 2–1 to Leytonstone, 6–1 to an Isthmian League team, and draw 2–2 against the Corinthian League. They went on to lose 1–0 against Dulwich Hamlet and 8–0 to the Athenian League. Their match against Bromley, winners of the Amateur Cup, occasioned a revival in the Nigerians' performance as they came from behind to win 3–1 (Vasili, 1995).

Despite the mixed fortunes revealed in the above list of results, the impression that the visitors made in terms of their style of play was generally favourable. The speed at which they played the game and their ability to control the ball, even though usually playing in bare feet, was subject to considerable scrutiny and praise. In addition to recording the analysis of the Nigerians' game, Vasili (1995: 63) also notes that the press occasionally referred to the need for floodlights 'because it's always difficult to find a black man in the dark' and excused the lack of attempts on goal made by one home team on the grounds that they had been instructed 'not to shoot until they saw the whites of their eyes'. Once more it appears that black players were being received in a highly contradictory manner: subject to considerable praise and taken seriously in terms of their tactics and skills on the one hand, but treated as somewhat exotic objects of curiosity who, whatever their sporting prowess, remained culturally inferior. However positively their talents as footballers were regarded they were finally unable to escape the confines that were placed upon them by a racist culture formed by long-experience of Empire.

One member of the Nigerian touring side, Tesilimi Balogun, made the transition to the English professional game when he signed for Peterborough United in 1955. Other notable footballers from the 1950s include Giles Heron, who was the first black player to appear for Celtic. Despite scoring on his debut in season 1951/52 Heron was criticised in Glasgow for apparently failing to display the physical strength and courage so often seen as essential to the British game (Sir Norman Chester Centre, undated). Perhaps this was one of the first instances in which a black player was accused of 'lacking bottle', it was certainly not to be the last. Another high-profile player from this period was Charlie Williams who made 158 appearances for Doncaster Rovers during the 1950s, and eventually became better known as a comedian. Williams recalled that he was often subjected to considerable curiosity from crowds who may not have encountered a black person before. He also recounted the racist abuse he received (Holland, 1993: 16):

> People shouted 'You black bastard!' at me but that didn't affect me, in fact it only made me stronger. I also used to get ridicule from players but after the game we shook hands.

The consolidation in the number of black professionals during the middle decades of the twentieth century served to indicate a number of themes that were to accelerate in the years that followed. The number of black players increased considerably from the 1960s, but the reaction that they often faced can be traced back to this earlier period in which a contradictory picture can be discerned. While black footballers may have been heralded for their skills and fêted as objects of curiosity, the reaction of supporters and the press often showed that they were ultimately regarded as inferior.

I.M. MARSH LIBRARY LIVERPOOL L17 6BD
TEL. 0151 231 5216/5299

Expansion, 1960–90

The post-Second World War labour shortages that had encouraged migration from the Caribbean to Britain provided a compelling reason why the number of black footballers began to rise in the late 1960s and early 1970s. Simply, the increasing black population meant that there was a greater pool from which successful footballers could emerge. There is clearly more to the expansion in black players than this, since subsequent increases in the Asian population – which is now larger than the African Caribbean – did not lead to successful Asian players emerging in numbers, but the particular history of postwar black migration to Britain provides the context against which black footballers emerged in the decades that followed.

Two of the greatest football legends of the 1960s were black players: the Brazilian Pele, and the Mozambique-born Portuguese striker, Eusebio. Although it has been suggested that the military authorities in Brazil consciously tried to 'whiten' the national team in the early 1970s in an effort to emulate what they regarded as a superior 'European model' (Arbena, 1988: 4–5), the success of both these players was seen by many to constitute a challenge from the marginal 'Third World' to the dominant European football élite.

Domestically, an important milestone from this period was that Tony Collins became the first black manager of a professional team in Britain when he took over at Rochdale in 1960 (Davage, 1995), a feat that few have repeated, even forty years later.[8] The black footballer who enjoyed most renown in the English game in the 1960s was Albert Johanneson, the South African signed by Leeds United in 1961. A powerful striker, Johanneson became, in 1965, the first black player to appear in the FA Cup Final and has been considered – wrongly, of course – to be the first black professional in the game (Whelan, 1998). Like black players before and after him, Johanneson was subject to racial abuse from crowds and, to some extent like Arthur Wharton, the malign neglect of history. Rarely does Johanneson feature in books or articles reflecting on the achievements of black players in the British game; even in those such as Hamilton's (1982) compendium *Black Pearls of Soccer* – which provides relatively lengthy player profiles – Johanneson receives only a fleeting mention. It was only when he was discovered living alone in poverty a few years before his death in 1995 that Albert Johanneson was even partially returned to public attention. The ignoble circumstances of his death were contrasted with the success of his playing career (Rivlin, 1995: 10):

For his body to be discovered in a council flat a few days after his death is cruel, because when I think of Albert Johanesson I think of an exciting and intelligent player in an era of cloggers. I think of Leeds' early and great European nights against the likes of Valencia and Real Zaragoza with Albert darting in from the wing, leaving a defender gasping for air.

One of the highest profile clubs in the English game during the late 1960s was West Ham United, largely because the side contained three members of the team that had won the World Cup in 1966: Geoff Hurst, Bobby Moore and Martin Peters. Perhaps the reputation of the club was one reason why Clyde Best, the Bermudan who signed in 1969, continues to be remembered as a pioneering black player. Many players who began their careers in the 1970s refer to the impact that Best had. One player who had extensive experience playing local league football in the 1970s described the positive model that Best became to him as a young boy:

My idol is Pele ... a lot of black supporters idolise black players and often that is Brazilian players. I have always looked to black players and I think I always will. I remember when Clyde Best played for West Ham – I used to watch them if they were on TV, just to see him. Without him I would not have watched it. I was always very choosy which clubs I watched.[9]

Another black player recalled (Highfield Rangers, 1993: 30):

It was important for me to see Clyde Best, a black man. I was proud to be black; I couldn't wait for West Ham to come down here to see this big, big black man, as a centre forward playing. The guy was a legend, a hero. Seeing a black man out there was tremendous. It was a good feeling to see one of you and be able to say, 'If he can do it, I can do it'.

When Ade Coker, a Nigerian, made his debut in the West Ham team in 1971, playing alongside Best, the team (and future England) manager, Ron Greenwood, forecast that the number of black players would increase and that within ten years there might be four or five playing at the top level of the game (Hamilton, 1982: 67). In the end of course, this prediction proved an underestimate. Best's experience of racist abuse was a precursor to the intimidation that many other black players were to endure during this period, and in his case this seems to have been one reason why he left to pursue a career in the United States after leaving West Ham in 1976 (Root and Austin, 1980: 31).

Another player who began his career in the late 1960s was Brendon Batson, who was with Arsenal until 1974, before transferring to Cambridge United and finally West Bromwich Albion. Upon retirement from the game, Batson became one of the relatively few black players to proceed into the administration of the game, becoming deputy chief executive of the Professional Footballers' Association. Reflecting on the racist abuse, monkey chanting and so on that he experienced throughout the 1970s, Batson recalls one occasion:

> when I was at Cambridge going to Bradford at the start of the season, and after the game, there happened to be a National Front rally up in Bradford, and their coaches were over-taking us on the way back down. When they saw me one of the things they were doing was spitting at me. It was ridiculous, they were spitting at me – and they were inside a coach – not very intelligent people! One year when we went to Chelsea, there were members of the National Front waiting for the coach to pull up, because we had three black players at the time. On reflection it makes you wonder why you put up with it without doing something about it – you know with the attitude well we are here you are not going to drive us away.[10]

Batson's determination to defy racist intimidation is echoed in the reaction of other players. Garth Crooks, for example, suggests that black players deal with the problem 'because sport offers an opportunity, one of the few areas where you can get on, doing what you do best, where talent is allowed to come through' (Harding, 1991: 362). Another high-profile black player of that period, Cyrille Regis of West Bromwich Albion and England, offered a remarkably similar perspective in an interview with the authors:

> Sport judges you as you are, on your ability and talent ... It is a form where you can go in and they can't say jack to you, because you have won the race, the match, the fight, whatever. You can't refute that. Sport is an avenue where you are judged on your talent. That is the nature of competition and sport.[11]

In addition to Best, Coker and Batson, other black players who appeared in the early 1970s include Cliff Marshall of Everton, Phil Walker and Trevor Lee of Millwall, Ces Podd of Bradford, John Chiedozie of Leyton Orient, Johnny Miller of Norwich, and Clive Charles of West Ham. The increasing visibility of black players was accompanied by a series of racialised concerns about their suitability to the game. A supposed inability to withstand the cold winters of the English season, to successfully conform to the conception of the ideal footballer that emphasised stamina, physical strength and commitment, and to develop the appropriate 'temperament' was often called into question by sections of the media, managers, and spectators. Root and Austin (1980: 31) noted that:

> Beliefs that Black players might be tricky, but lacked 'bottle' and wilted under close marking and heavy tackling; that they gave up too easily; couldn't play in cold weather; or lacked the necessary discipline for top-level training were all widely held.
>
> In a game where managerial expectations strongly affect a player's progress in the early years, these suspicions could be lethal.

In an era when the predominant reaction of clubs, the media and football authorities to the racist abuse manifest inside stadia was to either ignore it altogether or to equate it with the kind of criticism thrown at all players from time to time, it is perhaps not surprising that black players often sought to draw inner strength from their experiences, rather than to confront problems via the game's institutions. The accounts offered by players often suggest a perception that to confront racism, especially when it emanated from fellow players, would betray a lack of character, an inability to take the kind of 'stick' that all players were supposed to become used to. Much-travelled manager Dave Bassett argued in the *Guardian* (4 March 1999) that 'verbals between players are part and parcel of the game; always have been, always will be. It's human nature and doesn't just apply to football'. Garth Crooks observed that 'if you couldn't cope, you fell foul of the industry' (Harding, 1991: 362), suggesting an uneasy compromise between standing up to racism and maintaining a professional reputation.

Any escalation in the number of black players heralded in the early 1970s took sometime to materialise, indeed Root and Austin (1980: 24) suggest that there were no black players among the regular sides appearing in the First Division at the start of season 1976/77. Towards the end of the decade, however, black players were well-established in many sides, and in 1978 Viv Anderson became the first black player to achieve a full international cap when he made his debut for England at Wembley against Czechoslovakia. In 1979 George Berry became the first black player to appear for Wales since John Parris in 1938. Longmore (1988) details the tremendous media interest generated by Anderson's impending appearance in the England team – there had been speculation about a number of other black players who might have been considered by manager Ron Greenwood – and the manner in which the wider implications for 'race relations' were scrutinised. It seems that these were among the first episodes when the position of black players within the game was regarded as a metaphor for the place and progress of minority ethnic communities in British society. The prospect of a black person representing England in the national game, a possibility that seems to have been regarded as anathema to earlier generations of selectors, was often regarded as indicative that black people had become a permanent presence in Britain. In an era when extremist parties such as the National Front were relatively successful in electoral terms, standing on a platform that included 'repatriation' of black and Asian people, the appearance of a black person in an England team was widely regarded as a rebuttal to those who wished to perpetuate an exclusive white national identity.

In the event, Anderson acquitted himself well in a somewhat dull 1–0 victory for the home side. Longmore (1988: xii) commented on the implications which might have flown from a less impressive performance:

> If he had been sent off, given away a penalty or scored an own-goal, it would have confirmed the belief of householders up and down the country that West Indians were, of course, thoroughly unreliable. Imagine what Alf Garnett would have made of it.

Whereas black footballers featured in many sides during the late 1970s and early 1980s, West Bromwich Albion were one of the few who consistently used a number of black players. The most revered of these players were Brendon Batson, Laurie Cunningham, Remi Moses and Cyrille Regis – who received a bullet through the post when he was selected for the England team. That Batson was a formidable defender and Moses a strong midfielder served to refute, although not to dispel, racist stereotypes that maintained black players lacked the commitment and stamina required for the English game. By all accounts the players showed considerable fortitude in the face of racist abuse, and it is clear that the club were regarded as daring pioneers for including black players in numbers.

In other respects, though, media interest in the players served to cement their novelty status in a racialised manner that set them apart from their team-mates. Seeking to capitalise on a local appearance by the successful disco stars the Three Degrees, the West Brom manager, Ron Atkinson instigated a publicity campaign featuring Batson, Cunningham and Regis as the team's own 'three degrees', a label that remained attached to the players for years to follow. For Cunningham this kind of recognition continued after his transfer to Real Madrid, where he was dubbed 'El Negro'. One of the players involved at West Brom recalled that the interest in the black players served to detract from other members of the team and became counter-productive and tiresome:

> I don't know if it made me feel uncomfortable it was just that I felt that it went on for one or two publicity shots too long. It was great fun at the time, a little bit of publicity . . . had it finished, but it kept on rolling. It was a period you look back on and say well it was a bit of fun and even to this day, and you are talking now 19,18 years ago when it all happened – it was our year of the three degrees.[12]

Another episode during Atkinson's period at West Brom also courted the racialised debate about the ability of black players and their status *vis-à-vis* white footballers. In 1979 the club held a testimonial year for Len Cantello, a midfielder of ten years standing. To mark the occasion a 'black versus white' match was staged, involving select teams on both sides. In an era in which the relative strengths and weaknesses of black footballers were surrounded with racialised stereotypes and far-right political groups, including hooligans, circling the game, fears were raised that the match might attract unwelcome attention. It is interesting that players sought to deny a racial overtone to a game that seemed to echo the racialised debates about the qualities and attributes of black footballers. Garth Crooks, selected to play in the game, argued, for example, that 'politics should be left to the politicians. This is just a game of football played for a fellow professional'[13] – a game, however, predicated upon the novelty of black footballers.

Black players were becoming increasingly established in the game by the early 1980s – three black players appeared in the 1981 Centenary Cup Final between Manchester City and Tottenham

Hotspur,[14] and Hamilton's (1982) guide included more than 60 established black players, as well as a further 37 young footballers 'to watch out for'. In this period Justin Fashanu – a former Barnardo's Boy – playing for Norwich City became one of the most high-profile players of his generation. In 1980 he played for England under-21s against East Germany, before going on to score the goal of season 1979/80 against Liverpool. For most of the following season he was the leading goal-scorer and in August 1981 he became the first black player to be transferred for £1 million when he signed for Nottingham Forest. While some heralded football's example of 'racial integration', it is clear that a frequent response from supporters was racist abuse, 'monkey chanting' and banana-throwing. Holland (1993: 16) recalled the chant with which some Newcastle United fans greeted Howard Gayle when he played for the club in 1982/83, 'he's black, he's broon, he is a fucking coon, Howard Gayle, Howard Gayle', and Cyrille Regis similarly recalled being verbally attacked by supporters of his own side when he first went to West Bromwich Albion (Cashmore, 1982: 154). Williams (1992: 11) records the experience of Vince Hillaire, making his debut as a substitute for Crystal Palace at Port Vale in 1976:

> After about twenty minutes, the manager … Terry Venables, told me to go and have a warm-up. I came out of the dug-out, and I started jogging around the touchline. I couldn't believe the abuse that was coming at me … animal noises and all the names you could think of calling a black person. Any name under the sun. And it frightened me a bit, so I couldn't wait to get back in the dug-out.

An Arsenal fan recalled the extent of racist abuse meted out to players at Highbury in the early 1980s:

> it was always a common feature – every time a black player touched the ball he would be booed. Even though Arsenal had black players, the Arsenal crowd would boo the opposing black players when they got the ball. I remember John Barnes played for Watford, he had a bad time when he was going down the flank.[15]

That supporters of teams that featured black players would abuse those playing for opponents has been an issue of curiosity for many, and for some has been reason to deny that those engaging in monkey chanting and the rest are really motivated by racism. Instead, it is suggested, such abuse is akin to the usual vilification that most players, regardless of their ethnic origin, receive from opposing supporters. Regarding the apparent inconsistency of such behaviour, it might be pointed out that racism is rarely a rational or coherent set of beliefs, even though it may provide a 'practically adequate' understanding of the world (Miles, 1989: 80). Just as the racist who believes that all black people ought to be sent 'back where they came from' might enjoy good relations with their black neighbour, football supporters' racist abuse of black opponents is neither negated nor diminished by the presence of black players in the team they support. It has already been noted that the claim that racist abuse is equivalent to the insults offered to all players is often made, sometimes by black players themselves. The Wimbledon midfielder Robbie Earle, for example, commented in 1997:[16]

> it often intrigues me that when white players are abused by the crowd – Paul Gascoigne gets 'you fat bastard' all the time, Tony Adams used to get those dreadful donkey noises – you never see in-depth investigative reports into it.

As is argued elsewhere in this book, the suggestion that racist abuse and other obscene or personal insults offered to players are somehow equivalent denies the specific context and history of racism. An important characteristic of racist abuse, and racist violence, is that it seeks to reinforce white preeminence and to physically and culturally exclude minority ethnic communities. Claims that Paul Gascoigne could usefully lose a few pounds, however crudely expressed, simply do not carry the political or social resonance that emanates from racist abuse.

A qualitatively different response can be identified among players who, instead of denying the nature of the problem, have resolved to draw strength from and overcome the racism they have faced. A famous image of the game from the mid-1980s is a photograph of John Barnes deftly flicking a banana from the pitch with the underside of his boot in an act of quiet defiance of the racist abuse that dogged his career (Hill, 1989). While individual players were resolving not to be deflected from their careers, institutions within the game were slow to provide support. One player reflected how black players during the 1970s and 1980s often proceeded:

> with the attitude 'well, we are here and you [racists] are not going to drive us away', there was no tangible help that we were receiv-

ing from clubs or from the authorities and we didn't really make an issue of it – because it was enough us being there. At times I feel a little bit, maybe guilty isn't the right description, but I feel at times we didn't do enough to try to stem the problem at an earlier stage rather than leave it until the start of the 1990s.[17]

Reviewing the position of football authorities *vis-à-vis* racism during the 1970s and 1980s from the standpoint of the late 1990s, the cultural shift is stark indeed. Whereas anti-racist agendas have become *de riguer* among most clubs and agencies – even if their commitment remains superficial in most cases – ten, fifteen or twenty years ago comfortable complacency – or even outright hostility – was the more usual position. One extreme example of the suspicion that those who ran football had for anti-racist activity is that in 1979 Orient football club threatened legal action against a local pressure group, Orient Against the Nazis, for appropriating the club's name.[18] Thomas (1995: 98) recalls that anti-racism within English football during the late 1970s and 1980s was largely instigated by grassroots fans organisation, who were often acting in the face of active opposition of the clubs themselves:

> The response of Leeds United and the police exemplified the attitude of English football at the time [1987]. The police claimed in advance that we were likely to 'introduce political violence at Elland Road', even though the NF had been there for over a decade! And the club threatened to sue us for using its logo, though merchandise vendors had been using it without permission for years.

Of course some of those in powerful positions in the game were relatively sympathetic to anti-racism; as noted elsewhere in this book, two high-profile managers of the late 1970s – Jack Charlton and Brian Clough – endorsed the Anti Nazi League. However, the support offered to black players was piecemeal in the extreme and often they were simply expected to 'show character' by putting up with the abuse they received. The fact that so many of them did exactly this and showed considerable personal courage, provides irrefutable contradiction to one of the racist stereotypes within the game – that black players lacked courage – the prevalence of which was a central feature of the game during the 1970s and 1980s. Two of the most successful black players of the 1990s, Ian Wright – who became Arsenal's highest goal scorer – and Les Ferdinand – transferred twice for £6 million in a matter of years in the mid-1990s – were both 'discovered' playing for non-league clubs having been turned away from professional clubs as schoolboys. Of course the reasons why neither player was picked up sooner are likely to be complex and there are no doubt a number of white players with a similar experience. The role of scouts and their apparent reluctance to consider youngsters playing in Asian clubs and leagues is discussed more fully in a later chapter, and it seems that similar racist stereotypes have also been applied to the detriment of black players. Ferdinand recalled that (White, 1997: 3):

> when I was a kid there was a definite reluctance to look at black kids. Those words I hate and despise: 'They've got a chip on their shoulder'. You'd hear that all the time. No one tried to understand or work with us; the moment there was a hint of anything, we got dismissed as having an attitude problem.

Although the experience of the 1980s did not rid racism from football, it did finally see black players established in the game in numbers. At the beginning of that decade a few clubs, most notably West Bromwich Albion but also Crystal Palace, had a reputation for including black players in numbers, not just one or two 'flair' footballers on the wing or up front. By the end of the decade, however, what stood out was the few top-flight teams who had no black members. Even traditionally 'white' sides, such as Liverpool or Glasgow Rangers had included black players by the end of the 1980s. The other great change during this period related to crowd behaviour and hooliganism, which – although distinct issues – impinge upon the extent of racist abuse and violence within and around stadia. It is discussed in a later chapter of this volume, that the problem of football hooliganism reached its highest point on the political agenda following a series of incidents in the mid-1980s that resulted in English clubs being banned from European competition and an ultimately unsuccessful plan to introduce compulsory identity cards for football fans, which would have made it extremely difficult for the 'casual' supporter to attend matches. In 1989 poor crowd control measures and stadium design led to the Hillsborough disaster in which 96 fans lost their lives. Perhaps one impact of such terrible events was to prepare the way for a change in the culture of the game, improved safety procedures and stadia redesign that have been among the factors that encouraged anti-racist initiatives to gain momentum

I.M. MARSH LIBRARY LIVERPOOL L17 6BD
TEL. 0151 231 5216/5299

into the 1990s. That, however, is a matter to be considered at greater length later in this volume.

Conclusion

An important theme that has emerged from this chapter has been the ambivalent status of black footballers during the 100 years or so that separated Arthur Wharton from the high-profile black stars of the 1980s. In some respects the story of the intervening period has been a progressive one as the number of black players involved in the game increased dramatically and relatively steadily throughout the twentieth century. A series of milestones have been recorded here: from the first black professional, to the first black international to appear for Wales, the first black manager, the first black footballer to appear in the FA Cup Final, the first black player to achieve a full England cap. A superficial reading might suggest that there has been an unfolding tale of success, against many odds perhaps, but success nonetheless. To a degree this is true, of course, and many of the biographical details referred to above reveal the tenacity with which black players have overcome the racism that they have faced. Indeed it is indicative of the contradictory and inconsistent nature of many racialised attitudes that the myth that black players 'lacked bottle' was widely prevalent during the 1970s and 1980s when a great number of them were demonstrating week-in and week-out a grim determination to succeed in the face of racist vilification.

Against the progressive interpretation of the history of black footballers must be set the continuing evidence of racism in football – on the terraces and in dressing rooms and directors' boxes. Comparison of the extent of racism within the game in the early years of the twentieth century with those towards the end would be unhelpful even if it were possible. It seems likely that racist chanting, which is only one form of racism in the game, is more likely to be reported by the media in the contemporary period than it was in the 1890s or 1910s. The salience of racism is perhaps greater now than it was then, but – as with hooliganism – the absence of reporting in earlier times certainly does not mean racism was not present (Dunning *et al.*, 1987). It cannot simply be assumed that the increasing number of black players has occasioned a rise in the extent of racism. As Small (1994) has argued, such associations suggest that black people themselves are the locus for racism, as though it is a relatively automatic response of white people to the presence of different races. In fact, as the discussion of football and national identity in the colonial era that was briefly included earlier in this chapter indicated, purported links between the British character and the proper ethos of football were formed in an era before black professionals played the game. The nicknames bestowed on many black footballers also reveal the contradictory, but ultimately negative, reaction they have often received. While Arthur Wharton and Walter Tull both enjoyed considerable respect on and beyond the football pitch the sobriquet 'Darkie' by which they were both known indicated that, whatever their achievements, they remained different and inferior. Their fame was not colour-blind, but colour-conscious – part of the novelty was that they were tremendous players *and* they were black. That the black players who found success with West Bromwich Albion in the late 1970s and 1980s were collectively known as the 'Three Degrees' is especially revealing, associating as it does the prowess of black sports stars with the success of black singers – two areas in which black people have been relatively successful without fundamentally challenging racist assumptions grounded in the supposed physicality and musical ability of black people, properties that are held to reveal cerebral weaknesses. These themes will be considered at greater length in the concluding chapter of this book.

3
Standing Together? Charting the Development of Football's Anti-Racism

Introduction

The development of anti-racist strategies has been a notable feature of British football in the last decade. These schemes varied in size and scope from national programmes funded to the tune of hundreds of thousands of pounds, through to localised projects run by a few motivated individuals. Many have originated from professional football clubs, sometimes in conjunction with several other agencies. The diversity of these initiatives means that, in some respects, it is problematic to group them all under an all-encompassing banner of 'anti-racist strategies'. Indeed, some of the smaller initiatives have adopted the tactics similar to many single-issue pressure groups and have little in common, or indeed little liaison with, more high-profile national campaigns. Several club-based schemes have adopted educational aspects whilst others are more concerned with prohibiting racism within stadia through the imposition of rules and regulations.

Nevertheless, it is suggested here that it is important to assess the commonalities and diversities within the broad spectrum of football's anti-racism, and that the most successful of the campaigns have been those that have understood the complexity and diversity of differing *racisms*. It is contested that a number of schemes have a more simplistic notions of racism that undermine the good intentions behind them. Two related tendencies, to identify racism solely in conjunction with hooliganism, or with the activities of the far-right, can be seen in the responses of some agencies, including the police and fans' groups. It is argued here that these two notions fail to address subtler and more frequent forms of racism that may emanate from spectators not usually associated with fascist or hooligan activity. This point is developed more fully in the chapter that follows.

The response of football clubs to the issue of racism is a key aspect to this chapter. The importance of a club to its local communities has often been stressed (see for example, North and Hodson, 1997; Lansdown and Spillius, 1990), and yet before the advent of 'football in the community' schemes in the 1980s most were unconcerned with attracting minority ethnic spectators who were not viewed as being part of football's 'traditional' public. Over a decade later many clubs still display this ambivalence, creating the type of situation like that witnessed on Saturday afternoons in South London:

> On one side of the road streams of predominantly white football fans flock to support their club. Across the street the multicultural diversity of the area is reflected as residents from New Cross, South Norwood and Charlton go about their daily business. It seems as if these people pass each other by whilst almost living in different worlds. (Back, 1998: 1)

A common response from clubs to issues of racism has been to deny its existence at their stadium, although admitting that it may be present elsewhere in football. These clubs may have lent their support to national anti-racist campaigns but, it is argued below, have demonstrated little real commitment to them. In some cases, this reluctance to act has been justified by claims that such campaigns may actually *cause* racism, revealing a lack of understanding of the complexity and diversity of the issue, and therefore an inability to address the problem effectively. It is contested here that many of the stereotypes about the lack of interest in football among Asian communities still predominate at some clubs, causing them to develop schemes targeted at other social groups, even when the club may be based in an area with a high Asian population. On the other hand, a handful of clubs have made a commendable effort to encourage their local Asian communities to participate in club-related activities, and have developed closer ties with these groups as a result.

It is argued in the conclusion to this chapter that while the more positive interventions mentioned above are commendable, a common weakness is a failure to appreciate the nature and dynamic of heterogeneous *racisms*. This concern reflects more general debates about the need to theorise the complexity and diversity of the concept of racism and to recognise its contradictory character. Writers such as Hall (1992), Small (1994) and Solomos and Back (1996) have stressed the importance of moving away from singular conceptions of racism, which seek to explain it as though it were a unitary coherent phenomenon, and towards an understanding which recognises the plurality of racisms. Such diversity is one important reason for preferring the term racialisation, which, it is argued in this chapter, provides a more relevant and effective conceptual framework against racism.

There are a number of other important features of the racialisation approach. For example, it places emphasis on the fact that 'racial' identity is not a pre-given fact but is a socially constructed phenomenon with no independent ontological validity (Miles, 1989). The idea that 'race' is an artificially produced concept – socially rather than biologically or genetically based – has a number of important consequences relevant to the study of anti-racism in contemporary football. One such consequence is the contestable and changing nature of ideas about 'race' which evolve over time and provide a discursive legacy that impacts on contemporary understanding. In the context of football, long-established notions of black physical prowess continue to be influential in popular explanations of black sporting success, even though genetic and biological approaches to 'race' have been widely discredited (Cashmore, 1982; Rex, 1970). Asian participation at professional level has suffered through commonly-held assumptions of physical weakness and lack of stature, views held by many within the game that have seemingly prevented a breakthrough of Asian footballers into the top level of the sport (Lyons, 1996; Singh, 1990).

The argument that ideas about 'race' are generated in a particular social milieu is important because it means that the coterminous existence of contradictory, inconsistent and multidirectional discourses can be understood. Although attempts to develop theoretical systematic racist ideologies continue, they are in general confined to a minority on the extreme right fringe. However, that relatively few people appear to subscribe to fully-fledged racist 'theories' does not mean that racism is a rare or exceptional phenomenon. The unsystematic and ad hoc nature of much popular racism does not mean that it is less significant or malignant than would otherwise be the case. Recognition that racism is usually an incoherent set of beliefs is central to the racialisation approach and enables mutually contradictory beliefs to be explained. A common puzzle to many in debates about racism in contemporary football is the tendency for spectators to racially abuse black players on opposing teams whilst remaining loyal and supportive towards black members of their own side. This kind of behaviour is difficult to explain using conventional explanations of racism which, despite their diversity, tend to regard individual actors as consistently racist within the broad parameters of the social situation in which they find themselves. The racialisation approach, however, is much better placed to deal with such inconsistencies and to recognise the opportunity for anti-racist intervention that they offer. It is argued elsewhere in this book that a common tendency has been to assume that racism within the game is the preserve of a hard-core of extreme right activists who are committed to a full-blown ideology of racism. A preferable conception, central to the racialisation approach, is to recognise that the problem of racism within the game is a great deal more subtle and complex than has often been assumed.

Anti-racist campaigns

The diverse nature of football's anti-racist interventions referred to above means that they cannot easily be individually defined as being solely a 'club scheme' or a 'fan scheme'. Some have originated from a single source (a club officer or a supporters' group) and others have sprung from parties outside the game, such as Youth Against Racism in Europe. A number have involved a combination of organisations and have drawn strength from employing such a 'partnership approach'. For the sake of clarity, we have attempted to define broad categories so that the various programmes can be analysed sequentially. The schemes will be grouped into three separate but overlapping sections: national and regional; club-based; and fan-based. It is acknowledged, however, that these definitions are loose, and that strong cases could be argued for certain initiatives to be put into different categories from the ones in which we have placed them. It is also recognised that this chapter does not have the scope to cover *every* football-based intervention with an anti-racist agenda, and will instead concentrate on those which the authors consider to be the most significant.

   Quantifying the success of anti-racist projects is problematic as it entails assessing a range of indicators, including variables such as the frequency of racist chanting, the number of incidents involving players, the involvement of minority ethnic groups in playing and spectating, the activities of far-right parties in and around football grounds, and a host of other factors. Despite these methodological difficulties, evaluations of many of these schemes have taken place (AGARI, 1996; Garland and Rowe, 1996; McArdle and Lewis, 1997) and this chapter will draw upon these and other surveys, such as the annual *Carling Premiership Fan Surveys* and the 1998 Football Task Force report that investigated racism in the game. Whilst conducting research for this book the authors also undertook many interviews with key personnel within the game, and these will be used to try to attain an overall picture of the strengths and weaknesses of the campaigns cited below.

National and regional schemes

Let's Kick Racism Out of Football

The first of the high-profile anti-racist measures in the 1990s was the 'Let's Kick Racism Out of Football' campaign (hereafter referred to as 'Let's Kick Racism'), launched at the beginning of the 1993/94 season. It was developed by the Campaigns Unit at the Commission for Racial Equality (CRE) which was concerned by the number of incidents of racial harassment and violence at the time, including racist chanting at football matches and what the CRE viewed as the mounting efforts of far-right parties to recruit young people, especially in the environs of football stadia on matchdays (AGARI, 1996). The Unit recognised the significance of the sport for young people, and identified a potential conduit for anti-racist schemes:

> The first campaign we did was a football campaign, *Let's Kick Racism Out of Football*, because we looked at the whole area of young people and how to get to them, what medium we could use which would hold a message against racism and for equal opportunity and would also speak very clearly and directly to all people.[19]

The Professional Footballers' Association (PFA) was also involved in setting up the scheme which received support during its first season (and subsequently) from the Football Trust. The campaign urged clubs to declare their opposition to racism in their matchday programme and over the public address system, to display posters and deploy the 'Let's Kick Racism' advertising hoarding around the pitch perimeter. These measures were the first part of a nine-point action plan aimed at all professional clubs, asking them to:

1 Issue a statement saying that the club will not tolerate racism, and spelling out the action it will take against supporters who are

caught in 'indecent or racialist' chanting. The statement should be printed in all match programmes, and displayed permanently and prominently around grounds.

2 Make public announcements condemning any racist chanting at matches, and warning supporters that the club will not hesitate to take action.

3 Make it a condition for season-ticket holders that they do not take part in racist chanting or any other offensive behaviour, such as throwing missiles onto the pitch.

4 Take action to prevent the sale or distribution of racist literature in and around the grounds on matchdays.

5 Take disciplinary action against players who shout racist abuse at players during matches.

6 Contact other clubs to ensure they understand the club's policy on racism.

7 Make sure that stewards and the police have a common strategy for removing or dealing with supporters who are breaking the law on football offences. If it is dangerous or unwise to take action against offenders during the match, they should be identified and barred from all further matches.

8 Remove all racist graffiti from the grounds as a matter of urgency.

9 Adopt an equal opportunities policy in the areas of employment and service provision (CRE Communications Team, 1994).

By the time of the launch, the campaign had the support of 40 clubs throughout the four professional leagues in England and Wales, and by January 1995, 91 clubs had subscribed to the scheme (AGARI, 1996). 'Let's Kick Racism' was launched in Scotland in January 1994,[20] initially gaining the support of over half of Scotland's clubs (Reading Council for Racial Equality, 1998). The following year 'Let's Kick Racism' was taken over by the Advisory Group Against Racism and Intimidation (AGARI, originally called the Anti-Racism and Intimidation Group (ARIG)), a steering group tasked with developing and broadening the scheme. AGARI, a multi-agency body consisting of all of the game's main official bodies, as well as supporters' groups and local authority representatives, adopted the campaign slogan 'Let's Kick Racism – Respect All Fans'. Initially, AGARI focused upon producing an 'action plan' in a number of areas, including developing models of good practice, working with young people on anti-racism awareness and evolving local partnerships to tackle racism (ARIG, 1995).

A key aspect of the AGARI project was the evaluation of the progress of 'Let's Kick Racism', undertaken by a team of academics based at Goldsmiths College, London, as part of the 'Alive and Still Kicking' report (AGARI, 1996). The evaluation identified several weaknesses in the methods employed by the campaign, including poor execution of some regional launches and a lack of material aimed at an older audience (the two campaign magazines, *Kick It!* (1994) and *Kick It Again!* (1995), had been aimed at schoolchildren). The team also called for more guidance for clubs on the deployment of resources and materials, and urged the campaign to challenge the commonly-held stereotype of racist fans being 'skinhead hooligans' that was prevalent amongst many of the game's officials. Similarly, it also recommended that the 'Let's Kick Racism – Respect All Fans' slogan be dropped, as it was important to 'separate the issue of fan racism from its broader association with other forms of anti-social behaviour' (AGARI, 1996: 63).

In 1997 the coordination of 'Let's Kick Racism' was taken over by a new organisation, *Kick It Out* (KIO), with an initial three-year programme involving all of the game's key agencies.[21] At its inception, KIO targeted the following issues; development work with professional clubs, particularly those in the lower leagues; addressing the marginalisation of Asians; development of grassroots initiatives; production of educational material; increasing the involvement of minority ethnic communities in their local clubs; highlighting racism in European football (Kick It Out, 1998).[22] These priorities are important as they reflect the criticisms made of the campaign in some quarters: namely, that it had been too focused on top professional clubs, and overreliant on more superficial methods, such as poster campaigns (McArdle and Lewis, 1997).

At the time of writing, KIO appears to be developing a comprehensive programme and coordinating strategy, and 'Let's Kick Racism' has been hailed as 'football's flagship anti-racist initiative' (Football Task Force, 1998: 12). The scheme, in its various incarnations, has undoubtedly been responsible for raising the awareness of the issue of racism amongst supporters; indeed, the results of two small-scale independent surveys of fans (undertaken by the Football Supporters' Association in 1995/96 and by the authors in 1995) revealed that *all of the respondents* to both surveys had heard of the campaign (AGARI, 1996; Carver *et al.*, 1995). The campaign has also had the effect of making clubs realise that they had a responsibility to tackle racism, including some, like Norwich City, who were initially sceptical about the campaign when it was launched, yet subsequently adopted a highly-publicised anti-racist policy, and have acted against racist fans for the first time.[23]

However, it appears as though the scheme has been unevenly developed by clubs, and a suspicion lingers that many have merely undertaken the bare minimum asked of them (Garland and Rowe, 1999). A token effort to support the campaign is, in many ways, the easiest option for clubs, for by doing this they will not be criticised for a lack of support for anti-racism, yet they will not have to invest a great deal of time or money in developing strategies of their own. It appears as though many clubs have taken this 'easy option', and as McArdle and Lewis (1997: 1) report, of those clubs that responded to their survey about the extent of their involvement in 'Let's Kick Racism', only 15 per cent had implemented the three basic parts of the campaign (anti-racist statements in programmes and over the public address system, and the installation of Let's Kick Racism perimeter fence hoardings), whilst 45 per cent had only implemented one of them.

The adoption of 'Let's Kick Racism' does not therefore offer any true indication of a club's genuine *commitment* to developing anti-racist agendas. In February 1997 Wolverhampton Wanderers, who signed up to 'Let's Kick Racism' at the beginning of the 1996/97 season, invited Bernard Manning, a comedian with a reputation for racist 'humour', to appear at one of its social functions. This booking caused protests from sections of the local community around the club's stadium and raised serious doubts about the culture of an organisation supposedly committed to banishing racism from the game. One of Wolverhampton's Labour MPs requested that the club cancel the engagement, and local protesters argued that the event contradicted the club's support for the 'Let's Kick Racism' campaign (*Wolverhampton Express and Star*, 1997). A local councillor described to the authors the impact that the event had on relations between the club and local minority ethnic communities:

> The community is aware that this person was booked and the club didn't do anything about it. Wolverhampton Wanderers said the event did not compromise their anti-racist work, they do not have double standards. If they had cancelled, then that would have sent out very positive messages. But instead the message sent out by the club was negative. In terms of the *Let's Kick Racism Out of Football* policy ... they haven't done anything really, or the only moves have been minimal.[24]

LIVERPOOL JOHN MOORES UNIVERSITY
LEARNING & INFORMATION SERVICES

This one example illustrates an important limitation of anti-racist strategies which rely upon action at the local level. Whilst such strategies allow a relevant response to particular manifestations of racism, there can also be problems if local conditions do not encourage effective anti-racist responses. The failure of Wolverhampton Wanderers to appreciate that engaging a comedian such as Bernard Manning would prove offensive to the communities in the club's vicinity suggests that their anti-racism is merely superficial – after all, few institutions in the public eye would actually refuse to be associated with an endorsement against racism.[25] That some clubs apparently have little genuine commitment to 'Let's Kick Racism' has caused some current black players to be wary of tokenistic approaches:

> I'm sick of these trendy campaigns that seem to come around once every season, are in the spotlight for five minutes and still nothing changes. One season I was criticised for not giving my full support to a campaign, but then a fortnight later Arsenal were playing Barnsley in the Coca-Cola Cup and Glenn Helder and I were booed from start to finish, not just by handful of Barnsley supporters, but virtually a whole stand ... But how on earth is a trendy campaign going to stop such ingrained hatred? I don't pretend to know the answer, but putting posters up and waving banners around isn't going to do the trick. (Wright, 1996: 11)

The scepticism of some senior club administrators about anti-racist interventions is documented below, and it needs to be recognised that these key decision-makers have an important impact on the extent of the implementation of anti-racist measures. As McArdle and Lewis (1997) conclude, if these 'influential individuals' feel that anti-racism is 'something they want to get involved in' then this may have more of a bearing on whether anti-racist schemes are developed at a club than any other factor.

Nevertheless, 'Let's Kick Racism' has provided the impetus for many of the localised campaigns discussed in this chapter, and has helped to facilitate and precipitate others not included here.[26] Since the time of its inception in 1993, an unprecedented number of anti-racist programmes have been undertaken with football as their focus, and, whilst not all have been inspired by or involved with 'Let's Kick Racism', the campaign can take some credit for helping to develop a conducive atmosphere for anti-racism. As a campaign coordinator for the CRE commented to the authors:

[The campaign's] ... got a lot of people thinking about it, lots of media publicity and most heartening is the fact that there are about ten clubs who are making a tremendous effort which you would have been astounded at five or ten years ago.[27]

Regional schemes

One of the successes of 'Lets Kick Racism' has been its ability to act as a catalyst for other anti-racist work, and several significant regional initiatives have developed in its wake. Unfortunately there is neither the scope nor space to examine them all here, and it is a source of regret that not all can get the analysis they deserve. Instead, this section will focus on five projects that have employed a variety of methods to combat racism within their localities. These are: 'Football Unites, Racism Divides' and 'Streetwise' based in Sheffield; the 'Leicester Asian Sports Initiative'; 'Show Racism the Red Card' from the North East of England, and the Hounslow-based 'Equality Through Sport' project.

In 1996, 'Football Unites Racism Divides' (FURD) was launched with the twin aims of addressing concerns over incidents of racist abuse in the area around Bramall Lane (home of Sheffield United Football Club) and of encouraging greater participation by black and Asian young people in Sheffield United, as supporters, players and employees (AGARI, 1996). FURD, managed by the Sheffield Youth Service but run in conjunction with a host of other agencies (including South Yorkshire Police, fan and community groups, Sheffield United FC, and the local Race Equality Council) is described by the Football Task Force as being 'one of the most successful partnership initiatives' (Football Task Force, 1998: 42). The scheme has commissioned a research project into the experiences of Sheffield United fans and local residents (Pinto, Drew and Minhas, 1997); targeted coaching courses at minority ethnic young people; highlighted the career of the first black professional, Arthur Wharton – discussed in Chapter 2 – and helped to fund a memorial in his name; campaigned against racism in the Bramall Lane stadium; developed educational resource packs and provided opportunities for minority ethnic coaches to obtain FA coaching awards. In the autumn of 1997 a supporters' section of FURD was formed, so that fans could actively participate in developing the initiative.

The comprehensive partnership approach adopted by FURD and its focus on local issues has been helped by support from the club and fanzine *Flashing Blade*. The experience of the local authorities involved in working with Leyton Orient, for example (see below), demonstrates that fans respond better to 'outside agency' initiatives in football if they receive 'legitimation' through club endorsement. In the case of FURD, the combination of a partnership approach and support from fan organisations and the football club has undoubtedly been pivotal to its growth. One of the measures of the success of FURD is that, according to the Football Task Force, some home matches in the 1997/98 season produced 'the highest attendance of black supporters at Bramall Lane' (Football Task Force, 1998: 42), an indication that the project has achieved something tangible on matchdays. In a wider context, FURD has been involved in the co-ordination and initiation of Football Against Racism in Europe, launched in 1999 and involving over 40 anti-racist organisations from 13 European countries.

Another Sheffield-based project, the 'Streetwise Junior Football Coaching Scheme', was set-up in 1996 on the initiative of Sheffield City Council with the backing of several partners, including both local professional clubs, schools, sports centres, the local FA and South Yorkshire Police. Its aim was to develop a programme of football coaching for 8–16-year-olds in areas with a high percentage of minority ethnic groups and to identify and nurture any talented players unearthed through these schemes (Reading Council for Racial Equality, 1998). Within two years of its inception, 13 minority ethnic players from 'Streetwise' had gone on to have trials at professional clubs, and the project had developed two teams 'from players whose previous experience of racist abuse had prevented them joining local leagues' (Football Task Force, 1998: 24).

A similar scheme has been developed by the 'Leicester Asian Sports Initiative' managed by Leicester City Council in conjunction with the community office at Leicester City. The programme aims to increase the opportunities available to young Asian football players by providing coaching by qualified personnel, and by offering the chance to progress in local league football. The best players are referred to the Leicester City school of excellence. At the time of writing, around 200 8–17-year-olds attend the weekly coaching sessions, and according to the Football Task Force (1998), young Asian players are beginning to break into the youth team at Leicester City.

This 'direct link' from the Asian community to a professional club's school of excellence has also been developed by Guru Nanak Football Club, Gravesend (GNG) and Charlton Athletic. The link, aided by

Charlton through funding and coaching, aims to cultivate the talent at GNG, one of the oldest Asian football clubs in the country (formed in 1965) that boasts over 100 players and six teams (Kick It Out, 1998). The growth of the 'Show Racism the Red Card' project demonstrates that a regional anti-racist programme can become national and even international in scope. Initially based in the North East of England, 'Show Racism the Red Card' gained a national profile after the success of its two football-based anti-racist videos aimed at schoolchildren. The initiative, jointly developed by Youth Against Racism in Europe (YRE), the Independent Newcastle United Supporters' Association and the local race equality councils, evolved after YRE's anti-racist work in the north-east received the backing of local footballers. The project produced a video in 1996, featuring players discussing racism and football, and was accompanied by an educational resource pack, so that the video could be complimented by relevant classroom activity. The video was followed by a glossy magazine later that year. With the help of £20 000 funding from the European Union, a second video was produced in 1997 with a European focus, featuring over 50 footballers from 15 different countries. It was produced in four European languages, and proved so successful that it has been launched at football venues across Europe and has worldwide sales (Show Racism the Red Card, 1998).

The strength of the second video lies in its ability to capture the interest of young people in issues of racism by featuring famous footballers discussing the subject. Although the first video was criticised for focusing too strongly on the role of far-right groups in football (AGARI, 1996), both it and its successor have proved to be a success in engaging school children in debate about the effects of racism within football and in wider society. At the time of writing, a number of clubs, including Leicester City, West Ham United and Bradford City had bought hundreds of copies of the video each for distribution to local schools.

The Hounslow-based 'Equality Through Sport' programme also adopted an educational approach involving a number of agencies, including the London Boroughs of Hounslow and Ealing, Brentford Football Club and local industry, with the broad aim of developing curriculum materials relevant to sport. These materials, produced by local teachers, include a video about the project, as well as careers advice and GNVQ-level assignments.

Hounslow Council was also one of the first local authorities to utilise its position as owners of a large number of football pitches to

I.M. MARSH LIBRARY LIVERPOOL L17 6BD
TEL. 0151 231 5216/5299

promote anti-racism at a grassroots level (Football Task Force, 1998). The Council produced a poster for display in all local authority-owned dressing rooms that stated:

• We are concerned at the level of racism in sport.
• We believe that all the sports people in the Borough should be able to play and enjoy their sport in an environment free from the threat of intimidation, harassment and abuse.
• We believe that all sports groups should oppose racism and promote equality of opportunity.
• We want to play our sport in a borough where all communities are valued and respected (Hounslow Council, 1997: 58).

All local leagues and clubs were asked to sign up to this charter, and the Council amended its letting agreement with these clubs so that any complaints of racist behaviour reported to them by the local football association could result in the withdrawal of pitch facilities, and would also affect local authority and National Lottery grant applications. This model of compliance has been adopted by other local authorities, and the Football Task Force (1998: 20) recommended that it became 'standard practice in every local authority in England'.

As detailed in Chapter 1, racism at football's grassroots level is widespread, and local authority compliance conditions on football pitches could become an important part of anti-racist interventions at this level. The key to the efficacy of such compliance models may well depend on how efficiently they are managed. The local football association will need to play an active role in their implementation, something which, judging by the actions of some county FAs when tackling racism (discussed elsewhere in this volume), may be unlikely to occur.

An interesting feature of the regional schemes discussed above is the involvement of professional clubs. A key facet in the development of football-based anti-racism in the 1990s was the evolution of partnership projects involving clubs, local authorities and other agencies, and it is to an analysis of these that this chapter now turns.

Club-based schemes

The commitment of football clubs to genuine anti-racism has been widely questioned (Garland and Rowe, 1996; Horne, 1996; McArdle and Lewis, 1997) and their response to 'Let's Kick Racism' has, as discussed above, often been lukewarm. However, it is equally important to acknowledge the clubs who have developed extensive programmes, adopting partnership approaches and in some cases used educational tools as the main thrust of the schemes. The South London Initiative is an example of a multi-agency, multi-club initiative that has a long-term strategy for challenging racism and exclusion. Other clubs have developed educational packs for school children (Exeter City and West Bromwich Albion, among others) and even commissioned anti-racist plays for schools (Leyton Orient).

Some clubs have developed a close relationship with their local authorities, a relationship that may have come out of necessity (for example, Leeds United, who sold their stadium to the local authority in 1986 to ease crippling debts (Horne, 1996)) or out of an understanding that limited resources could be made to work better if pooled together (in the case of Leyton Orient, below). Whatever the reasons, some of the most significant anti-racist strategies evolved by clubs have utilised local authority support and expertise to generate long-term programmes of action. In the case of Northampton Town, the scheme is an example of a partnership approach that has, as a major theme, the development of a viable equal opportunities policy.

Equal opportunities at Northampton Town

The development of an anti-racist programme at Northampton Town was given initial impetus by the 'day of action' at the club that was part of the 'Let's Kick Racism' campaign in February 1996. A member of the board of directors (unusually in the footballing context, elected by fellow supporters) decided that the club needed an equal-opportunities policy as a way of demonstrating a long-term commitment to anti-racism.[28] The policy was formally adopted in October 1996, and was the first such policy at a professional club in England (Brown, 1997).

The club also instigated an anti-racism working committee consisting of representatives from the club itself, Northampton Borough Council, 'Kick It Out', the private company who manage the stadium, academics, community groups and the local police. Included amongst the strategies developed are a club policy statement against racism; the donation of tickets for first team matches for community groups; the distribution of thousands of anti-racist leaflets at home matches; and the provision of football coaching courses for minority groups.

The catalyst for one of the more unusual strands of this anti-racist work was a Northampton Town fan, Sean O'Donovan, who wanted to commemorate a prominent ex-'Cobbler',[29] Walter Tull (*Guardian*, 1998). As mentioned in Chapter 2, Tull, who played for the side from 1911–14, was one of the first prominent black professional footballers, and gained a degree of fame for both Northampton and Tottenham Hotspur. After the outbreak of the First World War, Tull served in the British Army and became its first black officer. He was killed on the Somme just a few months before the end of the war, and has no known grave.[30] The idea of commemorating Tull was backed by the working party and the club, and has taken the form of a garden of remembrance at the club's stadium in which the Tull memorial has prominence.[31] This gesture is important because it pays tribute to the contribution of black footballers to the sport in Britain, a contribution that, like other achievements by minority ethnic groups, has often been ignored or marginalised. The memorial is a reminder of the significant presence of black players throughout the twentieth century. It has also provided a pivotal point around which other initiatives at Northampton have been concentrated.

The measures taken at Northampton Town provide neat illustration of the more concrete steps clubs can take in order to reinforce public statements and declarations against racism. The establishment of an equal-opportunities policy reflects an approach to anti-racism often associated with local government and the public sector in general, and it may be that the close association between the football club and Northampton Borough Council (who own the stadium the club uses) has been an important factor behind the progressive work undertaken in this case. Certainly one Director of the club was keen to place their anti-racist work in the broader context of developing links with the entire community:

> The stadium for example, is the only stadium to have purpose built disabled facilities on all four sides of the grounds, so that disabled people have the choice of exactly where they want to sit. We have got a Supporters' Trust which raises money for disabled supporters, and we now have radio sets to assist the partially sighted with match commentary in the ground. They are portable and can be used anywhere within the ground. So they are all to me aspects of the same thing. It is all about being sensitive to the whole community and try to bring the whole community together.[32]

Although the 'municipal anti-racism' reflected in the developments at Northampton Town has itself been criticised in other contexts on the grounds that it offers only formal equality that may not be realised in practice (Ball and Solomos, 1990), there are reasons to welcome such developments within the context of contemporary British football. First, an equal-opportunities policy establishes the club's stance against racism on a firmer footing than at other clubs where public statements against racism are made but little action is subsequently taken. A further reason to welcome the establishment of such a policy is that it allows the anti-racist rhetoric directed at players, officials and spectators to be broadened and applied to other staff at the club as well. Whilst an equal-opportunities policy is not an end in itself, it does offer some scope for more effective anti-racism which extends beyond superficial publicity campaigns.

Similarly, the adoption of an equal-opportunities policy may help to promote understanding of issues of racism and anti-racism throughout the whole football club, rather than being seen as being the remit of the community office only. Watson (1997) describes the manner in which all telephone enquiries about football and racism were 'instinctively' directed to the community office at Leyton Orient by the club's switchboard operators. For Watson, all staff should have a grasp of these issues and be able to talk about them, not just those located in one office. The community office should not be seen as the club's 'conscience', nor should it be a 'get-out clause' through which a club can claim to be anti-racist when, in fact, little acknowledgment of the issue has spread throughout the rest of the institution.

This example is an illustration of the need to develop a thorough 'club culture' of anti-racism, something especially pertinent in the wake of the publication of the Macpherson Report that detailed the findings of the inquiry into the murder of black teenager Stephen Lawrence. Macpherson highlighted the issue of institutional racism within organisations, and defined it as:

> The collective failure of an organisation to provide an appropriate and professional service to people because of their colour, culture, or ethnic origin. It can be seen or detected in processes, attitudes and behaviour which amount to discrimination through unwitting prejudice, ignorance, thoughtlessness and racist stereotyping which disadvantage minority ethnic people. (Macpherson, 1999: 28)

This broader definition is helpful because it acknowledges the significance of *unwitting* prejudice and therefore moves away from equating institutional racism simply with deliberate acts by individuals who hold racist views. The absence of racist ideology therefore does not preclude an organisation from having procedures or policies that are discriminatory towards minority ethnic groups, a particularly useful notion to utilise when analysing the cultures and practices of football clubs. While undertaking research for this book the authors encountered senior club administrators who were clearly uncomfortable when discussing issues involving black and Asian communities. Officials able to talk fluently and convincingly on many issues relating to the game often become hesitant and uncertain when conversation moved on to racism or anti-racism. This wider tendency was unwittingly revealed by a former Premier League manager, who stated of his involvement with his local community:[33]

> We go to the garage where we get our petrol and they are Indian. You converse with them, you speak to them and you go down to the cornershop and it will most certainly be run by a coloured chap. So, the area we work in, daily, involves contact with other nationalities.

The discomfort felt when with dealing with 'coloured chaps' permeates other levels of many football clubs. The managing director of one Premiership club continually referred to his club's local minority ethnic communities as being from 'overseas', or being 'non-Londoners' or 'non-British' while being interviewed by the authors. Watson (1997) describes how a senior club official at Leyton Orient admonished a season-ticket holder who was shouting racist abuse by instructing him that if he wanted to use such language, he should do so from behind the goals and not from the season ticket area!

Even more perturbing were the views of the secretary of a Premier League club from a city with a large Asian population, who described to the authors how he thought his local Asian communities could become more involved in the sport:[34]

> I mean why are there no Asian footballers? Well first they have got to try and conform to our way of life, in my opinion. I mean they have religious things that hold them back, fasting and things like. Physically they are not as strong as English or white people are they?

There is some evidence that clubs have been reluctant signatories to anti-racist campaigns, displaying a lack of understanding of the dynamics of racism and the reasons for campaigning against it. Research for this book uncovered a suggestion amongst some administrators that anti-racist initiatives may actually prove counterproductive and attract greater levels of racism to an environment where the problem is relatively rare. This was illustrated by the secretary of a Premier League club, who commented to the authors:

> One of the things that worries me about them [anti-racism campaigns] is that if you are not careful you can cause a problem that wasn't always there ... if you start talking and banging on about racism, which we don't suffer from, we may then find that we've actually caused the problem.[35]

Just as the link between racism and the presence of black players exemplified wider perceptions about the origins of racism, this criticism of anti-racism also reflects broader debates. Several authors have suggested that the identification of anti-racists as the source of racism was a common feature of New Right politics in Britain during the 1970s and 1980s, especially amongst sections of the media (Searle 1989; Murray 1989). Gordon and Rosenberg (1989: 51) suggest that media assaults on anti-racism were part of a more fundamental political project, and argue that 'what such papers do is to deny, against all the evidence, that racism and systematic racial discrimination exist in Britain. Indeed, for much of the press, racism is a creation of the anti-racists who have manufactured the problem'.

The above examples demonstrate the dangers of pigeonholing the community office as being the only department that need understand 'race' issues, and are an illustration of how the good work of the community office can be undone by attitudes and actions in other sections of the club. The approach of Northampton Town, by developing and utilising an anti-racism group that involves workers from different offices within the club, is an example of how such problems can be tackled. Directors and administrators, as well as the community officer, are all involved in the anti-racism working party, and all have an input in developing the clubs anti-racism policy statement.

'We All Stand Together': educational anti-racism at West Bromwich Albion

A common theme of anti-racist schemes within the game has been the development of football-based educational projects, and prominent amongst these is the West Bromwich Albion 'We All Stand Together' initiative. The scheme follows on from previous work that the community office at the club had undertaken, including the 'Learning Through Football' package developed in 1997. 'Learning Through Football' is aimed at primary schools, and involves children visiting the club for a day and taking part in, amongst other activities, academic exercises with football as its central theme. Linked to this scheme are the various football coaching courses aimed at local children, and minority ethnic groups in particular.

The community officers spotted the potential of such a scheme and began to develop 'We All Stand Together', a larger programme aimed at older children in years 7, 8 and 9 of secondary school. The idea behind the project was to get the active participation in the football club of children from all minority ethnic groups, as the club itself was based in a multi-ethnic area yet these groups were conspicuous by their absence on matchdays. The project coordinator instigated a multi-agency working group, including local authority representatives and educational specialists, to develop the initiative. The aim of the programme is to construct an educational pack consisting of three main subjects – English, Maths and Science – that would be developed by a number of teachers from local education authorities and would therefore be consistent with the National Curriculum. The packs will be produced in several different languages and, funding permitting, will be available to all schools nationwide.

One of the many interesting things about this scheme is that those behind it realise that in order for the educational packs to be truly effective then the club itself must be seen to be doing something about racism within the stadium. Too often, as the authors have outlined elsewhere (Garland and Rowe, 1996), racist behaviour is ignored by those responsible for policing the game. To this end, a 'stewards' guide' is being developed that will offer stewards practical advice and procedures on how to deal with racism. Another working group, made up of representatives from the local communities, has also been set up to provide the club with feedback on the experiences that such groups have at home matches, which may provide a way for the club to evaluate the success of its projects.

Kicking Out in London's East End: the example of Leyton Orient

One of the most innovative and original 'football in the community' schemes has been the one developed over a number of years at Leyton Orient, a lower-league club situated in a multicultural area of East London. The programme itself began in 1991, and consisted of the local authority, Waltham Forest, employing an officer to develop stronger ties between the club and its local population. The scheme offered a large number of coaching courses and training sessions in a variety of sports, often at little or no cost to the participant, designed to involve sections of the community, such as women, people with disabilities and the elderly, that were not involved in activities related to the football club. By doing this, the programme not only enabled the club to become more integrated with its local communities, but also meant that the local authorities had much of their remit undertaken at a relatively cheap cost, as a council officer stated:

> [it] was enabling youngsters, girls, people with disabilities to get involved in a whole range of things [the community officer] started to develop and take further with the club. [The community officer] also, in a sense, educated the club along those lines. So, not only were the community getting involved outside the club, but within the club they were starting to provide facilities for people with disabilities, and family groups and so on. The Council, for a limited contribution, was getting all of this done.[36]

In 1995/6, the club's community officer decided to utilise the impetus generated by the national 'Let's Kick Racism' campaign in a local context, and felt that an anti-racist play may be the best way of communicating the sentiments of the scheme to school children. A theatre company, the Arc Theatre Ensemble, was commissioned to produce the play, *Kicking Out*, which went on to be performed 581 times and was seen by over 110 000 13–16-year-olds (Arc Theatre Ensemble, 1996). It told the story of a multi-ethnic five-a-side teenage team trained by a racist coach, and explored issues such as racist stereotyping and exclusion. Despite the coach being characterised as a 'violent skinhead', thus conforming to the stereotype all too prevalent in football alluded to elsewhere in this chapter, the play had a 'direct and engaging power' (AGARI, 1996: 30) that produced 'a kind of multicultural and anti-racist euphoria amongst young audiences' (*ibid.*: 31). The play was accompanied by an educational resource pack, and its success spawned a sequel, *Ooh Ah Showab Khan*, produced by the same team, that concentrated on the discrimination faced by Asian players within football. *Ooh Ah Showab Khan* also utilised educational material, with themes including racism experienced by Asian communities in Britain, racism in the police, and the 1960s Montgomery bus boycott in the United States.

The community scheme at Leyton Orient, instrumental in the evolution of *Kicking Out*, became a not-for-profit limited company in 1997 (Watson, 1997). It developed into a wider, community sports programme, seeking funding from private and public bodies. Although the achievements of the scheme over the last decade have been recognised by a number of awards, funding and resource problems faced by community offices at small clubs can affect what can be achieved, as the Leyton Orient community officer admitted:

> If you are at Tottenham and your crowds go down by 5000, then you just go and spend £3 million on a player and the 5000 will come back again. I'm sure that Klinsmann's transfer to Tottenham in the summer [of 1994] put more people on the gate than the best community scheme in the world.[37]

The financial difficulties besetting a small club like Leyton Orient necessitate an imaginative approach to fundraising from the community officers. Part of this approach saw the scheme gain some autonomy from the club by becoming a not-for-profit community sports programme. At larger clubs, where money is less of a problem, there *should* be more scope for developing community-based initiatives as these clubs generally have a higher profile within their local communities. However, although larger clubs have, in recent times, woken up to the potential of community work, extensive positive interventions amongst them are relatively rare. The example of Glasgow Celtic demonstrates how a large football institution can play a more proactive role within its locality.

Bhoys will be bhoys? Anti-sectarianism at Celtic

The importance of Celtic as a football club and as an institution to certain communities, and especially the Irish Catholic population of Glasgow, has been well documented (see, for example, Murray, 1988, 1998). When the club itself was formed in the 1880s one of its founding aims was to further the integration of the new Irish immigrant population into the largely Protestant community of the East End of Glasgow (Celtic FC, 1996a). With this history in mind, in 1996 Celtic launched 'Bhoys Against Bigotry', a programme designed to emphasise the positive role the club could play within its locality and also to challenge racism and sectarianism within football. The scheme included a Mission Statement that emphasised the club's wish to follow its founding principles of social integration and charitable work, whilst the 'Social Charter' emphasised inclusiveness and an opposition to racism and sectarianism in any form (Celtic FC, 1996b). Accompanying these edicts were more concrete actions to challenge racism and sectarianism. The club funded a number of projects, including several aimed at developing the integration of the nationalist and loyalist communities in Northern Ireland, and others with the local Asian community. In conjunction with Glasgow City Council the club produced a 'Working Against Bigotry' education pack for the city's primary and secondary schools. However, a proposal to discourage the singing of 'The Boys of the Old Brigade'[38] at home games caused a great deal of debate and disquiet amongst fans (Leadbetter, 1996), and perhaps reflected the fact that the club had a lot of work to do in order to tackle sectarian sentiments amongst a segment of its fan base.

Into the Valley: developing a partnership approach at Charlton Athletic

The initiative at Charlton Athletic demonstrates that many of the difficulties of developing a detailed anti-racist programme within the context of a football club can be overcome if the club itself is genuinely committed to promoting anti-racism. In 1992 the 'Red, White and Black at the Valley' scheme was launched by the Charlton Athletic Race Equality partnership (CARE), a multi-agency group consisting of representatives from the club, supporters' organisations, local authorities and race equality councils, the police, academics and community organisations. The principal aim of CARE was:

> to ensure that all people of whatever race, male or female, able-bodied or those with disabilities can be confident of a safe and welcoming environment at the Valley. (CARE, 1996: 1)

The CARE initiative involved the production of anti-racist leaflets, posters and programme messages, as well as tannoy announcements, the distribution of free matchday tickets to local groups, a variety of schemes from the club's community office and visits by players to schools and associations. A number of anti-racism days have also been hosted on matchdays. Since its inception, the scheme has managed to attract over £500 000 of local authority funding, enabling it to employ seven full-time workers. CARE also undertook a survey of over 1300 local school pupils in 1996, in order to gauge, amongst other things, if fear of racist abuse was deterring these children from attending home matches.

The commitment shown by the club is such that the scheme has enjoyed a high-profile throughout the organisation over a number of years. CARE also included diverse groups such as Victim Support Greenwich, Woolwich College and the Participatory Theatre (Patel, 1997), and this detailed, partnership approach appears to have paid dividends as the club had, by 1996, attained its 'best ever racial mix among its supporters' (CARE, 1996: 1) and was credited with attracting one-fifth of its home crowds from minority ethnic communities at some home games (Varley, 1997).

In mid-1997 Charlton entered the South London Partnership Against Racism, along with fellow South London clubs Crystal Palace and Millwall,[39] and a host of other agencies.[40] The aim of the Partnership is to make '. . . local football truly multi-cultural and representative of the diversity of ethnic groups that live in South London', both at professional and grassroots level (Back, 1998: 1). The scheme has a number of related activities, including a coaching programme targeted at inner-city areas that helps potential coaches gain recognised qualifications in their field. The 'Level Playing Fields' project is an anti-racist code of practice for all leisure facilities in each of the four London boroughs within the area, and is similar to the Hounslow model outlined above. Named the Sports Charter on Racial Equality (SCORE), the scheme has been developed by Greenwich Council in order to reward local teams for good practice, and punish those that have been found guilty of racism. Referees, leisure-centre staff and local team managers have been especially encouraged to report any incidents. If teams are proactive in ensuring that local minority ethnic groups are represented in their side, and constitute 10 per cent or more of the players, then the team is rewarded by the council.

At the time of writing, it is too early to see the benefits of the many projects undertaken by the South London Partnership. Nevertheless, its comprehensive multi-agency approach, coupled with the range and depth of its schemes, will almost certainly play an important role in tackling racism in South London. The involvement of supporters' organisations is, of course, a key component in the initiative, and reflects the part that fans have played in developing anti-racism within the footballing context. This chapter will now seek to examine the various measures and interventions undertaken by supporters in the last two decades.

Loyal supporters: fans and anti-racism

Part of the evolution of football's anti-racism has been the development of projects devised by supporters. There have been a number of such campaigns over the last 20 years, although the majority have occurred within the last decade. They have, on the whole, originated from fans with no broader political agenda, rather than being the products of established left-wing or anti-racist groups who may have seen football as a useful arena in which to become involved. One of the most high-profile and successful of these fan groups has been 'Leeds Fans United Against Racism and Fascism', which existed for nearly 10 years and, it is argued below, had a significant impact on the atmosphere at Leeds United's Elland Road stadium. This campaign inspired several others, including 'Foxes Against Racism' at Leicester City and 'Newcastle United Against Racism'. These groups, although following the lead set by 'Leeds Fans', also devised their own methods of combating racism based upon their own local contexts.

A number of other fans' groups have appeared across the country[41] and some enjoyed limited successes, but, as will be discussed below, also had failings caused by a narrow focus on a certain 'type' of racist – namely the skinhead thug stereotype, seen as being epitomised by members of far-right racist organisations. By creating a 'fan folk-demon' (Back and Crabbe, 1997), these fans identified a visible target for their actions and, in some cases, where far-right activists were evident on matchdays, this proved a successful idea. However, this sometimes meant that the more banal, individualistic forms of racism exhibited by 'ordinary' fans went unacknowledged, and indeed were rarely mentioned in some fanzine articles. All too often, the focus was on the far-right, with physical confrontation seen as the way to combat such groups. Whilst the efficacy of these tactics is debatable, they also reflect the 'macho' culture of football which alienates many fans from the game (Williams and Woodhouse, 1991). It is argued in the conclusion to this chapter that fans' groups need to develop a more sophisticated understanding of racism, necessitating a change in their campaigning agenda, if they are to be truly effective in reducing or eliminating racism within their locality.

The history of fan involvement in combating racism can be traced back to at least the late 1970s, when 'Football Fans Against the Nazis' became established at clubs across the country. These fans' groups were instigated by the Anti Nazi League (ANL), at the time also involved in the 'Rock Against Racism' campaign supported by many contemporary pop and rock bands. They were designed to challenge the presence of far-right extremist organisations at football grounds, who had an established presence at the time (Williams, 1992; Eimer, 1994), and by 1979, had established themselves at twenty stadia around the country (Sir Norman Chester Centre, 1997). However, these groups experienced a degree of mistrust and hostility from supporters, who viewed them as political 'outsiders' with little real grasp of the issues affecting the game. This hostility also was exhibited by some clubs, and, as mentioned in an earlier chapter, one, Orient, demanded substantial damages from 'Orient Against the Nazis' who, the club argued, were misusing the club's name (*Guardian,* 1979). Orient banned the organisation from the ground and demanded that all its badges and leaflets be destroyed. Such campaigning groups therefore struggled to establish a long-lasting foothold, and quickly faded from this environment. Almost a decade passed before another local-based fan group was seen in any real substance, at Leeds United, a club experiencing serious problems with racist incidents at the time.

Marching Altogether: Leeds Fans United Against Racism and Fascism

Probably the largest anti-racist supporters' organisation was 'Leeds Fans United Against Racism and Fascism' (henceforth denoted as 'Leeds Fans') that was established in 1987 by Leeds United supporters sickened by fascist parties selling papers outside the club's stadium on matchdays. A number of these anti-racist fans had been involved in the local Leeds Anti-Fascist Action (LAFA) group, itself founded a year before in response to an increase in the number of racist attacks in West Yorkshire and the growth of local extreme-right parties (Leeds Trades Union Council and Leeds Anti-Fascist Action, 1987).

The first football-related action undertaken by LAFA was the leafleting of Elland Road in October 1986. This initial work produced a degree of suspicion from the local police, who accused them of being likely to introduce 'a level of political violence' to the stadium, whilst the club itself threatened to sue the group for use of its badge (Thomas, 1993). The club was nevertheless concerned enough to ask LAFA to produce evidence of racist and fascist activity at the stadium, and consequently the group published *Terror on Our Terraces*, a report detailing the involvement of the local National Front and British National Party amongst the fans at Leeds United. The report made a number of recommendations to combat racism, including that the
ıb make, and display, a series of anti-racist messages in the

programme and on the scoreboard and advertising hoardings. The report also stated that the club should go out into the community to promote anti-racism. At the same time as the report was published, the Leeds United management and players issued an anti-racist statement, a significant step at the time for the club to take.

As 'Leeds Fans' developed, it decided that it needed to produce material that would appeal to 'ordinary' fans, and subsequently distributed *Marching Altogether*, a free Leeds fanzine featuring a mixture of irreverent articles and cartoons about the team, and the occasional item on racism, and in particular, fascism. Indeed, the fanzine often appeared to link racism solely with the activities of the far-right, and frequently carried cartoons depicting violence against nazis (see, for example, issue 13, 'Eric Le Hooligan de Football', pp. 2–3, and issue 18, '101 Things To Do With a Nazi Skin – Practice Your Heading: Nut the Bastard', p. 7). Whilst these illustrations were obviously lighthearted, they were carrying an important message that was reflected elsewhere in the publication.

Of course, the worth of campaigning against far-right groups is not being disputed here: merely the fact that the fanzine appeared to be falling into the trap of seeing racism as coming from a small section of the crowd, namely the identifiable fascist element. The racism itself, however, appeared to be spread amongst all sections of the crowd (Leeds Trades Union Council and Leeds Anti-Fascist Action, 1987), a fact infrequently acknowledged by *Marching Altogether*. This may be due to a number of factors, including, perhaps, that *Leeds Fans* originated from an Anti-Fascist Action group,[42] which was part of a loose national coalition that emphasises physical confrontation of fascists (see Anti-Fascist Action, 1994), and it appears that some of this strategy was included in *Marching Altogether*. It nevertheless should be acknowledged that by focusing its campaign against fascists, 'Leeds Fans' was specifically combating a known presence of such groups on matchdays, and was therefore justified in concentrating its efforts on tackling this 'fan folk demon'.

In any case, *Marching Altogether* and 'Leeds Fans' gained genuine 'credibility' amongst supporters (Thomas, 1995), and within a couple of years the presence of extremist groups had significantly diminished at Elland Road (Carver *et al.*, 1995). The campaign sustained itself for a number of years as racist abuse and intimidation decreased (AGARI, 1996), and by the early 1990s black Arsenal striker Ian Wright was moved to say:

We went to Leeds the other week – it was brilliant! They've got a thing down there petitioning the nazis and the racial abuse black players take. I think it's a giant step because Leeds were really bad ... it's changed a lot. (Bishop *et al.*, 1994: 11)

The winding down of 'Leeds Fans ...' in the mid-1990s coincided with birth of the national 'Let's Kick Racism' campaign and other anti-racist programmes, and it was hoped that the progress made by 'Leeds Fans ...' could be sustained at Elland Road. Unfortunately, two incidents of mass racist chanting involving Leeds fans, coincidentally against Leicester City in the home and away fixtures of the 1997/98 season (Pryke, 1998), suggested that much work still needs to be done there. It could be that, following the cessation of 'Leeds Fans', the lack of a supporter presence to challenge racist behaviour has caused certain people to think that they can get away with racist abuse. Or, it may be an indication that the club has not been fully committed to tackling the problem in the past, meaning that supporters do not feel that they will be punished if they exhibit racist behaviour within the ground. Either way, racism still appears to be a problem amongst part of Leeds United's following.

The early success of 'Leeds Fans ...' inspired a number of fan initiatives across the country, one of the most significant of which was 'Foxes Against Racism' (FAR) at Leicester City. Although only a small group, FAR gained a degree of local media attention after leafleting spectators at a home game in 1992. The principal aims of the group were to challenge racism within the ground, and to help to create an matchday atmosphere with which the city's large minority ethnic population would feel more comfortable. The group, in a similar vein to 'Leeds Fans ...', produced its own fanzine, *Filbo Fever!*,[43] and appeared to be a factor in spurring the club to produce its own anti-racist statement at the beginning of the 1993/94 season. Part of this statement read:

If you are discriminating against someone, or abusing them because of their race or colour, you bring shame upon yourself. Fortunately soccer is showing the way. There are multiracial teams playing to multiracial crowds. (Brain, 1993)

Contrary to this statement, and as we have highlighted elsewhere in this book, 'soccer' was not and currently is not being played in front of 'multiracial crowds'. As FAR were trying to argue (*Filbo Fever!*, 1993), a city like Leicester where the minority ethnic population is almost one-third of the total should have a similar proportion of minority ethnic spectators, although the figure for season-ticket holders for the 1996/97 season was estimated at just 1 per cent (Sir Norman Chester Centre, 1998).

Despite raising the profile of the issues of racism and exclusion, FAR struggled to make a sizable impact at Filbert Street, and remained a fringe organisation run by a small group of dedicated individuals. After an initial series of low-level meetings with officials at Leicester City, the group was largely ignored until it became part of the new anti-racist initiative launched in 1999 in the city, involving the club, the local anti-racist football task force and other agencies.

An idea that FAR could have developed was an action 'plan' for Leicester City to follow, in a similar vein to the 'Let's Kick Racism' example discussed above or the one devised by the Supporters' Campaign Against Racism and Fascism (SCARF) based at Heart of Midlothian in Edinburgh. This plan formed part of a concerted effort to challenge sectarianism and the overt racism directed by supporters at high profile black players such as Paul Elliott and Mark Walters in the early nineties. SCARF, a multi-club fan project, distributed leaflets at matches and involved other agencies in its work, including clubs and the police (Hewitt, 1992). As part of a concerted ten-point action plan for clubs, SCARF urged them to adopt policy statements against racism and take action against racist chanting, graffiti and the distribution of racist and fascist literature. This provided a framework around which SCARF could campaign, and helped to raise the profile of their efforts. Interestingly, the nine-point plan unveiled by the CRE a year later as part of the 'Let's Kick Racism' initiative was very similar to the one developed by SCARF.

Other fan initiatives

The use of fanzines as a campaigning tool by Leeds and Leicester supporters reflects the popularity of these publications amongst football fans (Taylor, 1992), a popularity that has soared since the mid-1980s to the extent that there are presently hundreds available, with often as many as half a dozen associated with a single club.[44] Although they do not always take themselves seriously and are often irreverent and humorous they have, on the whole, been a vehicle for alternative, independent comment and protest. They have been 'enabled by the rise of new, supporter-orientated social movements within UK football' (Giulianotti, 1997: 211) and have, for the most part, adopted a supportive stance towards anti-racism within the sport, being described by Horne (1996: 59) as an 'important part of the wider campaign against racism'. Some that emphasised the issue include *When Skies Are Grey* (Everton), *Our Day Will Come* (Celtic/ Manchester United), *Bluebird Jones* (Cardiff City) and the *Chelsea Independent* (Chelsea), although the fans that produce these fanzines may not actually be members of any specific anti-racist fans' organisation. *The Leyton Orientear* (Leyton Orient) effectively campaigned against the presence of right-wing groups in and around their stadia, as one club official at Leyton Orient described to the authors:

> The fanzine campaigned very hard to stop that [right-wing activity]. I think it was the BNP that came and leafleted outside the West Stand. I think the club was driven on by the fanzine *The Leyton Orientear*, who are a very well established organisation. They put a stop to this very quickly.[45]

Like the local initiatives originating from some clubs to cultivate closer relations with the community, these fan-based activities have the benefit that they are context-specific. They have appeal as they are written by genuine supporters, rather than appearing as an outside, non-footballing, intervention into the game. However, it is problematic to assume that the style and language many of the fanzines use necessarily reflect all football fan cultures. For example, as mentioned above, some reproduce macho and bullish facets of fan behaviour which may alienate supporters, or, conversely, as Moorehouse (1994) notes, some may actually *reinforce* certain reactionary fan cultures. Also, there is a suggestion that campaigning fanzines are, to a certain degree, 'preaching to the converted' as those who buy them are more likely to be left-of-centre in their political leanings.

The beginning of the 'boom' in the popularity of fanzines occurred around the same time as the birth of the Football Supporters' Association (FSA) in 1985. Formed in the wake of the Heysel Stadium disaster of the same year, the FSA has been an independent, national campaigning body that has prioritised the development of anti-racist strategies and has been involved in both localised and national programmes (Crabbe, 1994; Horne, 1996). The FSA advocates a multi-agency approach to combating the problem, within which prominent roles should be given to fans, coaches, players and managers. The organisation also recognises the dangers of pricing disadvantaged groups out of the game, and fears that extortionate ticket prices may affect the numbers of minority ethnic groups that attend matches (Reading Council for Racial Equality, 1998).

The FSA has been active in the 'Let's Kick Racism' campaign, and was responsible for producing the *United Colours of Football* fanzine in 1994. 110 000 copies were distributed outside stadia free of charge at the beginning of the 1994/95 season, as fanzines were utilised as an anti-racist media in a similar vein to how Leeds fans used *Marching Altogether* (see above). *United Colours* contained articles about the contribution of black players, both professional and amateur, and addressed the issue of the lack of Asians in the game. It also avoided the trap of portraying the perpetrators of football's racisms as being stereotypical skinhead hooligans.

The FSA campaigned for an amendment to the original version of Section 3 of the 1991 Football (Offences) Act (see Chapter 4), and has been part of the AGARI project's anti-racism monitoring scheme. It was also invited to be a constituent of the Football Task Force which investigated racism in the game in 1997/98. One of its most innovative projects has been the development of 'fan embassies' at major international football tournaments involving the England national side. These embassies offer free advice on ticketing, policing issues and accommodation, and have helped to diffuse confrontational situations between local populations and visiting supporters. For the European Championships held in England in 1996, the FSA produced fan guides in the languages of the competing nations.

However, it needs to be acknowledged that not all fan organisations and fanzines have been receptive to anti-racist initiatives within football, and one or two have been sceptical and at times hostile to such interventions. Although a comprehensive survey of fanzine articles is beyond the scope of this book, perhaps typical of the attitudes of a section of fans to the initial anti-racist interventions are the sentiments expressed in an article entitled 'Racism' in the Everton fanzine *Gwladys Sings the Blues* (Pearson, 1994). In this piece, Pearson defends accusations of racism made against his club by arguing that 'racism is no more of a problem for Everton FC than it is for any other club' (Pearson, 1994: 16), seemingly taking offence not at accusations of racism, but by accusations that his *own club*, Everton, have a *worse* problem than others. Thus, in some ways, his argument reflects difficulties the authors of this book have had of trying to locate racism within football. Whether it's because of a desire to protect the image of a club in the case of its officials, or because of almost 'instinctive' defensive reactions by fans to criticism of *their* club, racism is either located 'elsewhere' or is excused as being no worse than elsewhere. Developing coherent anti-racist interventions is therefore, of course, made even more problematic in these conditions.

Opposition towards anti-racist legislation has come from the fans' group 'Libero!' which opposes Section 3 of the 1991 Football (Offences) Act because 'the banning of racist chanting is an assault on the civil liberties of everyone, including ethnic minorities' (Brick and Allirajah, 1997). The group sees such legislation as being part of the 'excessive regulation of behaviour at football matches' and that the anti-racist element of the legislation 'continues to be used as a justification for eroding the civil liberties of football fans' (*ibid.*). In the context of the legislation and the way it is framed, 'offensive' fan behaviour (in the form of swearing and indecent chanting) is linked with racist abuse, and 'Libero!' argue that the former, being 'normal' fan behaviour, is restricted because the latter is restricted. Fans are being 'criminalised', the organisation maintains, 'for doing what they do best, supporting their team' (*ibid.*).

The group develops its argument further by maintaining that people have the right to hear and judge viewpoints that they may disagree with, including racist chants and abuse, and that it is 'patronising' for minority ethnic groups to assume that they need to be 'protected' from racist views. 'Libero!' sees racism as being:

> the systematic denial of equality to black people. Racist chanting is at most an expression, but not the cause, of racism. The criminalisation of racist chanting is a symptom of the collapse of the anti-racist project which aimed to achieve social equality. Anti-racism has been reduced to a mechanism for regulating personal behaviour. (*ibid.*)

Sentiments like these do, of course, take 'Libero!''s argument away from the 'sanitisation of football' debate, and into other, more complex realms. Is the philosophy behind 'Libero!' merely one that wants to reclaim the game for the genuine, passionate fan, or does it have other agendas? The debate about the 'gentrification' of football, which is central to 'Libero!''s remit (Libero, 1997) has been reflected and debated in other places (see, for example, Horton, 1997; Redhead, 1997; Taylor, 1997), and the group may find it has a degree of support for this stance. Yet it appears that the group is mapping the issue of racism directly on to arguments about broader changes in the game, and it may be problematic if one particular context of racism is overlooked. By failing to draw a distinction between swearing and racist abuse, 'Libero!' deny the specificity of racism, and fail to see the difference between 'passion [of fans at matches] that's historically exhibited and unacceptable levels of racism' (Powar, quoted in Kliman, 1997). Like others involved in the game, 'Libero!' appear to see the campaign against racism as more of a problem than racism itself.

Also, the suggestion that it is patronising to protect minority ethnic fans from being subjected to racist abuse appears to ignore the experience of black and Asian fans, many of whom cite racist abuse as a significant reason for not attending professional football matches (Garland and Rowe, 1995; Holland, 1992; Pinto, Drew and Minhas, 1997). Research conducted by the Charlton Athletic Race Equality Partnership found that around 40 per cent of black and Asian schoolchildren surveyed stated that racist abuse was a factor in their non-attendance (CARE, 1996), even though the same survey showed a high level of interest in football amongst these communities. This experience is mirrored by minority ethnic supporters at other clubs (Holland, 1995) as one of the black supporters interviewed for this book stated:

> I heard the racism at my home ground and it made me feel sick as I hadn't heard it for so many years, and the ground is like a second home to me. So it feels like someone coming into your own home and abusing you. It really did upset me.

Conclusion

That there have been successes in challenging racism in football is a point that should be acknowledged. Although there are problems with many of the anti-racist interventions discussed above, a number have had a significant impact. Racism within the game is now high on the sport's agenda, and was one of the Football Task Force's areas of investigation. How long this topicality lasts is, however, a moot point, and, as is outlined above, there are some within the game who feel that anti-racism is a 'trendy' issue that that clubs are complying with as a short-term, public relations exercise. Genuine, long-term programmes need proper resources, and a commitment by clubs that they will persue such policies even when anti-racism becomes 'unfashionable' once more.

However, if further progress is to be made then many involved in football need to develop better conceptions of the nature of the racisms evident within the game. Whilst it is, of course, unrealistic to expect practitioner-oriented initiatives to become fully informed of recent theoretical developments, a better understanding of the problem would obviously lead to a better development of solutions. It is not being argued here that those involved in football need to become fully conversant with specialist academic theories, but that anti-racist efforts that were more informed about current debates would be better placed to develop and sustain more meaningful programmes.

The problem of the *denial* of racism also needs to be countered by those developing anti-racist agendas within football. The specific nature of racist abuse and intimidation needs to be acknowledged as a section of the football community still sees it as being no different from abuse heaped upon players with easily identifiable physical characteristics, as one professional player commented to the authors:

> I think it [racist abuse] can be blown out of proportion ... I mean, what about all the fat players and thin players, they all get abuse as well. Why not try and put that issue out, rather than focusing all the time on black people?

A related conceptual factor is the multiplicity of racisms and their inconsistent and contradictory character. It is suggested here that the framework provided by the concept of racialisation best enables this since it recognises the changing nature of racism over time. It allows the consideration of diverse manifestations of racism directed at different minority groups and offers the analytic space to intervene. While the issue of racism had a relatively high profile during the 1990s, the nature and extent of this racism is often denied by associating it solely with the activities of a minority of extremist fans. Whilst these groups have maintained a presence at international matches, at most domestic league stadia their influence has been minimal. However, a number of anti-racist initiatives have concentrated their efforts upon these groups, even when evidence of their presence has been negligible. This reflects the mistakes of groups in other contexts, as Malik (1996: 191) noted: 'anti-racist organizations have characteristically exaggerated the political or physical threat posed by far-right groups, and at the same time portrayed racism as largely emanating from fascist organizations'.

Also, there is a tendency by some clubs to perpetuate the image of 'racist hooligans' as being the sole purveyors of racism in order to claim that racism has died down concomitantly with the reduction of hooliganism inside stadia in the 1990s. Isolating the problem within an easily identifiable 'pariah' group marginalises it rather conveniently for club officials, who can admit to there being a problem of racism, but can claim that this problem is located amongst a tiny minority of 'demonised' fans. This misconceptualisation of racism leads to low-key, yet perhaps more ingrained, individualistic forms to go relatively unchecked by anti-racist groups and other agencies such as the police. As these types of racism are now more prevalent than incidents of mass chanting, they need to become more of a focus for anti-racist schemes.

Football clubs see the problems of racism and the lack of minority fans and players as eminating from external sources: either ignorant racist 'boneheads' – who are unwelcome anyway in the new era of football – or within communities who are different, and culturally or religiously disinclined to participate in the game. If the former could be excluded, perhaps policed, out of football and the latter persuaded that there is something in it for them then the problems would be resolved. Both steps might – arguably – in themselves be welcome, but there is a conceptual blindspot hidden in this 'commonsense' reasoning – the organisational nature of the clubs themselves. Rather like traditional conceptions of the state contained in political science textbooks, football clubs seem to regard themselves as 'neutral arbiters' somehow removed from these issues. Rarely it seems – and Northampton Town is a notable exception – do clubs even begin to acknowledge that they may have to critically consider their own policies, procedures and practices. Black or Asian people might be relatively absent from football crowds, but they are almost entirely absent among senior club administrators or in the boardroom.

A common excuse often advanced by key actors within the game is that the sport does not have a problem with racism but that society does. Although this was often an excuse for inaction, it does contain some truth and the broader influence of a racialised social context must be considered by those who wish to make football accessible to all ethnic groups. This means that social, political and economic obstacles need to be addressed, perhaps in conjunction with other authorities, just as importantly as direct manifestations of racism which serve to exclude. Thus some of the more successful anti-racist interventions have entailed the adoption of partnership approaches involving a number of key local agencies that are fully conversant with prevailing local conditions. These interventions are more flexible and adaptive than less sensitive national campaigns, and have the advantage of not being perceived by fans as being outside interventions.

Clubs, as part of these multi-agency programmes, need to develop community-related schemes that understand their local populations, and take into account their expectations. Instead, they often appear to fall victim of what Bains with Patel (1996) describe as the 'colour-blind approach', whereby the needs of minority ethnic groups are ignored by clubs whose idea of anti-racism is to deny any social or cultural differences between them. The clubs therefore develop community schemes that lack diversity or insight, under the banner of 'all groups being treated equally'. This point is developed by Verma and Darby (1994: 155), who noted the problems of such approaches:

> Sport and physical recreation do not take place in a vacuum. For the participants it is part of their lives which provides its own particular rewards but is none the less consistent with the general thrust of their culture ... [yet] these activities are firmly located in the mainstream provision designed to meet the needs and expectations of a white, liberal, essentially Protestant society.

Finally, as discussed above, there is evidence that fear of racist abuse and intimidation discourages minority ethnic groups from attending professional matches. It is therefore vital to understand the culture of spectating at football matches if anti-racist interventions aimed at fans are to be successful. Fan groups such as 'Libero!' may find some resonance amongst supporters for their notion that certain fan rituals, such as abusing visiting supporters, are an integral part of spectating. As the AGARI (1996) report noted, the slogan 'Let's Kick Racism – Respect All Fans' briefly adopted by the 'Let's Kick Racism' initiative was unsuccessful because it failed to keep the notions of racist intimidation and non-racist abuse separate, thus once more denying the specificity of racist behaviour. It needs to be acknowledged by those devising anti-racist actions that such programmes need to comprehend the difference between 'racist abuse' and ritualistic abuse of opposing fans. The demonstration and enactment of club rivalries is important for the construction of fan-group identities, and all agencies involved in challenging racism within football need to realise that racist abuse need not, and indeed should not, form part of this.

4
Policing Racism in Football

Introduction

In the months leading up to the 1998 World Cup considerable concern was expressed in the British media that the French authorities lacked the experience and know-how to ensure that the tournament passed off without major crowd disorder. To some extent dire warnings in the media about impending violence at football tournaments were par for the course, as the experience of Euro '96 indicated, but concern about hooliganism was also fuelled by the limited amount of tickets available via legitimate outlets to non-French supporters. As most of the tickets for each game were reserved for French nationals and corporate sponsors there were fears that large numbers of supporters would flock to the host cities and seek to obtain tickets illicitly. An unintended consequence of the European internal market, it seemed, was that football hooligans enjoyed the same free movement around the Union as legitimate travellers.

Against this background the British government went to some length to establish its anti-hooligan credentials. Stern warnings were issued by the British government in order to dissuade English and Scottish supporters from travelling across the Channel without match tickets, including television adverts which emphasised the stringent security measures designed to eliminate the activities of ticket-touts. In February 1998, while Britain held the EU Presidency, the Home Secretary chaired a seminar designed to bring together experts from across Europe to prepare effective policing measures for the summer tournament. Although this preparation clearly involved multi-national efforts, the British government was keen to stress that 'the UK was keen to share its world beating expertise in the policing of

I.M. MARSH LIBRARY LIVERPOOL L17 6BD
TEL. 0151 231 5216/5299

football and take a lead in tackling hooliganism' (Home Office, 1998). Subsequent events suggested that the English disease had not been cured but was merely in remission – in March 1998 a fan was killed at Gillingham, and a match between West Bromwich Albion and Bristol City led to serious disorders inside the stadium in 1999. Despite incidents such as these, and these are by no means the only examples, the fact that a British Home Secretary could seriously claim expertise in tacking hooliganism demonstrated the extent of the transformation of the national game. As is discussed in more detail below, a series of events in 1985 saw English football reach its postwar nadir, culminating in the prohibition of clubs from all European competition. Ten years later, contrary to doom-laden predictions from sections of the press, Euro '96 passed off without major disorder, although certainly not without any violence whatsoever (Garland and Rowe, 1999). Commenting on plans for the policing of the 1998 World Cup, the Director of Security claimed that 'the English model is fantastic! ... The English may have invented the poison of hooliganism, but they have also invented the remedy for this poison' (*Le Monde*, 1997). Similar sentiments were expressed in publicity materials for the Football Association's bid for the 2006 World Cup, which suggested that '... England's new breed of fully trained safety officers, inspectors and stadium managers have ensured that "fortress football" is no more. Our new generation of welcoming, fan-friendly and family-oriented stadiums are safe, secure and accessible to all' (Football Association, 1997). While events including those outlined above cast doubt upon such effusive comments about the eradication of disorder from English football, that they could be entertained in this manner demonstrates the extent of the transformation of the image of the national game. Indeed one feature of the press coverage of the violence that did eventually occur during France '98 was to draw a contrast between the occurrence of those disorders and the relatively peaceable recent experience of the domestic game.

The issue of football hooliganism has been widely discussed in a range of books, from the academic analyses of Humphries (1981), Taylor (1990) and Williams, Dunning and Murphy (1988, 1989), to Home Office and other official reports ('Popplewell', 1986; Taylor, 1990; Home Office, 1995). More recently a spate of titles purporting to be first-hand accounts of those involved in hooliganism in the 1980s have appeared (Brimson and Brimson, 1997; Ward, 1989). Whether marked by bravado or penitence the frequent publication of such reminiscences suggests that hooliganism – like many other forms of deviance – continues to exert a powerful hold on the public imagination. This book does not seek to add much to this body of literature and only refers to football hooliganism because very many of the policing initiatives which have been used to tackle racism within the game were originally designed to counter the distinct problem of football-related violence. Although we are critical of attempts to conflate the problems of racism and hooliganism, since they marginalise the importance of less-overt forms of racism, the association between the two is so widespread that it is all but impossible to consider many of the policing initiatives against racism independently of those designed to curb disorderly behaviour.

The previous chapter explored various initiatives which have attempted to undermine cultures of racism within football. Many of the campaigns and schemes outlined were designed to confront racism and to engender an environment at football matches in which the expression of overtly racist sentiments would no longer be considered an appropriate form of behaviour. Another important dimension discussed was the various attempts to utilise the game as a vehicle for anti-racist education and youth work in a more general setting. In terms of the dichotomy in anti-racism identified earlier in this book, such efforts are primarily intended to effect the values and beliefs which underpin racism and to challenge the assorted myths and stereotypes which allow it to flourish. This chapter explores the other dimension of anti-racism, that is the steps which have been introduced to influence the behaviour of football supporters within and around grounds so that racist attitudes and beliefs are not manifest in 'antisocial' or disorderly behaviour.

Simply put, the measures reviewed in this chapter are not concerned with educating football fans about the evils of racism or encouraging them to recognise the benefits of an inclusive multicultural society. Instead the focus is on a wide range of steps that have been taken to prohibit racist abuse, harassment or violence. The concern in this section is with the steps that have been taken to police racism from the game, and the term 'police' is used deliberately to refer to a broad range of activities and the work of diverse agencies, including the use of closed-circuit television, private stewards, legal provisions, disciplinary measures within the rules of the game, and local-authority interventions in the amateur and professional game. The starting point for this discussion is the role of extreme-right groups in English football. Although subject to considerable exaggeration, it is clear that organised fascist groups have played a part in the related problems of football hooliganism and racism in the game. Before considering in detail the nature and efficacy of policing measures against racism in football something of the history of far-right activity in the game is recounted below.

Fascism and football

A recurring theme of this book is that efforts to challenge racism within football have frequently relied upon an unhelpful assumption that the problem can be reduced to that of football hooliganism, and especially to far-right infiltration of the game. Our argument is that such an association between racism and hooliganism is unhelpful at best and potentially counter-productive, since it may allow racism of a less overt and physically threatening nature to go relatively unchecked. Although we remain critical of the conflation of racism and fascism in football and argue that a more complex understanding of the diverse and contradictory dynamics of racisms should be adopted, it would be naive in the extreme to ignore the links between racism, neo-fascist groups and Britain's national game. This chapter is concerned with policing strategies – in the broadest sense – which play a role in combating racism within football. One concern we express is that many of these are of limited use because they were primarily designed to counter the related but distinct problem of hooliganism. Before moving onto examine the policing initiatives in detail it is important to discuss the relationship between football and fascism in Britain during recent decades. In this section something of the history of extreme-right activity around football will be charted and related to the broader problem of football hooliganism. We suggest that the extreme right have targeted football in Britain for three main reasons: to further their political programme, to generate and sustain international networks of the far-right, and as a potential means to attract new recruits. However, in keeping with our insistence that this is but one dimension of the racism within football, we also raise a number of crucial issues which demonstrate that the extent of far-right involvement in the game often will remain a matter of conjecture and supposition rather than fact and evidence.

Throughout much of the 1970s and 1980s, before the game entered its latest renaissance, a common image of the football fan was of the bone-headed thug – an ignorant, lager-swilling lout more interested in violence than the game itself. As mentioned in Chapter 6, this stereotype of the football fan remains a staple of much media coverage of the game. In the mid-1980s, following the Heysel stadium disaster in which 39 Juventus supporters were killed prior to their team's European Cup Final against Liverpool, the *Sunday Times* argued that football was a 'slum sport' watched by 'slum people' (*Sunday Times*, 2 June 1985). Representations of football supporters in popular culture were also dominated by images of toilet-roll-throwing morons responsible for the destruction of countless 'football special' trains. A report from the House of Commons Home Affairs Select Committee (1992: ix) reflected upon the

> pervading impression that soccer stadia are nasty, cold, wet, windswept places where crowds are herded together on concrete terraces, where the lavatory facilities are minimal and dirty, where the catering facilities are virtually non-existent, where, in short, people are treated like animals and consequently, not surprisingly, act like animals. Even the words used ('pens', not 'enclosures', for example) show how badly fans are regarded.

A central plank of the conception of football fans as 'animals' has been the close association drawn by many politicians and sections of the media between football supporters, hooliganism and far-right political activism. As discussed in greater detail in Chapter 6, sections of the media continued to raise the spectre of neo-fascist violence in the weeks and months prior to the Euro '96 tournament in England and before the France '98 World Cup, a fear that self-consciously reflected the continuing legacy of the far-right hooliganism in Britain. In his analysis of racism in the press, Van Dijk (1992) refers to the notion of a 'script', an unwritten popular memory or consciousness which makes stories presented in the media intelligible. When it was suggested, sometimes with scant evidence, that neo-nazis were planning to disrupt a major football competition, folkloric images of marauding skinhead hooligans served to make otherwise vague threats seem more plausible. That such concerns continued to enjoy relatively widespread currency in the media after a period of many years in which far-right activity and hooliganism in general had been relatively absent demonstrates how ingrained such imagery had become.

To some extent the association between football hooliganism and the far-right has been drawn in the aftermath of disorder at international fixtures involving both club and national teams. As Table 4.1 shows there have been a number of violent incidents involving

English fans abroad that have been wholly or partially blamed on the malign influence of neo-fascist groups such as the National Front (NF), the British National Party (BNP) and Combat 18.[46] Following disorder at a Denmark versus England match in Copenhagen in 1982, the *Daily Mail* commented that 'the NF seemed to be everywhere'[47] and the Front's newspaper *Bulldog* boasted that English fans 'booed and jeered every time Black players touched the ball'.[48]

Table 4.1   Far-right involvement in football: a select chronology

Date	Comments
late 1950s	Colin Jordan's White Defence League targeted football grounds to sell their newspaper *Black and White News*.
late 1970s	The 'League of Louts' first appeared in *Bulldog*, the NF newspaper: 'in many ways this offensive and aggressive publication was the first football fanzine, as its style was deliberately pitched at the young fans on the terraces' (Thomas, 1995: 96).
1978	NF members blamed for violence at FA Cup match between Millwall and Ipswich (Fielding, 1981: 183).
1981	NF activists assaulted two men who declined their leaflets outside a match between Barnet and Peterborough (*Searchlight*, 1985).
1982	NF involvement in disorder at Denmark *vs* England, Copenhagen, reported in the press.
November 1984	'Chelsea NF' fans were pictured 'sieg heiling' at Turkey *vs* England match in Istanbul.
1985	The secretary of Oxford United demanded fans remove a banner emblazoned with a swastika (*Searchlight*, 1985).
May 1985	John Smith, chairman of Liverpool FC, claimed that NF supporters had boasted to him of their role in the Heysel stadium disaster in which 39 Juventus fans died.
September 1987	Chelsea-supporting members of the NF attempted to 'build bridges' with Glasgow Rangers – a purportedly Loyalist club – and pledge to support them in European competition (*Searchlight*, 1987b).
October 1988	Walsall FC chairman, Barrie Blower, threatened drastic measures, including possibly stopping games, if the 'fascist element' in the crowd persisted with 'heil Hitler' chants (*Birmingham Evening Mail*, 1990).

January 1990	Local newspapers reported that the NF were planning to buy shares in Aston Villa FC (*Birmingham Evening Mail*, 1990).
August 1993	Reported that police intelligence suggests far-right targeting of football grounds in a recruitment drive, focusing on Chelsea, Aston Villa, Blackburn, Oxford United, Glasgow Rangers and Hearts.
October 1993	Combat 18 members identified amongst those orchestrating violence in Rotterdam as England fail to qualify for 1994 World Cup: 'Combat 18 has always seen events like this as ideal for their purposes' (*Dispatches*, 1994).
November 1993	'... it has been alleged that the BNP and other racist groups are stepping up efforts to recruit support from among football supporters, targeting in particular members of known hooligan groups' (*When Saturday Comes*, 1993).
February 1995	Claims were made that the BNP and Combat 18 were at the centre of violence which led to Ireland vs. England match being abandoned (*Sunday Times*, 1995).

The association between the national team and the far-right seems to have persisted despite a perceived decline in the influence of such groups at club level. There are several reasons why such politically-motivated groups may have actively maintained their association with the national team more vigorously than with individual clubs. Three possible motivations are discussed here – the desire to make political or symbolic capital from hooliganism; furthering international contacts amongst neo-nazi networks; and the opportunity to recruit new members from a section of football supporters perceived to be particularly dedicated to their national football team and so, it is assumed, aggressive nationalism more generally.

First, the symbolic position of the national team may mean that political capital can be made by far-right groups anxious to promote their views. As discussed in Chapter 2, the 1978 selection of Viv Anderson as the first black player to appear for England (in a match against Czechoslovakia) was widely acclaimed, with a degree of self-congratulation, as evidence of the permanent presence and progress of black people within British society, and, as such, was vigorously opposed by groups who preferred a 'racially homogenous' national team. In its extreme form such opposition was manifest in the death threats far-right activists reportedly sent Anderson (Longmore, 1988). More recent examples also illustrate the political capital the far-right believe they can secure via football violence. One issue around which the far-right group Combat 18 have sought to mobilise football supporters and football hooligans has been Ulster loyalism and hostility to Irish nationalism.[49] A television documentary from 1994 revealed police surveillance footage of a counter-demonstration against a 'Troops Out' march held in London in 1993 on which police-identified football hooligans were in abundance (Dispatches, 1994).

Links between the far-right and Ulster loyalism were vividly forced onto the political agenda following clashes between England supporters and Irish fans which led to the curtailment of the Ireland versus England friendly match in Dublin in February 1995. Media reports focused on the role that the BNP, and its off-shoot Combat 18, had played in orchestrating the disturbances as a vehicle to air their opposition to Anglo-Irish efforts to achieve a peaceful settlement in Northern Ireland.[50] One factor which was widely cited in the media as evidence of extreme-right involvement in the disorders was the chanting of 'no surrender to the IRA', a common refrain of groups such as the BNP and a theme occasionally heard from England supporters.[51] In an article which referred to the links between the BNP, Combat 18 and extremist Ulster Loyalist groups, the *Guardian* reported that:

> As the cameras panned across the upper terraces of Lansdowne Road [the stadium where the game was played], it was never more apparent that a hard core of politically-motivated activists could stampede England's violent fellow travellers into mob confrontation...Two groups are once again being blamed: the fascist fringe parties and the broader strata of young – often racist – white male fans who simply enjoy inspiring mayhem and fights.[52]

Scoring political points is not the only reason why the far-right have targeted football. Other incidents referred to in Table 4.1, such as the Heysel Stadium disaster of 1985, provided an opportunity for Italian and English neo-nazi groups to develop mutual contacts and further enhance a pan-European network of extreme-right groups (Bjørgo, 1995; Merkel, 1997). Jensen (1993) argued that recent decades have seen the development of a pan-European network of neo-fascist groups which is committed to a programme of terrorism and is organised around football violence and the skinhead music scene. The quasi-paramilitary nature of such groups clearly requires subterfuge and secrecy and it is evident that organised football hooliganism is occasionally used as a smokescreen for even more sinister activities. In

1987, for example, the anti-fascist magazine *Searchlight* reported that Chelsea-supporting members of the National Front were planning to follow Glasgow Rangers in European competition as a means of developing contacts with their far-right counterparts abroad, and that such links had already been made via football hooligans from Sweden and Germany (*Searchlight*, 1987a). Later that year it was reported that a team of academics from Leuven University in Belgium, having conducted research into the causes of the Heysel stadium disaster, concluded that fascist groups across Europe were using football as a cover for networking, exchanging information, and recruitment (*Searchlight*, 1987b).

The third reason why far-right groups seem keen to target football matches is in order to attract recruits. Several of the incidents referred to in Table 4.1 highlight this activity and it has been suggested that as long ago as the 1930s, Mosley's British Union of Fascists focused on football crowds as a potential source of Blackshirt recruits (Anti-Fascist Action, 1994). A number of the anti-racist campaigns discussed in Chapter 3 were initiated by fans worried by far-right publicity and recruitment drives at their grounds (Leeds TUC and Leeds AFA, 1988). The major reason for this has been the 'traditional' demographic make-up of football crowds as overwhelmingly male, large numbers of whom are young and from lower-working-class backgrounds (Malcolm, Jones and Waddington, 2000). Whilst it is simplistic to generalise about either the potential political allegiances of such broad sections of the population or the typical socioeconomic background of a fascist, it remains the case that the stereotype of the football fan seems to overlap quite broadly with that of the far-right street activist. This point was well-made by Williams *et al.* (1989: 73) who, whilst noting that far-right groups had been largely unsuccessful in their attempts to mobilise football supporters, commented that:

> The attitudes and beliefs which underlie the stance taken by extreme right-wing groups towards what they regard as alien races are similar in many ways to those which play a large part in generating disturbances between geographically distinct groups of white lower-working class youths at football matches.

In rather more uncompromising terms this analysis is shared by some extreme neo-nazi groups themselves. Boasting of the potential to recruit followers of the England national team to their organisation, Combat 18 suggested that 'ninety nine per cent of football thugs are

white and ninety nine per cent of those are nationalistic and patriotic
... White youths displaying the warrior instincts which made Britain
and our race great' (*Dispatches*, 1994).

While the selected events charted in Table 4.1 provide some indication of the range of incidents that the far-right have been associated
with, and three broad motives have been identified to explain these
activities, it is important to note that there are serious grounds for
caution in judging the extent to which such groups are implicated in
the distinct but related problems of hooliganism and racism in football. Firstly, the accuracy of the reported involvement of neo-nazi
groups can be questioned since many agencies have a possible interest
in either magnifying or depreciating their involvement. It may be, for
example, that far-right groups have an interest in amplifying the
extent of their role in football hooliganism as a means of inflating
their more general level of support and political influence. The 'league
of louts' that the NF paper *Bulldog* began to print in the late 1970s
seemed to be one way in which rival groups within the extreme right
in Britain, which is riven with factions, could seek to establish their
credentials. In amplifying their capacity to organise extensive football
hooliganism, neo-fascist groups in Britain, which usually appear
small-scale and rather shambolic, are able to inflate both their
strength in numbers and their capacity for concerted activity.

As with many forms of deviance, it is as well to remain skeptical
about the accounts of those who participate in it as a reliable source
of information. Other parties to the deviant behaviour may also have
an interest in exaggerating or denying its extent. For example, anti-
fascist groups may perceive some benefit from highlighting the degree
of fascist influence in hooliganism as a means for garnering support
for their broader political agenda. Football authorities may share an
interest in focusing on the degree to which extremist groups are implicated in violence since this helps reinforce the frequently-heard claim
that the problem is caused by those beyond the game, the outside
agitator rather than the 'genuine' football supporter. Policing authorities may also perceive some interest in concentrating on the
involvement of the far-right in football hooliganism as a means of
asserting the importance of their role in surveillance and intelligence-
gathering, especially during a period of fiscal constraints and role
redefinition (Johnson, 1992; Morgan and Newburn, 1997). The media,
too, may tend to overplay the degree to which football hooliganism is
coterminous with the extreme right. Chapter 6 provides further analysis of the media coverage of the game and illustrates how the press

have conveyed images of neo-nazi-inspired disorder. The notion of an organised neo-nazi conspiracy to create disorder at high-profile football matches provides a sensational angle for the media to pursue. A frequently heard reaction from football clubs to suggestions that the game might have some problem of far-right activity is to recognise the issue as a general concern, whilst maintaining that it is not one which applies to that club in particular. The insistence that specific clubs do not have a problem of fascist activity in or around their stadium is an attempt to establish some distance between the club and antisocial or criminal behaviour. In many respects the equation of hooliganism and racism with the actions of a small tight-knit organised faction performs a similar function of disassociation. As Back *et al.* (1996) argued, the conflation of racism, hooliganism and the far-right enables an understanding of the problems, and an agenda for tackling them, behind which a wide-range of otherwise disparate groups can readily coalesce. Whilst this may provide some strategic benefits it should not be assumed without question that it is a wholly accurate portrayal of the role of far-right groups in football hooliganism.

Another reason for suggesting caution in considering the links between football and the far-right in Britain is the lack of emphasis placed upon football-related activity in the broader literature on neo-fascist political groups. Whilst it is undeniable that parties such as the National Front and the British National Party have had some involvement in football hooliganism, accounts of their more general activities tend to make little mention of the game. A considerable literature on far-right groups in Britain in recent decades has now been published, some of which are academic analyses, while others are politically-motivated exposes, and yet more are journalistic accounts. Although football is mentioned in a number of these, most of them convey the impression that activity surrounding the game is of relatively minor import. Fielding's (1981) account of the National Front, for example, described the establishment and membership of the party but makes no reference to attempts to infiltrate the game for recruitment or other political purposes. Walker's (1977) volume on the NF also made light of the significance of football to their activities. *Searchlight's* (1995) account of an antifascist 'mole' who had been working inside the BNP does refer to a number of 'Chelsea headhunters' involved in the party, but this is very much overshadowed by the importance of the skin-head music scene to far-right activism, reinforcing Jensen's (1993) view referred to above. An earlier expose of the BNP (Hill, 1988) also made no more than passing reference to football hooliganism.

One implication of the marginal role of football hooliganism in accounts of the far-right is that other areas of political and social life must also be considered in discussions of contemporary neo-fascism. It is an important though uncomfortable truth that the far-right in Britain, although relatively small compared to mainstream parties or to neo-nazi groups in other countries, is not confined to the activity of football hooligans who are easily dismissed as 'mindless criminals'. Indeed, during the 1970s the National Front adopted more traditional democratic methods and enjoyed relative political and electoral success (Solomos, 1993: 188–90), indicating that other apparently non-deviant areas of life in Britain are also important to far-right politics, and that this problem is not confined to pariah groups such as football hooligans. Just as the stereotype of the football hooligan as a nazi is misleading and counter-productive, antifascists need to remember that fascism is not the sole preserve of any one section of society and that not all far-right activists are bone-headed thugs.

Another reason for treating accounts of the extent to which extreme-right groups are involved in football hooliganism with some caution is raised by Williams *et al.*'s (1989) study of England fans at the 1982 World Cup. Whilst this account recorded the breadth and depth of racism and xenophobia amongst many followers of the national team and the extent to which National Front insignia and chanting were on display, it also warned of the danger of treating such evidence simplistically. The extent to which football hooligans who adopt something of the trappings of far-right ideology, uniforms or slogans actually do so out of genuine, if desperately misplaced, political conviction is open to doubt. It may be instead that some of those who regale themselves in swastikas or NF banners do so in order to shock or to comply with subcultural norms (Dunning *et al.*, 1988: 182). This difficulty in establishing the significance of far-right insignia to football hooliganism also calls into question the role of the media in reinforcing stereotypical images of disorderly spectators. The extent to which 'hooligan gangs' adopt the paraphernalia of the far-right in order to comply with established media images of 'football thugs' is open to question. That football hooligan gangs in other European countries often adopt the imagery of English gangs bears testimony to the scope of the stereotype of the English hooligan.

Whatever the need for caution in evaluating the evidence outlined here, it is apparent that neo-fascist groups have been widely involved in violence at football matches and remain heavily implicated in some of the most infamous forms of racism within the game. On an international and club basis groups such as the NF, the BNP and Combat 18 have actively pursued violence as a means of asserting their political agenda, networking with other similar groups across Europe and recruiting new members. The degree to which any of these objectives have been achieved seems to be negligible and it seems that previous observations that the far-right have enjoyed little success in the context of football remain valid. This should not be regarded as an excuse for complacency as it is evident that extreme-right groups have been at least partially responsible for some of the worst incidents of hooliganism in recent decades. However, in advocating some degree of caution in this area, we are maintaining that other forms of racism, for example those that are less well-orchestrated and overt, must also be acknowledged and addressed. Whilst many of the imaginative attempts to do just this are described elsewhere in this book, the next section of this chapter will focus on the legislative and policing measures which have been developed to counter the particular forms of racism and disorder sketched above.

Policing racism in football

Although the extent to which the far-right are responsible for the racism and disorder that has disfigured football in recent decades is open to question, it seems that strategies to tackle hooliganism have enjoyed considerable success. As was mentioned at the beginning of this chapter, not very many years ago it would have been unthinkable that British officials could offer advice to other nations on how football-related disorder might be countered, and yet this idea was seriously entertained in the months leading up to the 1998 World Cup in France. In the rest of this chapter some of the key policing developments utilised against racism and against hooliganism will be considered.

As has already been outlined, although the term 'policing' is most obviously associated with the activities of particular public agencies known as police forces, the term actually has a much older provenance which refers to wider processes of societal regulation, and it is this broader sense that is being utilised here. Given this, technological forms of social control, legal interventions, the role of the private sector and the impact of non-police agencies such as local authorities are included in the discussion alongside an analysis of the actions of public policing agencies. In recent years the responsibilities and functions of the police in Britain have come under increasing scrutiny as escalating crime rates, coupled with more general pressures on public expenditure, have called the postwar tradition of public policing into question. The independent report into the role and responsibilities of the police, commissioned by the Police Foundation and the Policy Studies Institute (1996), identified at least four other major inquiries into similar matters in the 1990s. Whilst these reports arrived at diverse conclusions, the privatisation of various aspects of policing was a fairly consistent theme, and sporting and other leisure activities have often been highlighted as areas where the hard-pressed public police can withdraw.

Technological interventions against racism in football

As debates continue about the efficacy and cost-benefit of installing closed-circuit television (CCTV) in town centres, it seems that the value of cameras in football stadia is now recognised by nearly all of those involved in the game. Virtually all safety officers, police football liaison officers, stewards and stadium managers agree that cameras have had a beneficial effect (Garland and Rowe, 1996). Fans surveys[53] suggest that supporters also welcome this development, as other surveys have suggested the public more generally welcome its introduction.[54] CCTV began to be introduced in the mid-1980s and is now present in most major grounds, to the extent that one report stated that 'football supporters are probably more accustomed to being subjected to camera surveillance than most other groups in society' (Home Office, 1993). During the same period, levels of violence within grounds have declined enormously. It is not possible to determine whether the two are closely linked or if other factors have played a more important role in reducing disorder. It seems certain that the introduction of all-seater stadia has enhanced the detective capacity of CCTV because the police can now pinpoint individuals more easily than they could in the era when fans were packed together on terracing.

That hooligans now know that they may be arrested outside the ground as they leave (or even weeks later) after disorder has occurred, suggests that CCTV may have a deterrent effect. One officer interviewed went so far as to suggest that, of the fans of the club he polices:

> they are now very wary of cameras. Point a camera at our lot and they don't like it. And that's true about a lot of the 'top lads' from

other teams, because a lot of them have been convicted by the use of CCTV.[55]

Improvements in 'Photophone' technology allow pictures and information available from CCTV and other sources to be transmitted through telephone and computer links from force to force, so that information about troublemakers is instantly available to those who need it on matchdays.

A concern, however, is that violence has simply been displaced following the introduction of CCTV and now occurs in city centres, railway stations or even motorway service stations rather than inside grounds. The violence before the FA Cup semi-final between Crystal Palace and Manchester United supporters in season 1994/95 occurred several miles from the stadium, which seems to suggest that there is some degree of truth to concerns about displacement. Of course, rioting fans may be wary of CCTV inside grounds and yet not realise that they can still be identified via other cameras in city centres.

Although it might be widely claimed that CCTV has had a deterrent effect on those who might otherwise engage in disorder inside football grounds, there are enough instances of violence within stadia to suggest that the CCTV offers only a partial solution. When Chelsea fans engaged in violence during a game at Leicester in season 1996/97 or when Barnsley supporters invaded the pitch in a match against Liverpool in 1997/98, or those engaged in violence at the Ipswich Town *vs* Norwich City fixture in 1998, they were presumably aware that their actions were being recorded – given the preponderance of cameras inside and around grounds. Perhaps these incidences indicate that the deterrence approach at the centre of claims about CCTV is flawed and that crime cannot be eradicated via such means alone. In many respects this point illustrates our more general concern about the policing initiatives against racism, which is that they focus upon addressing the manifestations of individual's racist beliefs and values rather than developing an anti-racist agenda which could address these racist attitudes on a more fundamental basis. This point will be returned to later, in the conclusion to this chapter.

Another problem with CCTV in regard to tackling racism in football is that verbal abuse cannot be detected by video cameras. The lack of any audio capacity means that closed-circuit television is of limited use against the most common expression of racism within grounds, which is isolated abuse or occasional mass chanting. This drawback can be overcome via other technological means. Some clubs have placed 'professional witnesses' near to those engaging in racist abuse in an effort to record audio evidence which can be used to support further disciplinary action, such as the withdrawal of season tickets or club membership. Of course such undercover activity is entirely reactive in as much as it can only be mounted once perpetrators of racist abuse are identified. They allow action to be taken after the event but do little or nothing to prevent it occurring in the first instance. What is more such activities are labour-intensive and may not be viable on anything other than a small scale, although it may be that a few high-profile instances might have some broader deterrent effect.

One method by which clubs can seek to glean information about spectators who engage in racist abuse – or other forms of antisocial behaviour – is via confidential telephone 'hotlines'. Such hotlines have been established in a number of contexts in Britain over recent years, including efforts to gather information about football hooliganism. A study conducted by McArdle and Lewis (1997) suggested that no more than a handful of clubs make use of such schemes, but those who have done so reported that they had led to individuals being warned against repeating racist abuse. One concern about clubs establishing hotlines to encourage spectators to provide information about those engaging in racist abuse is the reliability of the information gleaned. Of course this applies to all such anonymous reporting systems and it is clear that clubs need to supplement such methods with others that can provide more reliable evidence. Perhaps clubs could effectively use telephone hotlines as a method of identifying likely subjects for the covert collection of audio recordings of fans engaging in racist abuse.

Technological developments of various kinds have been introduced with considerable success against those participating in football hooliganism. Although the suspicion that such activity has been displaced into other venues such as town centres or motorway service stations remains, there is a widely-held perception that technological developments have provided invaluable assistance in policing the game. This may lead to an unthinking assumption that racism too has been reduced via similar means. In concluding this section we argue that there are several reasons to be extremely cautious about the role of these new technologies in tackling racism at football matches. The first reason for caution is that CCTV, the primary technological development, is unable to record audio evidence and so is of very limited use against racist chanting by crowds or abuse by individuals. It can be usefully supplemented by other techniques such as the professional witness schemes mentioned above, however this is resource-intensive and is unlikely to be used on anything other than an occasional basis. A key factor in the successful deployment of CCTV has been the advent of all-seater stadia whereby individual offenders can be identified via their seat number. This facility may not always apply since some grounds continue to include unrestricted seated areas where season ticket holders or club members, whose names and addresses could be obtained from computer records, can sit in any position and are thus much harder to accurately pinpoint.

To some extent the debate about the impact of CCTV seems likely to remain inconclusive as firm research into this issue would be very difficult to conduct. Whatever the situation, it is inconceivable that CCTV will not retain a key role in anti-hooligan initiatives. Its usefulness in tackling racist chanting and abuse is less obvious, however, and it seems that the role of personnel is more important in this respect.

Private policing

Whatever the potential of technological means to prevent or detect racism, the degree to which they are effective clearly depends upon the willingness or otherwise of the personnel who are responsible for utilising the cameras or other devices. A major recent debate within police studies has been about the privatisation of policing and football grounds have been a particularly ripe arena for the developing security industry.[56] For financial and other reasons football clubs now rely largely on private stewards to control fans inside grounds. The increasing use of such personnel inside grounds is one reason why the ratio of police to supporters decreased from 1:74 in 1985 to 1:132 in 1992.[57] Several clubs such as Chelsea, Ipswich Town and Leicester City have no police on duty inside grounds for what are perceived to be low-'risk' matches, and one club, Scarborough, went as far as playing most of their home games in the 1992/93 season without a police presence inside the ground at all. Whilst this may be an unusual case, the experience of policing football throws into relief a variety of issues of wider relevance to debates about the private security industry. The shift from reliance upon public police to the use of private stewards is perhaps the major factor behind what the Football Association (1997) have proclaimed as the decline of 'fortress football'.

The training and recruitment of stewards to work at football matches is one issue of concern, both to the prevention of racism and the broader question of disorder. Serious questions have been expressed about both of these aspects of stewarding.[58] The suitability of stewards who support the club that employs them to supervise away fans has occasionally been questioned. Anecdotal evidence suggests that on rare occasions it has been claimed that stewards have provocatively celebrated home goals in front of the away fans, and even attacked visiting supporters! A less stark but probably more common difficulty is the employment of stewards who are unsuitable, for a variety of reasons, for the job.[59] One journalist who reported on his experience of stewarding at an England fixture suggested that his colleagues were typical casual workers, who might not be dedicated or trained as stewards (Lee, 1998):

> Everyone I spoke to had come to see the game and certainly not for the money which, at £3.50 an hour failed to generate many feelings of job responsibility. Our minibus included temping agency lifers, drifting from order-picking jobs in the supermarket warehouses to early starts 'on the bins', and students, either struggling to balance night-shifts and engineering degrees – or those just out for a laugh.

Most clubs claim to provide training for their stewards. At the moment, though, there is no recognised standard for such training and it seems to be determined in an *ad hoc*, club-by-club, basis. In 1995 a number of bodies responsible for running the game combined to produce a guide to assist clubs in the training and management of stewards (Football League *et al.*, 1995). Whilst this document established some useful principles surrounding the role of stewards, and drew specific attention to the need to combat racism, it remains the case that the agreed common standards remain to be established, and local authorities retain considerable discretion in certifying that clubs provide appropriate training. Given this it continues to be the case that the likelihood of a steward intervening against illegal racist chanting, abuse or assault seems to depend upon the club and the steward in question. National initiatives designed to highlight the problem of racism in football can only be undermined if they are not translated into firm action at the local level.

The Football Task Force (1998) reflected the general concerns with the quality of stewarding and made a number of recommendations as to how the standards might be improved – including the creation of a National Vocational Qualification in stewarding and a greater willingness from local authorities to use their licensing powers to encourage best-practice. Although welcome in themselves, it seems likely that such measures will also remain piecemeal given the great diversity in relations between football clubs and local government. Clearly the potential for local-authority involvement will be very different at Northampton Town, where the local council own the stadium the club use, compared to the case of Islington council and Arsenal FC whose relationship has been relatively fraught in recent years as disputes about ground developments have continued.

Legal provisions against racism in football

Although the use of 'obscene and foul language' at football games had already been outlawed by the 1989 Football Supporters' Act, racist chanting was not explicitly made illegal until the advent of the 1991 Football (Offences) Act. Section 3 of the Act decreed that 'chanting of an indecent or racialist nature' was an offence, and that anyone caught doing so could now be prosecuted.

However, there was a loophole in the way the legislation was framed that made prosecutions for racist abuse difficult. An individual engaging in racial abuse could not be convicted under the Act unless they were acting 'in concert with one or more others', as the wording of the Act required. However, the charge that the Act failed to deal with the problem of racism in the game is in some respects misplaced, since it was never intended to address the wider problem of racism in the sport and focuses on those manifestations which may incite or amount to hooliganism. Again the conflation of racism and hooliganism is apparent. Although it does specifically prohibit racist chanting, the other provisions of the legislation are aimed at disorderly behaviour and the background context to the law was clearly concern with the more general problem of hooliganism. Other football-related problems that were prohibited include running onto the field of play and ticket-touting, which led to 196 and 216 arrests in season 1995/96, compared to 19 arrests for 'racialist chanting'.

The Football (Offences and Disorder) Act 1999 amended the 1991 Act such that individuals who are engaging in racist abuse on their own can be acted against. While this is welcome in itself, it will not prove effective unless police officers, stewards and safety officers are encouraged to enforce the legislation. Even without an extension of this Act, there are legal measures which might be used to arrest spectators who indulge in racist behaviour. The 1986 Public Order Act, for example, can be used against fans who shout racist abuse, and other laws might be used against the 'incitement of racial behaviour'. The introduction of more stringent legal measures will not make any difference to the extent of racism within football grounds unless such provisions are enforced by police officers or stewards. A study by Maynard and Read (1997) found that many officers were unaware of the legal provisions that they could use against racist abuse and harassment. One recent review of racist violence in the United Kingdom observed that (Human Rights Watch, 1997:1):

> There is a widespread impression among victims that the responsible authorities are failing effectively to investigate crimes against them ... Hostile or ineffective policing leaves many ethnic minorities frightened with no place to turn for protection. Eventually, many lose trust in the police and stop calling them for assistance, even when they are subjected to ongoing violence and harassment.

Given this broader context in which the police are seen to be unwilling to intervene against instances of racist violence and harassment it seems untenable to argue that greater legal powers alone will enable them to eradicate racist abuse in football grounds. What is at least as important as the provisions of the law is the will to intervene against such behaviour. If the police or stewards are not interested in tacking racist abuse which is already illegal it seems unlikely that extending their powers in this respect will make any substantial difference.

Local authorities

The role of local government in encouraging or requiring professional clubs to act against racism has already been hinted at in relation to the training and management of stewards. In recent years some local authorities have broadened their role to include efforts to tackle racism within amateur and recreational football. In particular, local authorities are able to use contractual procedures to 'police' the game at this level and to act against amateur teams who habitually engage in racist abuse or harassment against opponents. As the Football Task Force (1998: 19) noted:

> More than three-quarters of football pitches in England are council-owned. As landlords for thousands of teams, local authorities have the power to influence the behaviour of their tenants and, by extension, play a positive role in tackling racism in grassroots football.

Most of the anti-racist initiatives discussed in this book have targeted the professional game. Whilst this is understandable in many respects and makes sense if the high profile of football is being exploited in order to propagate a broader anti-racist message, it does mean that many aspects of the game have often been ignored. In particular, amateur and recreational football, which engages innumerable teams and players,[60] has generally been overlooked by the anti-racist interventions described here – although, as outlined in Chapter 3, this omission has been addressed to some extent in recent years. The relationship between local authorities and professional clubs varies considerably, whilst some areas include no major professional teams all will oversee at least some recreational facilities used for the amateur game. It has been in this respect that the 'Hounslow model' has been developed to address racism in the grassroots game. As discussed in the previous chapter, the borough council, in association with Brentford Football Club, has developed educational packages designed to exploit the game's popularity in order to convey anti-racism to young people. A key element of the Hounslow model is that the contracts which the local authority issue to teams which hire their pitches include clauses which provide for the withdrawal of facilities from teams which persistently engage in racist abuse or harassment. Although it has rarely, if ever, been necessary for the Borough to take such action, the fact that the provision is there to reinforce their public commitment against racism is an important factor which returns to the point made earlier in this chapter which is that public pronouncements against racism are of limited use if not backed up with concrete measures to deal with instances which may arise.

Conclusion

Although football clubs and related associations are often regarded – with some justification – as rather insular and parochial institutions, the various schemes and initiatives detailed in this chapter illustrate that there has been considerable progress in efforts to rid the game of the problem of racism. Early on, such developments were closely related to the need to deal with the more specific issue of far-right groups' involvement in football hooliganism and this chapter has made a number of criticisms of the continuing assumption that racism and hooliganism within the sport are two dimensions of the same problem, a point that is returned to below. The widespread use of

LIVERPOOL JOHN MOORES UNIVERSITY
LEARNING & INFORMATION SERVICES

police surveillance – including CCTV – and the private security industry have important implications for attempts to combat racism in the
game, and yet they are of limited use in themselves and the public
should be suspicious of those clubs who can claim only such developments as testimony to their anti-racist credentials.

Other initiatives designed to rid football stadia of racism have also
been outlined, including the use of confidential hotlines, legal provisions such as the Football (Offences) Act, the Football Supporters' Act,
and the Public Order Act and the stringent application of ground regulations so that those who engage in racist abuse or harassment are
excluded. In many respects such measures are welcome since it is vital
that clubs, local authorities and the police intervene against racism so
as to ensure that public declarations of anti-racism are reinforced by
concrete action against those who persist in the belief that such
behaviour is an acceptable part of the culture of the game. Given that
many football supporters of a minority ethnic background are put off
attending live matches for fear of racist abuse and intimidation
(Holland, 1995), it is clearly imperative that the authorities take firm
action. Having said that, a number of concerns arising from this tough
stance against those who engage in racist abuse need to be addressed.
First, clubs must make greater efforts to ensure that their policies to
eject or prohibit fans who engage in racist behaviour include scope for
individuals concerned to challenge their treatment. Summary justice
whereby fans are banned on the basis of slender evidence and with no
possibility to appeal against such a decision is no more acceptable
when applied to those accused of racism than in any other circum-
stance. Tough measures against racism are unlikely to receive
widespread public support if they are seen to be unfair or arbitrary. Of
course, the insistence on just procedures may provide an excuse
against action on racism, but if the football community is seriously
committed to dealing with the problem then the inclusion of safe-
guards must be ensured.

Second, another advantage to developing thorough procedures to
deal with alleged racists is that equitable treatment of cases can be
more nearly ensured. The suggestion that some clubs have particular
problems with racist supporters or are prone to be targeted by far-right
groups has been outlined and the development of a coherent and
consistent procedure common to all clubs, if properly applied, would
ensure that such perceptions were diminished. The issues of equitable
treatment is also raised when the treatment of racist supporters is
compared with others who engage in other forms of offensive or

disorderly conduct. One Millwall fan who was prosecuted for racially abusing an opposition player contrasted his treatment with that of another fan (*Talk Radio*, 1997):

> The punishment that I received for making racist and indecent chants was a five-year exclusion order from all football within England and Wales. How they can justify giving me a five-year ban, I don't know. I'll give you an example, a mate I know who goes to Millwall, he threw a coin at Ian Wright who played [there] in the Coca Cola Cup a few years ago ... he was caught doing it, he got a twelve-month ban. Now that coin could have gone in his eye or anything, he's physically attacked someone. All I've done is verbals and I've got a five-year ban, so where's the equality in that?

While it is impossible to make any definitive comment on the validity of this complaint, and it is important to recognise that most of those who engage in racist abuse or violence in football stadia or anywhere else never receive punishment of any kind, it remains the case that the punishment of offenders ought to be relatively equitable. Making examples of a few offenders by giving them harsh sentences is unlikely to provide much of a deterrent when supporters are aware from their own experience that intervention by stewards or the police – let alone prosecution through the courts – is extremely unlikely.

The third objection sometimes made to the harsh punishment of racist supporters is that the sentiments they express, whilst reprehensible, are merely an expression of frustration and that they are unlikely to be 'real' racists. The supporter quoted above claimed in his defence that he was racially abusive as a means of distracting an opposition player from his game and that he was not otherwise prejudiced against black people. The notion that football stadia are an arena in which hard-pressed individuals can seek relief from the trials and tribulations of everyday life is a common and romantic way of understanding football fandom. Early theories of crowd psychology embedded this notion in popular explanations of mass behaviour, and Le Bon's (1895: 32) famous expression of this process continues to enjoy wide currency:

> By the mere fact that he forms part of an organised crowd a man descends several rungs on the ladder of civilisation. Isolated he may be a cultivated individual, in a crowd he is a barbarian – that is a creature acting by instinct. He possesses the spontaneity, the

I.M. MARSH LIBRARY LIVERPOOL L17 6BD

TEL. 0151 231 5216/5299

violence, the ferocity and also the enthusiasm and heroism of primitive beings, whom he further tends to resemble by the facility with which he allows himself to be impressed by words and images.

Despite widespread criticism of this simplistic psychological account of crowd behaviour (see, for example, Reicher, 1987), the notion that individuals act differently when part of a mass of people continues to be referred to by those who argue that the expression of racism within a football crowd is fundamentally different and distinct from such behaviour elsewhere. Prohibiting the expression of racism in football grounds will not – of itself – serve to change the attitudes of spectators, and it is difficult not to agree that many of those who make monkey chants or shout out their opposition to the 'black bastard' centre-forward are probably not active racists or supporters of the NF or BNP. Nonetheless, the idea that such expressions should be tolerated as 'heat of the moment' aberrations of no great significance can be rejected. Given that minority ethnic groups are put off from attending matches because they dread such incidents, it is in nobody's interest, except perhaps some of the far-right groups referred to earlier in the chapter, to smugly accept racist abuse as part and parcel of the game.

The principles behind efforts to tackle racism within stadia have been broadened to address problems within the game more widely, including attempts to rid the amateur recreational game of racism, and to tackle incidents between players, managers, coaches and administrators. The high profile of these problems was evident is the publication of the first report from the Football Task Force created by the government soon after the 1997 general election. The Task Force findings, published in March 1998, considered many of the initiatives described in this chapter and corralled them behind the broad principle of 'zero tolerance' of racism within the game. Such a strategy, the Task Force argued, could be extended from local councils using their powers to prohibit racist players of park football through to the insertion of clauses into the contracts of professional footballers allowing them to be sacked if they racially abuse fellow professionals or officials. The philosophy of 'zero tolerance' was developed primarily in the context of policing in New York and became current in the United Kingdom in the mid-1990s. It was strongly associated with the approach to criminal justice Tony Blair tried to develop as Shadow Home Secretary and one that was central to redefinition of 'New' Labour. During this period the phrase has been subject to considerable scrutiny, and is criticised by many as an empty slogan, Given that it has fallen into disrepute, to some extent, it is perhaps ironic that it should be extended to efforts to tackle racism within football. Although many of the recommendations of the Task Force appear imaginative and beneficial, if occasionally naive – it is hard to imagine some of the professionals recently alleged to have racially abused opponents being sacked by their clubs – there are several reasons to advise caution with the broader notion of 'zero tolerance'.

First, as we clearly identified earlier in the chapter, all of the initiatives discussed here are essentially reactive, they respond to racist abuse, harassment or violence but do little or nothing to challenge attitudes which cause them. It should not be forgotten that many of the other campaigns and strategies we discuss in this book do attempt to do so, but the policing agenda, which was reinforced by the Task Force report, relies upon the unspoken assumption that racist attitudes are relatively fixed and the most appropriate action is to ensure that actions which arise from such beliefs is firmly controlled and repressed. To some extent it might also be argued, as is often the case with other crime prevention measures, that the developments outlined also serve to deter individuals from engaging in racist abuse or violence. Given that we argued earlier that many of those who do join in monkey chanting and banana throwing are unlikely to be committed racists or fascists, and it is more probable that they are simply behaving in a way they misguidedly feel is appropriate in the context of a match, it seems likely that the measures discussed will have some deterrence effect. If many of those engaging in racist banter do so casually and without much forethought then perhaps they can be deterred from doing so by high-profile messages that such behaviour will be penalised. These messages will only prove effective in the long term if they are backed with consistent procedures to deal with offenders, which is why we argued that clubs must take firm action to deal with these problems.

However, we have also been keen to stress that whilst many of the forms in which racism is manifest within football grounds are specific to that context, monkey chanting for example rarely seems to feature anywhere else, the fundamental nature of racialised attitudes are no different in stadia than anywhere else in society. Although often used rather lamely as an excuse for inaction, the familiar argument that racism is society's problem, not football's, is essentially true. We have been critical of simplistic psychological arguments which suggest that people gathered in crowds shout racist abuse and slogans simply because they are irrational beings stripped of their identity as individuals. Despite media images of neo-nazi hooligans, most of the racism in the game, especially when one looks beyond the supporters and considers the problem more extensively, is not that different from other environments. 'Zero tolerance' of racist behaviour will do little to counter the ignorance, stereotypes and prejudices which marginalise or exclude altogether black and Asian people from many areas of contemporary football.

Following on from the problem of concentrating on countering racist behaviour instead of beliefs is the issue of displacement of racism away from football stadia and into other fields. If racist behaviour does not occur within grounds but is simply transferred to the street, the factory or other areas where it continues to be expressed relatively unhindered, then little has been gained except that football clubs and the industries that share a stake in the game's success can congratulate themselves on their efforts and forget about the problem. This is not an argument for tolerating racism within the ground, though, as we reject the idea that football matches provide an isolated 'safety valve' via which unpleasant and objectionable attitudes can be exorcised. It does raise the question, however, of what is really gained from a zero tolerance strategy if it only serves to relocate racism from one arena to another. A more fundamental approach to challenging racism on social, political and economic levels is preferable, a challenge to racism which does not assume that the problem is solely about the reprehensible behaviour of an extreme deviant minority but which recognises the subtle, contradictory and pervasive nature of a diversity of racisms.

The condemnation of 'race thugs' by the media is welcome, and it is remarkable how the press have focused on the problem within the game. However, it does fit with prevalent conceptions that hold racist views to be the preserve of a minority of ill-educated impolite extremists. The corollary of this is that the mainstream, the middle-class families who are apparently the new generation of football fans, are immune from racism.[61] Clubs must tackle the problem of racism, that is skinhead troublemakers who shout abuse or throw missiles at black players or rival supporters, because the problem is offensive to middle-class groups and alienates the TV and advertising companies. Like swearing, racist views are unacceptable in polite society. Of course such views concentrate upon very narrow forms of racism and do nothing to challenge structural or institutional matters. The failure of most clubs to operate effective equal opportunities policies; the fact that black and Asian people, like women of any ethnic background, are noticeable by their absence from managers' benches or boardrooms; that local football associations have few minority ethnic members, and that the press and television journalists who report on the black stars of the game are usually middle-aged white men; all these dimensions of the problem are overlooked by the prevailing view that racism in football is the preserve of racist hooligans. Of course organised groups of politically motivated troublemakers are active within the game, and wider sections of football supporters may become embroiled in similar behaviour from time to time. Such activities must be effectively policed and many of the initiatives described in this chapter have made some considerable progress in this regard during recent years. In many ways these anti-hooligan measures have had the added effect of confronting racist behaviour within football stadia. They have not eradicated it though, and the policing approach offers very little scope for concerted action against indirect or covert racism. If football really does wish to transform itself in order to reflect more closely the reality of a multicultural plural society, then it must complement the kind of measures outlined here with other strategies to ensure that all sections of society are represented in the governing bodies and boardrooms of the game.

5

A Design for Life: Deconstructing the Game's National Identities

Introduction

> Which side do they cheer for? It is an interesting test. Are you still
> harking back to where you came from or where you are? I think we
> have got real problems in that regard.
>
> (Norman Tebbit, April 1990)

The controversies surrounding issues of sport and national identity
encapsulated by Norman Tebbit's infamous 'cricket test' quoted above
resurfaced in 1999 in England during the cricket World Cup. The
support for Pakistan, India and Bangladesh during this tournament
from Britain's Asian communities was significant, and many of these
fans were quoted as being only too happy to fail Tebbit's 'test' (Reid,
1999). Whilst for Tebbit and others not just of the political Right, to
be English is to identify with, and assimilate into, the dominant white
culture, for many British Asians the cricket World Cup offered the
opportunity to affirm and display their own cultural and sporting
identities.

This chapter will discuss the construction of national identities
within British football and will argue that many are too narrow, and
exclude minority ethnic groups in a similar fashion to Norman
Tebbit's 'test'. For instance, the tendency to sentimentalise the
England that featured in two world wars flavours the nostalgia
surrounding England's only World Cup triumph in 1966. The
perceived national characteristics that helped win the wars are
portrayed as being those which won the World Cup for England,
something reassuring for a nation seeing its global influence shrink-
ing. It is argued below that the dominant imagery surrounding this

nostalgia is of an ethnically homogeneous all-white England, with little acknowledgement of the role and influence of any minority ethnic communities.

In the case of Scotland, media analysis of national identity is often focused as much on the behaviour of Scotland's travelling support, the Tartan Army, as it is on the team's performance. The Tartan Army's 'ambassadorial' role is enacted by the exuberant and friendly nature of its constituents, in an attempt to forge an identity in opposition to the perceived hostile and hooligan English following. For Wales, football often takes second place to rugby union, especially in the south of the country. Its identity as a separate football nation has been questioned by other national associations, principally from Africa and Asia, who wonder why it is that the United Kingdom, one nation-state, should have four separate representative sides, in contravention of FIFA rules. Whilst this pressure also affects the other UK nations, some commentators (for example, Duke and Crolley, 1996) have argued that the establishment of the League of Wales in 1992 was as a direct result of the vulnerability felt by the Football Association of Wales. The former Sports Minister Tony Banks's championing of a single UK team only complicated matters further.

The debates surrounding issues of national identity are complex. Cohen (1994: 192–3) argues that it is impossible to assess general characteristics of a particular nationality for three broad reasons: first, because these assessments would assume a genetic blueprint for the population that is 'radically different' from that of other nations, or a unique set of 'traumatic' experiences that occurred uniformly across the population; second, because any notions of national traits should be temporally contingent, and not fixed in any particular era; and third, because such generalised characteristics fail to recognise identities based around gender, ethnicity or a myriad of other aspects of society. In this chapter, we will seek to utilise Cohen's standpoint in order to analyse how English, Scottish and Welsh identities are represented through football, and how, repeatedly, those that are involved in the game offer outdated or stereotypical ideas about what constitutes these identities. It is argued below that many of these constructed identities are exclusive, in that they fail to reflect the contemporary, multicultural and fragmented nature of the separate nations.

Therefore, we are not trying to establish what actually constitutes 'Englishness', or 'Scottishness' or 'Welshness', but rather to examine how these notions have developed in the context of football – after all, to talk of a definitive 'Scottishness', for example, is to fall into the trap of ideas of fixed national characteristics so articulately dispatched by Cohen. Rather, what we are seeking to do is to provide a framework through which the problematic construction of national identities in a sporting environment can be seen, and how some of these are over-reliant on popular mythologies or 'invented traditions' (Hobsbawm, 1983: 2) that try to link the present with a suitable version of the past. Maudlin reflections on the 1966 World Cup win are especially relevant here.

That we are discussing the expression and construction of three separate national identities, rather than one single 'British' identity, reflects our assertion that the idea of 'Britishness' is increasingly problematic in the developing political climate. The recent vote by the populations of Scotland and Wales for a measure of devolution, resulting in the holding of elections to the Scottish parliament and Welsh Assembly in 1999, throws into debate the whole idea of 'Britishness'.[62] A significant percentage of the electorate appears to be rejecting the idea of a shared identity with the English, something reflected in the growth in support for nationalist parties like the Scottish National Party and Plaid Cymru during the 1990s. The Tartan Army's construction of its own identity as being the 'polar opposite' of that of England's fans is a manifestation of this feeling.

The idea of a 'British' identity can be traced back to the expansion of British imperialism in the eighteenth and nineteenth centuries. For Houlihan (1997: 130):

> The conceptualisation of the British nation was an English elitist construct designed to rationalise direct rule over the Scottish, Welsh and Irish and also to provide a cultural *cordon sanitaire* to protect the English upper class's notion of its social and cultural superiority and exclusivity from being tainted through direct association with the colonies and dominions.

The English identity therefore became the dominant aspect of Britishness from the latter's first inceptions. Aspects of this identity were constructed as being the antithesis of the perceived characteristics of certain national or ethnic groups opposed by the British state, in particular the French, Irish, Catholics and Jews. For Cesarini (1996) this was an aspect of the overall racialisation of national identity, part of a process that differentiated Britons from the populations subject to British imperial rule. The employment of racist stereotyping was also used against immigrants from the late nineteenth century onwards: the 1905 Aliens Act, the first legal restriction of immigration into Britain, came mainly from concerns over Jewish immigration to London's East End. Solomos (1988) suggests that the series of postwar acts that have restricted immigration into Britain have done so with a view to creating a racially-exclusive British identity. This perceived 'threat to Britishness' has recently resurfaced through issues such as the 'borderless Europe' and, in the case of football, the Bosman ruling.

The European Union and the challenge of the Bosman ruling

The 'Europeanisation' of British football has been a key development in the 1990s. The name itself is, of course, a misnomer, as it seems to suggest that before this process began, England, Scotland and Wales were themselves something different and apart from Europe. However, the number of players from other European Union nations playing in Britain has risen dramatically, directly as a result of the 'Bosman ruling' of December 1995 which opened up the European 'player pool' to British clubs.[63]

The case centred around a Belgian footballer, Jean-Marc Bosman, who fell into dispute with his club, RFC Liege, when he was out of contract in 1990. Liege retained Bosman on a quarter of his previous salary, conditions that prompted the player to ask for a transfer. When his club placed him on the transfer list at an exorbitantly high price that precluded any offers from other clubs for him, Bosman began litigation proceedings at the European Court of Justice in Luxembourg. He was seeking damages of £300 000 from UEFA, the Belgian Football Association and RFC Liege for restraint of trade, citing Articles 48, 85 and 86 under the 1957 Treaty of Rome. He also challenged the 'three foreigner rule' that had previously placed restrictions on the number of overseas players that played for a club in European competitions to three – something that had, for example, seriously hampered Manchester United's team selections for the Champions League in the 1990s as, under this rule, 'foreigner' meant anyone who could not be selected for the club's national side. For Manchester United, this limited the selection of Welsh, Irish and Scottish players, as well as those from other parts of the European Union.

In December 1995 the Court upheld the Advocate's decision to find in Bosman's favour, meaning that footballers from any nation in the European Economic Area (EEA), could, like workers in other industries, move freely from one nation in the area to another at the end of their contracts, and in the case of football with no transfer fee attached. This has resulted in large numbers of EEA footballers playing in all of the four professional leagues in England, a consequence of which has been an often heated debate as to whether these 'foreign imports' are good for the game, or whether they deny opportunities for home-grown talent. This chapter will examine the impact of these players, the reaction to them from fellow professionals, coaches and football authorities, and whether they have challenged the insular traditions and ideas that have historically characterised English football.

This post-Bosman transformation has mirrored broader political developments in the European Union, including the closer integration of national economies through the development of the single European currency, and closer political and social ties through the signing of the Maastricht Treaty in 1991. These developments have provoked a debate about national sovereignty within Britain, and whether the 'British way of life' is imperiled by these changes (Lunn, 1996).

Euroscepticism, on occasion tinged with xenophobia, discussed more fully in Chapter 6, played a significant part in the formation of the Conservative government's relations with its European neighbours, and has featured in tabloid press coverage of the subject. As we shall argue below, these sentiments have been reflected in some aspects of the football industry's response to the influx of foreign footballers. Stereotypes of 'fancy-dan' foreign footballers not being able to withstand the rigours of the English league season, particularly applied to southern Europeans, have been directly challenged by the influence of the playing and coaching styles of the new EU imports. However, it is interesting to note that much of the debate has not centred around new football 'cultures', but instead has focused on *numbers*, an approach which characterised the political response, in the form of controls, to postwar immigration to Britain. As will be suggested below, this emphasis on the threat to British jobs posed by immigrants has not been a million miles from the response to the influx of EEA players from the Professional Footballers' Association.

Fair play and invented tradition: how English football cannot escape the past

The defeat of the England team at the hands of the Argentineans in the second round of the 1998 World Cup was a bitter pill for the

English national press and public to swallow. The match itself had been something of a roller-coaster ride, with England coming from 1–0 down to lead 2–1, before eventually being level at 2–2 at the end of extra-time. The resultant penalty shoot-out produced victory for Argentina, an early exit from the tournament for England and, in the days that followed, vilification for David Beckham, sent off during the second half, in certain sections of the national press.

Unsurprisingly, however, the press coverage told only half of the story of the match. For example, much attention was paid to Michael Owen's spectacular solo goal, although little was given to his role in the penalty that England were awarded when he appeared to exaggerate the effects of a challenge from an Argentinean defender in order to win the penalty. By doing this, Owen had contradicted notions of 'fair play' and honesty that, as will be detailed below, are still regarded by many involved in English football as being quintessential national characteristics. Owen's actions sat uncomfortably with these traditions, and were seen by some as a reflection of a type of cynical professionalism directly opposed to the old chivalrous Corinthian spirit where winning was considered secondary in importance to 'how you played the game'. It was apt, after all, that at the end of a previous tournament where the England team had lost on penalties, in the 1990 World Cup, it was awarded the tournament's Fair Play trophy by FIFA.

The elimination of England at only the second stage of France '98, and its overall record (two wins, two defeats) was an unexpectedly poor performance from a team that had finished top of its qualifying group. Indeed, the main news stories surrounding the English at France '98 centred around the outbreaks of hooliganism from a minority of England supporters, particularly in the days around the team's first match against Tunisia in Marseilles (see Chapter 6). Pictured graphically in the *Mirror* (16 June 1998: 5) as being a central figure in the disorder was James Shayler, a tattooed, shaven-haired, white, working-class male: in other words, the archetypal hooligan 'folk devil'. Symbolically, Shayler represented another form of English identity – that of the 'bulldog' male who was prepared to fight for his country and would never run away from confrontation.

The disorder in Marseilles was a representation of the kind of nationalistic violence typical of a section of England fans abroad for a number of decades (Dunning, Murphy and Williams, 1988). Just as the Tartan Army uses the media to demonstrate its own projection of a gregarious, exuberant Scottishness (see Giulianotti, 1991), so a rump of England supporters use it to project their own ideas of Englishness. As an anonymous England follower stated:

> With England, we think the team is detached from us. However, we have something in our control: we can remind those who 'want to know' that, if need be, we're still those mad bastards who fight like fuck and don't give up until we win. If I'm running with an England crew ... we know that just for once an England that means something to us is all around us – something we can believe in, fight for, get hurt for, wreck for, live for and die for. (Brimson and Brimson, 1997: 35)

Although caught on film as being in the 'front line' of the trouble in the old port region of Marseilles, Shayler was loyally defended by his friends in his home town of Wellingborough as being: '... a proud man. You can't walk away when there are a crowd of Tunisians after you. He's a good guy, a family man' (Armstrong, Blackman, Young, Daniels and Disley, 1998). It was almost as if the people interviewed 'back home' could not really see that Shayler had done anything wrong, and appeared to share some of his 'bulldog' values. After all, he had not run from the confrontation, had he? In the eyes of some, that *really* would have been reprehensible.

Within the media, there were also debates surrounding the reasons as to why the trouble occurred, and in particular why hooliganism was 'back' after apparently having disappeared during the 1990s. The contrast between the press coverage of the riots in France and that of the disorder during the Euro '96 tournament in England was striking. For the most part, the English press sought to 'deamplify' the disorder surrounding the clashes involving the home side's supporters and those of Scotland and Germany in 1996, and instead portrayed the tournament as being essentially peaceful (Garland and Rowe, 1996).

For England's games at Wembley during Euro '96, the atmosphere was, generally, peaceful and celebratory. The profile of far-right groups, who have traditionally targeted England home matches, was small, as fans projected a more positive identity by the wearing of England shirts *en masse*, painting their faces with the cross of St George, which supplanted the Union Jack, and the communal singing of 'Three Lions', the defining song of the tournament.

Nevertheless, despite the lack of presence of extremist groups, an editorial in *When Saturday Comes* noted that during the semi-final with Germany, England fans taunted their opponents with the chant

'Are you from Dresden?', whilst the refrain 'I'd rather be a Paki than a Jock' featured at the Scotland match (Back, Crabbe and Solomos, 1998: 77). This was a recognition that, as mentioned in Chapter 3, xenophobic and racist chanting is evident in fan-friendly, 'family' crowds, and is not just the preserve of stereotypical 'hooligan' fans like James Shayler. As Davis noted of a family group he saw in Marseilles:

> The England-supporting family we saw in the city centre kitted-out in 'No Surrender/Spirit of Drumcree' T-shirts may like to think they're not part of the problem, but clearly they are. (Davis, 1998: 19)

Carrington (1998) is also critical of the nature of this newly constructed English fan identity and its portrayal in the media and other popular discourse during Euro '96. Essentially, Carrington argues, this identity was depicted as uniformly white and England itself seen as being culturally homogeneous. This was exemplified by the 'Three Lions' anthem so enthusiastically sung by England supporters, which spoke of the 'thirty years of hurt' endured by fans since England last won a major football tournament in 1966. In the video for the song, all of the English players and supporters featured were white.

Carrington identified other concerns with the dominant imagery of Euro '96, including ITV's tournament coverage (prominently featuring the White Cliffs, in a fashion almost identical to that of an election broadcast a year later by the British National Party), and the pervasive nostalgia for the 1960s, and in particular England's World Cup triumph of 1966. For Carrington, the lack of acknowledgement of the multicultural aspects of contemporary England produced an effect of 'cultural and racial exclusion from the constructed national community that was inadvertently more powerful than anything the BNP could have achieved' (Carrington, 1998: 117).

Many of the key images of England's progress in the 1966 tournament, such as the stoicism and grit of Nobby Stiles or Geoff Hurst's hat-trick in the Final, appear to have passed into contemporary football folklore by a mythologising process often evident in representations of Britain's efforts in the two world wars. The aspects of national character so often championed as having won the wars – the bravery of 'The Few'; the 'spirit of the Blitz'; 'We will never surrender' – were also, as Clarke and Critcher (1986) argue, seen as

I.M. MARSH LIBRARY LIVERPOOL L17 6BD

TEL. 0151 231 5216/5299

being evident in England's World Cup win, something reassuring for a nation that had suffered postwar austerity and decline. The triumph was a way of reemphasising the virtues of English 'national characteristics', and nobody represented this better than the Charlton brothers, summarised by Harris (1971: 86) as:

> Bobby graceful, cultured, creative, conveying some sort of artistic instinct; and in the English tradition, a sense of restrained emotion, a faint air of diffidence overlaying his talents and his endeavour. And Jack the honest artisan, straight as a gun barrel, stiff as a sentry, solid, stout-hearted, dependable. Foreigners must have seen it too.

Interestingly, Harris's description of these supposed aspects of the English character – creativity, modesty, honesty and valour – was peppered by the use of military metaphors. Not only this, it was implied that foreigners were somewhat in awe or even afraid of these characteristics. This populist nationalistic nostalgia for past glories is present in television programmes such as the perennial *Dad's Army*, *Allo Allo* and the 1990s comedy *Goodnight Sweetheart*, all of which paint a cosy picture of the Second World War, and in sports programmes such as *A Question of Sport* [64] and *They Think It's All Over*, which takes its title from the BBC commentary of England's fourth goal in the '66 Final.

The reality of England's tournament win in 1966 was, of course, somewhat different from the myth. During the match against France, for example, England defender Nobby Stiles brutally fouled French captain Jacques Simon, and while Simon lay injured England took advantage of their numerical superiority in order to score the game's second goal. After the quarter-final against Argentina, Ramsey referred to his opponents as 'animals', something which, to the Argentineans, smacked of English colonial arrogance. When the Argentine captain, Rattin, was sent off during the match, the Wembley crowd abused him with cries of 'Dago! Dago!' as he left the pitch (Hill, 1996). The dubiousness of England's third goal in the Final hardly needs underlining.

Of course, celebration is integral to the football experience, and the point here is not that England as a nation should never recall or celebrate the 1966 win. However, the exclusive and ethnocentric content of much of the popular culture that surrounds the 1966 win is problematic. The images conjured up by John Major, when he was Prime

Minister, of an England of 'county grounds, warm beer, invincible green suburbs . . . and old maids cycling to Holy Communion through the morning mist'[65] is mirrored in the jingoism surrounding 1966. Both represent an introspective national contemplation rooted in a version of British society essentially monocultural and previous to the economic and political crisis of the 1970s that accelerated national decline.

This retrospective portrayal of England and English football marginalises the role and presence of minority ethnic groups. Back, Crabbe and Solomos (1998) describe the experiences of a black England fan who, before the Euro '96 encounter with Scotland, was 'accepted' as being 'on the same side' as white England fans, because the focus of the day was on establishing English identity as being separate from, and opposed to, Scottish identity. Temporarily, his Englishness was not being questioned, as in the eyes of the white fans his normative identity was constructed as being English first, and black second. On another day, and with different opponents, this construction, as the black supporter recognised, would be reversed.

This experience was endorsed by a number of supporters interviewed for this book. One, a black Arsenal fan, explained that while he felt comfortable going to matches at Highbury, he was wary of watching England because of the presence of far-right groups, and the almost exclusively white nature of the crowd at Wembley. He also had a problem identifying with the England team, stating:

> Even in cricket, with my family being from the West Indies they always want them to win when they play England, and so did I because I identified with the players. You could say the same about football. During the 1978 World Cup Finals I remember, even though my parents weren't into football, they supported Brazil and Peru because they had black players. Maybe that's why I don't support the England football team, I don't identify with them. There were no black players in the team when I was growing up.[66]

Datar (1996: 11) claimed that during Euro '96, whilst large sections of the white population supported the English side, a majority of black people rooted for other nations in the tournament. Johal (1998) found himself in a similar situation. As a teenager of Asian origin born in England, Johal described himself as being 'enmeshed' into English youth culture and an ardent supporter of the national side during the 1986 and 1990 World Cups. However, during the latter, while watching the quarter-final match involving England and Cameroon on television in a local pub, Johal was subject to racist abuse as the game, temporarily, went sour for England. He was made to realise that for many of those white England fans he was not English, but an 'estranged and marked foreign other' (*ibid.*: 118), in spite of his own identification with the England side during this period. In some respects this reflects the point referred to earlier, that for many the presence and status of minority ethnic people in English society remain ambiguous and negotiable. If Norman Tebbit's 'cricket test' were reversed, it seems clear that English society would fail it. By the time of Euro '96, Johal, too, was supporting 'anyone but England'.

As Gilroy (1987) notes, identity is not fixed, but is subject to a constant state of construction and change. Through the various anti-racist measures outlined in Chapter 3 football in England currently has an opportunity to provide a more inclusive sense of English identity. Yet, it seems, significant sections of the English football industry and media return time and time again to the 1966 tournament, relishing an ethnocentric view of Englishness. Whilst English identities continue to change and develop, influenced by a myriad of global and ethnically diverse sources, the notion of English identity projected through its national sport remains based in the past, trapped by an insular sense of nostalgia. As Hobsbawm (1983: 2) suggests, nations have 'invented traditions' which try to establish links from the present to a certain, constructed, view of the past. In the case of English football, these traditions are, seemingly, based around a mythologised World Cup win from over thirty years ago. As the English side frequently struggles to keep pace with nations to whom the English supposedly once 'taught the game', so ever-more comforting become the images of '66. The possibilities of constructing an inclusive English identity through football that more closely reflects a multicultural society thus become remoter, typified by the unquestioningly revere in which Alf Ramsey was held by sections of the press, even though it is claimed that he 'largely despised ... all outsiders and most foreigners' (Glanville 1999: 8).

England at home: Bosman, politics and the globalisation of the game

The attitudes of many involved in English football outlined in the previous section are, of course, in part the product of an historical development of the game in the broader context of the evolution of football into a global sport, and England's often problematic relationship with that process (Tomlinson, 1986). This has involved a steady erosion of the paternalistic and Anglo-centric view of the game's origins (although some of these attitudes remain) coupled with England's reduced influence in global football politics. In the 1990s, after the Bosman ruling, the influence of continental European coaches and players has brought an increased awareness and adoption of tactics that have altered the traditionally physical and unsophisticated 'English' way of playing, at least at the highest levels of the domestic game. At the same time, the development of football in Africa and Asia, and the increasing influence of these countries within FIFA, has resulted in a shift in power away from football's 'traditional' power base of Europe and South America (Sugden and Tomlinson, 1998).

As was discussed at some length in an earlier chapter, although there is evidence that different forms of games loosely comparable to football were played in a number of European countries, the sport was first developed in its modern form at British public schools in the early part of the nineteenth century (Wagg, 1995). During this period, sport was viewed as being an essential part of the training for the prospective 'lieutenants of the Empire' (Holt, 1989: 204) as it helped to induce courage, stamina, leadership and sense of duty. A set of rules was devised at Cambridge University in 1848 that formed the basis of those adopted by the English Football Association on its formation in 1863 (see Table 5.1). A decade later saw the formation of the Scottish Football Association, with Wales following suit in 1876 and Ireland in 1880. England drew 0–0 with Scotland in the first official international match in 1872. Indeed, such was the prominence of the British game that it was not until 1901 that a match between Argentina and Uruguay constituted the first international not involving a team from Britain.

In 1904, under a French initiative, the Fédération Internationale de Football Association, FIFA, was formed, comprising seven nations – France, the Netherlands, Denmark, Spain, Sweden, Switzerland and Belgium. Conspicuous by their absence were the British associations, who were invited to join, but declined – the English FA responded by stating 'The Council of the Football Association cannot see the advantages of such a Federation, but on all such matters upon which joint action was desirable they would be prepared to confer' (Tomlinson, 1986: 85). Despite this statement, this isolationist stance was only to last one year: the English joined in 1905.

Table 5.1   The development of British football, 1863–1950, selected
milestones

1863	English Football Association formed.
1872	Scotland 0 England 0 – first official international match.
1873	Scottish Football Association formed.
1876	Welsh Football Association formed – First Welsh international fixture versus Scotland (0–4 defeat).
1886	International Football Association Board formed.
1904	Fédération Internationale de Football Association (FIFA) formed: British associations decline to join.
1905	English FA joins FIFA.
1910	Scottish and Welsh FAs join FIFA.
1913	FIFA officials join the International Football Association Board.
1920	British FAs withdraw from FIFA in a dispute over a proposed boycott of Germany and its former allies and set-up an alternative body, the Federation of National Football Associations.
1924	British FAs rejoin FIFA.
1928	British FAs withdraw from FIFA again due to a dispute over the definition of 'amateurism'.
1930, 1934, 1938	First Three World Cup finals; England, Scotland and Wales absent as their associations are not in FIFA.
1946	English, Scottish and Welsh FAs rejoin FIFA.
1950	England team is first British national side to compete in World Cup finals, losing two out of three matches.

This problematic beginning to the English FA's relationship with
FIFA (and, indeed, those of the other British nations) was an early
indicator of the difficulties that lay ahead. In 1920, all four associations withdrew due to a dispute over whether to play Germany,
Hungary and Austria, with the British objecting to competing against
the nations they had so recently been at war with. A separate international organisation, the Federation of National Football Associations,
was formed, but after four years the association was disbanded as the
British rejoined FIFA. However, in 1928, as the result of further
disagreements regarding the definition of payments for amateur
players, the British nations withdrew from FIFA once more, not rejoin-
ing until 1946.

Wagg (1995) notes that during this period of isolation from international football politics, the myth of England being the 'unofficial
world champions' began to emerge, despite a number of defeats
against European opposition. As none of the British teams entered the
three competitions held in the 1930s, as their associations were not

then part of FIFA, this myth remained untested in World Cup finals until 1950. In those finals, England were humiliated, losing two out of three matches, including a 1–0 defeat by the USA.

The real shock for English complacency came three years later, when the national team was thrashed 6–3 at home by the skillful and tactically more adept Hungarians. This reversal was followed by a 7–1 away defeat at the hands of the same opponents later that year. The realisation that English football did not have a divine right to be the best in the world was slowly dawning. The English game, in isolation, had become too reliant on the 'myths of Northern male working-class culture' (Wagg, 1995: 10), revolving around the idea that players had learned their skills playing in the streets, rather than needing to be properly coached. These myths persisted, in some form, for decades: Bobby Charlton pointedly recorded in his autobiography that he and his brother were not, contrary to accepted fact, taught their foot-balling skills by their mother in their back yard.

Under the coaching of Walter Winterbottom (who still had his teams picked by an FA committee) the national side enjoyed mixed fortunes in the World Cups during the 1950s, never reaching the semi-finals. During this time, the press began to focus on Winterbottom's tactics, often painting a picture of him as a 'theory-bound boffin chalking on a blackboard while the Brave Lions of the England team looked away in embarrassment' (Wagg, 1998: 34). Domestically, the advent of European club competitions had been met with suspicion and caution from England's football administrators, who initially did not permit England's club sides to enter. Glanville (Leviathan, 1997) described Alan Hardaker, then Assistant Secretary of the Football League, and allegedly responsible for forcing Chelsea to pull out of the first European Cup competition in 1955/56, as 'very xenophobic' and that Hardaker told him that he did not like visiting the continent because 'there were too many wops and dagos'.

During the 1950s and early 1960s, the expansion of football in Africa and Asia resulted in a number of these nations seeking to join and influence the politics of FIFA. Up until this period, the game had been dominated by Europe and South America, but the possibilities of turning the African and Asian nations' disaffection with this state of affairs into their representatives acting *en bloc* had occurred to João Havelange, who gained their support for his campaign for the FIFA presidency in 1974 (Tomlinson, 2000).[67]

Following Winterbottom's resignation in 1963, Alf Ramsey became England manager with, for the first time, full responsibility for team tactics and selection. However, the sides fashioned by Ramsey tended to be functional, pragmatic and hard-working, with emphasis placed upon team work and rigid tactics, rather than individual flair. This attitude was exemplified by England midfielder Alan Ball, described by Miller (1970, cited in Critcher, undated: 7) as:

> All the adjectives, the superlatives as well as the clichés which surround the modern game apply to Ball – the 90-minute man, genius clothed in sweat, perpetual motion, the essential team-man, hating to lose, living and breathing the game, awesome opponent and valued colleague, selfless.

Ball's work ethic, commitment to the collective effort, his sense of *duty* even, are championed here: attributes which fitted perfectly into Ramsey's playing system. The success this system generated is undeniable, with England's 1966 World Cup victory, now having passed into folklore, as described above. What is debatable here are the long-term benefits for an English footballing culture which, as sketched above, was prone in the boardroom and on the pitch, to insularity and wariness of 'foreign' ideas. Ramsey's playing legacy of 'caution and dullness' (Clarke and Critcher, 1986: 115) had proven effective and, arguably, continued to influence the selection of England sides through the next three decades.

For example, Bobby Robson, perhaps England's most successful postwar manager after Ramsey, shared many of the 'traditional' ideas of his illustrious predecessor and, like Ramsey, had enjoyed club success with Ipswich Town. Although his successful side of the 1970s and early 1980s featured Dutchmen Arnold Mühren and Frans Thyssen, much of Robson's success was based on playing a fairly rigid 'English' 4–4–2 system, which he tried to adapt at international level. England defender Tony Adams, in his autobiography *Addicted* (1998), outlines his frustration at the lack of tactical awareness of Robson, and the inflexible nature of his team formations whereby each player had a limited role and function in comparison to many of the other sides competing in the European Championships in 1988.

Davies (1990) describes how during the 1990 World Cup in Italy, some of the senior England players had to *persuade* Robson to adopt a sweeper system instead of the less-flexible formation he had been insisting upon. Robson, somewhat reluctantly it seemed, agreed to this more 'continental' approach, yet could not resist describing Bryan Robson, the England captain, in familiar terms:

Robson's outstanding, the captain – you could put him in any trench and he'd be first over the top. He'll go into the unknown, wouldn't think about it – he wouldn't think, well, Christ, if I put my head over there it might get shot off. He'd say c'mon, over the top. (Davies, 1990: 89)

Contentiously, Kuper (1994) argues that when coaching PSV Eindhoven in Holland, Robson never really earned the respect of the Dutch players, despite winning the league title twice in two years. For many of them, Robson lacked detailed tactical knowledge, being too reliant on the tried and tested methods that he'd used before. Kuper argues that a different culture exists amongst players in Holland, who openly debate and discuss tactics with their coaches, but who were critical of Robson for not being able to teach them anything.

Robson also had difficulties coping with players who were articulate in their views and independent-minded enough to express them. He was used to the English dressing-room environment where players call the manager 'boss' and do not question his authority. In this environment, team-spirit and camaraderie are all-important, and peer-group pressure decisive. Pearson (1996: 22) compares the atmosphere to that of a school classroom, a 'land of japes and banter. The dormitories of Billy Bunter and Winker Watson with the addition of sex and lager'.

Reng (1999) describes the difficulties that some of the post-Bosman EEA players have had in coming to terms with the 'dressing-room culture' of English clubs, and in particular the lack of debate between players and coaches regarding tactics. This situation is replicated in dealings with the media, with which, for example, German players have been used to dealing with frankly and articulately in their own country. This approach has clashed with that of English players, who are encouraged to speak to the press only in the most uncontroversial of terms. Therefore, overseas players who do 'speak out' in England, such as Didi Hamann and Uwe Rösler, are subsequently labelled as 'foreign whingers'.

Some of the media debate regarding the growth in the number of overseas players at English clubs has centred around notions of how the imports are damaging the game. Much of the discussion has questioned whether 'the foreigners' have influenced 'our game' for the better, and there has been concern voiced by some within football, including the Professional Footballers' Association – the players' 'trade union' – about the numbers of continental European players that have arrived post-Bosman. The PFA has also become alarmed over the proposed changes in employment laws that, at the time of writing, could lead to larger numbers of non-European Economic Area players being recruited by English clubs.[68] At the moment, a club manager wishing to buy such a player would have to satisfy a number of Department of Education and Employment criteria in order to fulfill work-permit requirements.[69] If these restrictions are weakened or abolished, then the number of players from the United States and Africa, for example, could rise dramatically.

Whatever the proposed rule changes, the globalisation of the player market has already changed the outlook and playing style of a number of English sides. Tony Adams (1998) argues that it was not until the influx and consequent influence of overseas players into the English leagues in the 1990s that English players and coaches began to develop a more sophisticated tactical awareness. He also describes the influence of Arsenal coach Arsène Wenger, someone credited with not only bringing a number of high-class continental European and African footballers to Arsenal, but also with changing the playing style of the club away from the traditional 4–4–2 English 'long-ball' style. Although this style had proved successful for the club in the past (evidenced by its championship wins in 1989 and 1991), these tactics were becoming outdated in the post-Bosman Premier League, with its increased emphasis on sophisticated tactics more suited to achieving success in European competitions, and especially the lucrative Champions' League.

Wagg (1998) outlines the current influence of continental European coaching ideas on English Premiership clubs as they seek to emulate the methods of successful Italian, Spanish and French clubs. He cites the case of ex-Liverpool manager Roy Evans, whose association with the powerful 'boot room' mythology at Anfield appeared increasingly anachronistic to the more sophisticated coaching needs of top clubs competing on the European stage. In the pre-Bosman era, Evans's background would have been an asset, but post-Bosman it was seen as old-fashioned for a club seeking to compete with Europe's élite. Evans was replaced by a French coach, Gerard Houllier.

The difficulties experienced by overseas players in the laddish environment of English football have been mirrored by those of English players when transferred to clubs in continental Europe. The insularity of English football has been reflected in the attitudes of many of those who have been transferred abroad. Whilst some, including Ray Wilkins and David Platt have enjoyed a measure of success, others, like Jimmy Greaves and Luther Blissett, have met with little reward and returned home disillusioned. Indeed, Blissett had found it so difficult adapting to conditions in northern Italy, where he was playing for Milan, that he apparently remarked 'No matter how much money you've got, you can't seem to get any Rice Krispies' (Kuper, 1994: 72).

Paul Gascoigne, it seems, fared little better than Blissett in Italy after being transferred from Tottenham Hotspur to Lazio in 1992. On his arrival in Rome, Gascoigne was presented to the Lazio supporters at the Olympic Stadium, where it seemed as though his reputation went before him as he was greeted by an enormous banner proclaiming: 'Gazza's boys are here, SHAG women, DRINK beer' (Nottage, 1993: 72). Yet, despite possessing an 'un-English skill and tactical intelligence' (Kuper, 1994: 73) on the field of play, Gascoigne's behaviour off it mirrored that of many young English males on package holidays abroad, centring as it did around drinking, sexual innuendo and practical jokes (Nottage, 1993). This type of behaviour bewildered Lazio officials, who were used to their footballers possessing, on the whole, self-discipline, sensible diets and drinking habits more fitting to élite professional athletes.

With the advent of the Bosman ruling in January 1996, avenues have also opened up for lesser-known English professionals to play in leagues in continental Europe. Ball (1996: 27) outlined the difficulties faced by two English players Jamie Pollock and Robert Ullathorne adapting to the social and footballing cultures of Spain. Whilst Ullathorne appeared to be learning the language and was actively interested in the new environment he was in, Pollock had adjusted less well. When describing the difference between the drinking culture which was a feature of his professional footballing life at home and the stricter environment of Spain, he exclaimed: 'I need discipline. Nothing against the lads back home, but fucking hell (he mimes slaking a pint). Here we can't be seen in bars, like. We'll get fined'.

In many ways, Gascoigne was himself a conundrum of English identities. Although his technical ability and footballing intelligence were considered adaptable for the more sophisticated and tactically deft Italian *Serie A*, and atypical of many workhorse English midfielders, he exhibited the parochialism characteristic of some of the lads who follow England abroad. Indeed, in spite of the many cultural attractions available to him in Rome, it was said of him that he was never happier than when he was back home, drinking with his friends and family in the working mens' club in Dunston.

Coming up for air: the submerged nations, football and national identities

Moorhouse (1991) describes Scotland and Wales as being 'submerged nations' within a UK dominated by England and outlines the importance of sport as an expression of national pride and identity for nations in this situation. Recent devolution for Scotland and Wales suggest that, to a certain extent, these 'submerged nations' are 'coming up for air', and maybe asserting their independence more confidently than before. The role that football can play in reshaping new Scottish and Welsh identities will be discussed in the following section and it will be suggested that, as in the case of England, these identities are often constructed in a fixed, exclusive fashion that rely on romanticised versions of history.

The importance of football for a large section of Scotland's population has been well-documented, being succinctly described by Cosgrove (1986: 99), for example:

> The Scottish national experience finds its richest and most complex expression in football. The support for the national team is intensely patriotic, a reflection of the distinct sense of nationalism to be found in the character of most Scots.

Scotland's ability to sustain its own league (formed in 1890) reflects this enthusiasm for the game, and also Scotland's status as a more independent nation than Wales, exemplified by, for example, its own separate legal, judicial and education systems. The Scottish Football Association was formed in 1873 (see Table 5.1), although Scottish clubs continued to play in the English FA Cup until 1887. Scotland's initial high profile on the international football stage (the national team played in the first official international fixture, versus England in 1872) was boosted by the Association's decision to join FIFA in 1910. The SFA was, however, to undergo the same problematic relationship with FIFA as both the English and Welsh FAs were until the mid-1940s.

The complex relationship between Scotland, Scottish identity and perceptions of England and Englishness in Scotland is thrown into sharp relief by the ideologies of the national team's travelling support, the Tartan Army. Taking its name from a small but militantly nationalist political faction (Cosgrove, 1986: 106), the Tartan Army has become integral to the way that Scottish national identity is projected through football, and, on occasion, has symbolically become more important than the performance of the team. That the fans have an 'ambassadorial role', and that they appear to take this role seriously, is central to constructions of Scottish identity (Finn and Giulianotti, 1998), and it is interesting to trace the cultural and behavioural developments of Scotland's support.

The migration of large numbers of Scottish supporters to Wembley for the fixture versus England began in earnest in the 1920s and 1930s, and during the following decades the 'taking over of London' every two years for the Home International match by tens of thousands of Scots became a matter of pride and an important and defiant way of proclaiming national identity. The occupation of Trafalgar Square had a special symbolic resonance, and a key aspect of the whole process was to ensure that the English were vastly outnumbered inside the stadium itself.

The Scottish victory in 1967 was of vital significance as it came a year after England's World Cup win, achieved in a tournament that Scotland did not even qualify for. The Scottish triumph was greeted with a celebratory but disorderly pitch invasion. Ten years later, a similar invasion brought widespread media condemnation, and the labelling of the Scots as hooligans by sections of the English press. An estimated 80 000 Scots had made the trip that weekend (Cosgrove, 1986), when the celebrations for the Queen's Silver Jubilee were in full swing. As was the case a decade before, the timing of the Scottish victory was crucial for expressing Scottish pride in the wake of outpourings of English patriotism and jingoism.

During the 1970s and 1980s spectator disorder had become a feature of the England–Scotland fixture. Violence in and around Wembley and Hampden Park increased to such a level that by the mid-1980s the game was switched to a Wednesday night in an effort to prevent fighting between fans. However, after 1989, when there were 240 arrests at Hampden Park, the annual fixture was scrapped by the English and Scottish football associations, under some political pressure from the Conservative government.

Giulianotti (1991) traces the cultural change in the Tartan Army, away from hooligan behaviour and towards an overtly friendly internationalist outlook, to the late 1970s/early 1980s. During this period, Scottish supporters' perspectives shifted from basing their identity around notions of violence, towards reacting *against* the hooligan behaviour and xenophobia of England's support by being non-violent and friendly with fans of other teams, and local populations. By doing this, the Tartan Army sought to establish Scottishness as being distinct and separate from Englishness, a distinction not always made by those that the Scots encountered abroad. This transformation relies on a degree of self-policing and a number of informal rules within the Tartan Army. For example, the wearing of club colours, and especially those that may prove controversial or potentially divisive (those of Glasgow Rangers, for example) is banned. Excessive consumption of alcohol and noisy, exuberant behaviour are encouraged. The supporters won a special award from UEFA for their good behaviour at Euro '92 in Sweden, in direct contrast to the violent behaviour of a part of the English contingent.

The Tartan Army's 'carnivalesque' rituals are now well-established at international matches and especially at the major tournaments. They are played out to several different audiences, including, crucially, the national and international media. The Scottish press has been complicit in building the Tartan Army's myth, with the *Daily Record* going as far as to associate images of Scotland fans 'taking over' Trafalgar Square as being the 'definitive representation of being Scottish, and to herald the new Scotland to come' (quoted in Finn and Giulianotti, 1998: 199). That the Tartan Army can manipulate the media, to a degree at least, is important to the overall mission of establishing their, and Scotland's, identity to a wide audience. The creation and presentation of positive images, the complicity of the media and the wider public's perceptions of the reality, is, Finn and Giulianotti (*ibid.*) argue, as important as the reality itself.

Underpinning the Tartan Army is a collective anti-Englishness that has acted as a way of unifying its members under a common banner. These sentiments came under attack from parts of the Scottish press during the 1998 World Cup in France. The *Daily Record* stated before the England–Argentina match (which occurred after Scotland had been eliminated from the tournament): 'Let's Not Cheer Too Loudly if England Lose – Why the Tartan Army Should Grow Up and Stop Putting the Boot into the Old Enemy' while a post-match article in the *Sun* argued: 'Any Scot who supported the Argentineans should be ashamed of themselves ... what happened to our claim to be the friendliest nation on Earth?' (MacGregor, 1998: 21).

The implication of the above pieces was that Scottish identity should involve more than a collective anti-English sentiment. In a political climate of further integration of the European Union, to express national identity in such a parochial and insular way may appear incongruous, and it could be argued that this anti-Englishness contradicts the Tartan Army's 'internationalist' outlook. It also fails to take into account that English fan cultures are changing. Although England's travelling support has not fully undergone the type of transformation undertaken by the Tartan Army, there is evidence that it is moving away from the type of behaviour that the Tartan Army defines itself against. As Perryman (1998) and others noted, in spite of the impression given by some sections of the press (see Chapter 6), the vast majority of England fans in France for the 1998 World Cup were non-violent and were there solely to enjoy themselves, mixing happily with other supporters. Arguably, this process began at Italia '90 where the English fans' behaviour exhibited signs of exuberance and 'daftness' similar to the Scots, and continued through Euro '96. The face-painting and wearing of fancy-dress that have characterised some aspects of the English support in the 1990s are similar, at least in spirit, to that of the Scots, presenting a challenge to the Tartan Army's stereotypical view of England supporters, and therefore to its own counter-identity.

It is also suggested that the very narrow Scottish identity portrayed by the Tartan Army acts to exclude significant sections of the population. Bairner (1994) argues that it is almost exclusively male, with females forced either to be passively sidelined, or to exhibit the 'laddishness' that characterises much of the Army's activities. It also seems to allow little room for the incorporation of other Scottish identities, such as those of minority ethnic groups who see themselves as Scottish (Bains and Johal, 1998). Although the Tartan Army likes to think of itself as being outgoing and not xenophobic, there is an argument that this is based upon a myth that the Scottish are tolerant of others and are not racist, assumptions challenged by Dimeo (1995) and Dimeo and Finn (1998) in their analysis of racism within the Scottish game.

Towards the end of the 1990s the debate surrounding the Tartan Army's role had spread to the Scottish press, in a form that implied that the Army's own constructed identity was becoming outmoded. In the week following the World Cup qualifying game against Estonia, James Traynor of the *Daily Record* exclaimed: 'Call Time on the Sporran Legion – We Have to Stop Making Fools of Ourselves On and Off the Park', and Stuart Cosgrove commented: 'Scottish football is keen to preserve its last pathetic myth – that a bedraggled army of travelling fans can seduce the world' (Donnelly, 1997: 12).

It is also relevant to acknowledge the divisions within the Tartan Army. As well as being male-dominated, Scotland's support, despite its best attempts at unity, still unsurprisingly reflects club and ethno-religious loyalties. For example, Bradley (1994) outlines the difference in the levels of support given by the fans of clubs to the Scottish national side, with Celtic fans in particular being less committed to supporting Scotland. One of the most pertinent aspects of Bradley's research is his assertion that supporters of Aberdeen and Dundee United developed a strong Scottish identity in the 1980s and 1990s, in opposition to Rangers (perceived as having pro-English sentiments because of the club's unionist political stance) and Celtic (regarded as having strong affiliations with Ireland). He also describes the importance of political, cultural and religious affiliations that supporters across Scotland feel with the two big Glasgow clubs.

The dual Scottish–Irish identity of many Celtic fans is an important aspect of the complex construction of national Scottish football identities. Boyle's survey of Celtic fans in the early 1990s (Boyle, 1994) showed 43 per cent of respondents demonstrating a stronger commitment to the Irish national side than the Scottish team, reflecting the cultural and historical roots of the club. As one young fan interviewed by Boyle commented (*ibid.*: 86):

> I'm Scottish, I'm thinking about it in two senses. If I go abroad and meet someone, they'll ask me where I'm from, and I'll say 'Scotland' and I'm Scottish 'cos that's where I've been born and brought up, but there is always in your mind that most of your characteristics are portrayed through the Irish way of feeling, you've got that.

Moorhouse (1994) argues that the sectarian divisions within Scottish football as popularly described are not as deep or as pervasive as many suggest. He conceives of identity having five levels, through which people:

1 may know an identity exists;
2 may understand what that identity involves;
3 may believe in what that identity involves;
4 may allow that identity to affect behaviour;
5 may make that identity one of their main identities (Moorhouse, 1994: 191).

Moorhouse suggests that, although generally media and academic discourse claims that most Scots adopt Catholic and Protestant identities at levels four and five, the vast majority of the population, if it adopts them at all, does so at the first two levels only. He does acknowledge that these identities are situationally contingent, and on rare occasions can rapidly be taken up at the highest level. This appears to have happened in a number of incidents involving those playing in Celtic–Rangers matches. Most famously, Englishmen Graham Roberts and Paul Gascoigne have been involved in controversial sectarian incidents during Old Firm matches,[70] but, as these were relatively spontaneous, it is difficult to place the players on one of Moorhouse's levels. The adoption of the 'Protestant identity' was probably no more that a fleeting occurrence. However, Terry Butcher, Rangers's English centre-half, appeared to adopt the unionist and loyalist politics associated with his club, stating:

> I don't like U2, that's rebel music, Southern Irish. And Simple Minds – I found out Kerr was a Celtic supporter, so all my Simple Minds tapes, they went out the window. Celtic, you hate 'em so much. (Davies, 1990: 45)

The violence at the end-of-season Celtic–Rangers match in 1999, including widespread disorder and an assault on the referee, is indicative of the deep emnity between the two clubs that still appears, at the very least, to have a sectarian element to it. Indeed, these disturbances were referred to in a BBC television documentary as the 'worst sectarian violence seen in Glasgow for 20 years' (BBC2, 1999). Significantly, when celebrating Rangers' cup win over Celtic in 1999, one of the club's directors, Donald Findlay, a prominent anti-devolution Tory, resigned after being caught on camera singing sectarian songs.

Rugby union in Wales is, for Holt (1989), a symbol of 'celtic nationalism' more potent than that of football. That it became established as the dominant code in Wales, and popular among the working-class communities of the south, is all the more surprising given that the sport itself is so often associated with the upper and middle classes of England, and with English public schools. Holt (*ibid.*) traces this development through the expansion of the coal industry in the 1880s, which brought around 1.5 million immigrants into the area. These came mainly from places without, as yet, an established football culture, including south-west England where rugby was already popular, and Ireland. The game itself, which resembled the old Welsh game cnappen, suited the isolated communities of the valleys which

I.M. MARSH LIBRARY LIVERPOOL L17 6BD
TEL 0151 231 5216/5299

were too small to sustain professional football and so used amateur rugby as a conduit to channel intense local rivalries.

At the same time, a new form of Welsh identity was establishing itself in the south. This construction had a number of political and cultural components that reflected a more modern, industrialised nation: socialist activism, social activities centred around the coal pits, including male-voice choirs, and a thriving club rugby scene. This 'new Wales' was distancing itself from the outdated, 'bardic' Wales that the new immigrants found little resonance with.

By contrast, in the north, football was more popular, as the area was influenced by its geographical proximity to north-west England, already a football stronghold (Wagg, 1995). The first Welsh professional clubs were established there, at Wrexham and Ruabon, and early cup competitions were dominated by north Walean sides. The 1920s saw the growth of the professional teams of south Wales, with Cardiff, Swansea and Newport joining the English league. The same decade saw the only major trophy won as part of the English structure by a Welsh team when Cardiff won the FA Cup in 1927, beating Arsenal 1–0. Until relatively recently, Cardiff were the only Welsh team to have played in the top division, until Swansea gained promotion to the old First Division in the early 1980s. The Welsh Cup, established in 1877, has since the 1950s been dominated by the clubs playing in the English Football League.

The Football Association of Wales (FAW) was established in 1876 and joined FIFA in 1910, following the lead of the English FA. After this it split from, and then rejoined, FIFA in the same pattern as the other British associations (see Table 5.1 above). The national side has only qualified for the World Cup Finals once, in 1958, via a play-off, and eventually reached the quarter-finals, losing 1–0 to Brazil.

The British associations enjoy disproportionate influence within FIFA due to their presence on the International Football Association Board, the rule-making body of football founded by the British in 1882. Despite this favourable historical legacy, the comparative lack of success of the clubs and national side put the FAW under increasing strain as the pressure grew within FIFA, and particularly from nations in Africa and Asia, for the UK to have one representative side, and hence one voice in FIFA, rather than four sides and therefore four FIFA votes. FIFA rules state that a nation-state should be represented by one national team, something directly contravened by the four UK teams.

The unique situation involving the status of UK national teams and clubs was underlined in bizarre fashion in the early 1980s when

Swansea City qualified for the UEFA Cup by finishing in sixth place in the old Division 1 in England. In the same season, the club won the Welsh Cup, and therefore found itself with the peculiar prospect of simultaneously representing England in the UEFA Cup, and Wales in the European Cup Winners' Cup.

The insistence from UEFA and FIFA in the early 1990s that the newly-independent states of the former Soviet Union and Yugoslavia should have their own established leagues as a prerequisite to joining, placed greater pressure on Wales than on England and Scotland, nations who had leagues that were over 100 years old. As a result, the FAW formed the League of Wales in 1992, but the birth of the League was fraught with difficulties. The three clubs, Cardiff City, Swansea City and Wrexham, playing in the English league, and at the time the only fully professional clubs in Wales, negotiated exemption and eight others opted to stay in the English non-league 'pyramid' structure. The machinations of the politics between the FAW, UEFA, FIFA and the clubs that did not want to participate in the League of Wales have been well-documented elsewhere (see, for example, Duke and Crolley 1996), but, overall, the establishment of the League of Wales can only be called a partial success. Despite a perceived rise in the standard of play in the League (Crockett, 1996), none of its winners have made any significant progress in European competition, and the championship itself is being dominated by one club, Barry Town. In addition, attendances are still, for the most part, less than a thousand for matches.

In the light of this, and the dominance of rugby as the sporting expression of Welsh patriotism and nationalism, it would be all too easy to make the assumption that football is not important as an expression of Welsh identity. This would be to ignore the achievements of the league clubs, who, after all, have enjoyed significant success in European competition in the past,[71] and who regularly attract attendances that put their rugby union equivalents in the shade. Haynes (1999: 141) claims that it is football, not rugby, that is the Welsh national game, citing as evidence the fact that more people play football than rugby in Wales.

The proliferation of Welsh flags amongst the supporters of these clubs at away matches is also indicative of the fact that, for many fans, it is impossible to separate their club's league encounters with English sides from feelings of national identity. Lewis and Haynes (1999: 133) go so far as to claim that the Welsh 'have an aggressive hatred for all things English'. To what extent these feelings are shared by football supporters in Wales as a whole, or the Welsh public in general, is questionable. The vote for a measure of devolution in 1997 was dubbed 'Yr Ie Bychan', or 'The Little Yes', as the electorate voted for an assembly only by the smallest margin. Tellingly, the turnout for this vote was only 50 per cent, a figure barely improved upon for the actual elections to the Welsh Assembly in 1999. These figures do not, on face value at least, appear to show a population of strongly nationalist sentiment.

It is important to acknowledge, though, that the vote for devolution varied considerably between regions, with, generally speaking, the constituencies near the English border being lukewarm or even hostile to devolution, and those furthest from it more supportive of the notion. Tellingly, perhaps, Cardiff, the nation's capital and the location of the proposed Assembly, voted against its establishment. Welsh nationalism, according to Cohen (1994), is more cultural than economic, and is based around ideology and myth rather than hard economics. It may be that these feelings were reflected in the devolution vote, with the more Anglicised section of the population being less susceptible to romantic nationalism and more focused on the benefits of being fully integrated into the English political system. Whatever the realities, and there is not the space to do the discussion justice here, the fragmentation of the electoral base of nationalist support is indicative of the regional splits and differences that exist in Wales.

This parochialism is exemplified by the most intense and bitter football rivalry in Wales, that between Cardiff City and Swansea City. This fixture, and its associated violence between groups of fans, appears to contain more ill-feeling than any match against English teams. This is not to say that both clubs do not have a hooligan element that follows them to matches in England, and, indeed, Cardiff have an especially notorious and violent minority of fans who figured in significant amounts of disorder in the 1990s. As both clubs have spent the recent past out of the top divisions, and hence out of the national football spotlight, it could well be the case that, away from south Wales, the only occasions that the public becomes aware of them is when their supporters are involved in high-profile incidents of disorder. It could therefore be argued that the Welsh identity most prominently projected through football is one of hooliganism and insularity, symptoms, paradoxically, of what many call the *English* disease.

Conclusion

Throughout the chapter we have been considering the complexities of identity construction, through football, of Englishness, Scottishness and Welshness. That we have been looking at the latter two in terms of their relationship with England, rather than with each other, is testimony to England's historical dominance within Britain. That these relationships are complex, and constantly being reformulated, is crucial to how new identities are also redefined.

The fact that both Wales and Scotland have a measure of devolution, in the form of an Assembly and a Parliament respectively, is also a symbol that these submerged nations may be 'coming up for air'. This is an indication that nation-states are themselves, in many instances, fragmenting, something which Billig (1995) regards as inevitable in postmodern times. For Billig, nations are a product of the modern era, and are now being attacked both from 'above' and 'below' by the processes of globalisation: 'above', from supranational organisations like the European Union, and 'below', from the assertion of a number of local identities, some of which, like those related to gender or lifestyle, are also transnational. Therefore, the old style of politics based on ideas of nationhood are being replaced by the politics of identity, as Billig notes (1995: 133):

> national identity no longer enjoys its pre-eminence as the psychological identity that claims the ultimate loyalty of the individual. Instead, it must compete with other identities on a free market of identities.

In the British example, the expression of local nationalisms in Wales and Scotland has begun a process that may ultimately lead to full independence for these nations. As this process unfolds, the necessity for the development of new forms of identity, rather than ones based on images and myths from war or other conflict, becomes ever more pressing. It is therefore important to recognise that the assertion of other non-national identities, such as those based on ethnicity, is also a part of contemporary developments and needs to be recognised whenever notions of national identity are thrown open for debate and development.

The globalisation of British football, evidenced by (among other things) the advent of the post-Bosman European player 'pool', the proposed European Super League and the development of the

Champions League, is no more exemplified than by the case of Manchester United. That its support is national and transnational is oft-remarked,[72] but that it is developing its multinational corporate profile through a series of burger bars, retail outlets and other marketing avenues in Southeast Asia has been less well-analysed. These markets (there are estimated to be over 500 000 Manchester United 'supporters' in the region) are potentially a considerable source of revenue for a club that has seen sales from merchandise decline in recent years in England.[73]

These developments illustrate the complexities of regional and national allegiance and identity, and also the newer, market-driven priorities of football. The globalised marketing of the sport is reducing the relevance between club and locality. That it is apparently less and less important to ever attend a live match of your club, or even have much of an idea of the local identities and fan cultures of the area where your club is based, is significant. For Redhead (1997) this is the notion of 'post-fandom', marked by the privatised nature of football culture and the 'style-surfing' notion of what it means to be a football supporter. Thus, new forms of football consumption are appearing, whether through satellite television at home or in bars, or through the Internet or other media.

The watching of matches in pubs and bars in Britain has become a feature of 'Sky era' nineties football. This has had a number of effects, including the creation of a culture of collective participation that at one time was confined to the stadium itself. As Redhead notes (1997: 30):

> The traditional soccer culture of yesteryear of participatory, largely male, fandom of the terraces – threatened by small all-seater stadia, steeply rising prices of admission and the embourgeoisment of the sport – has effectively transformed itself to the already existing male 'pub culture' which in large part it created in the first place.

However, the other side of this development has seen widespread disorder spilling out from pubs and bars after a match has finished 'unfavourably', such as that witnessed after England lost the Euro '96 semi-final against Germany. Also, the kind of xenophobia and racism witnessed and experienced by Johal (described above) is indicative that this 'new style of football consumption' is, in some ways, still as exclusive as the old one. Indeed, Johal's assertion that there is a higher than average take-up of satellite television in Asian households, and that this is the form in which many members of minority ethnic groups watch the game, is instructive of the need to assess the complexities of how football is consumed in Britain. If, as outlined in Chapter 3, minority ethnic groups still find football stadia intimidating, and this is replicated in the atmosphere of the pub, then it can be of no surprise that, for excluded groups, the 'new style of football consumption' is the same as the old one: watching it at home.

As was evidenced during the 1999 cricket World Cup, large sections of the black and Asian communities still have strong allegiances to the nations of their antecedents, and express this passionately through sport. This illustrates the complexities of issues of national identities, and is indeed indicative of the way in which multiple identities, which are situationally and temporally contingent, are formed and reformed. Yet it is instructive to note the description given by Holt (1989: 173) of nineteenth-century football values:

> The team symbolized the men who supported it ... Football was a celebration of intensely male values: 'grit' was the great virtue ... but there was also sticking at the task, persisting and never letting your mates down even if you were injured or dropping with tiredness. Football was a saga in which skill and cunning were valued, but, hardness, stamina, courage and loyalty were even more important.

Even in an era when football is becoming globalised, and when national and regional football identities are being challenged and redefined, these values *still* seem to reflect those of many involved in the contemporary game, from the managers, through to the players and fans, and even those supporters that engage in disorder. These values are those that, as described above, are often used simultaneously to describe national characteristics that supposedly won two world wars and the World Cup. As Gilroy (1993) notes, they evoke notions of Churchill's 'island race', a homogeneous 'race' that excludes from this constructed national identity Britain's visible minority ethnic groups.

6

Mad Dogs: England, the Media and English Supporters during Euro '96 and France '98

Introduction

The similarities between the England national team's performances in the 1996 European Championships (Euro '96, held in England) and the 1998 World Cup (held in France) are worth noting. Both competitions saw the team struggle initially, then progress to the latter stages only to come unstuck in penalty shoot-outs. Euro '96 and France '98 also saw England compete against nations, Germany and Argentina, with whom Britain had been at war with in the relatively recent past. To the indignation of the national press and in a manner underlining the wider decline in influence and power of the country on the international political stage, England lost both matches.

This chapter will critically analyse the English press's reaction to the unfolding events of both of these competitions, in relation to the England team's achievements, its fans and the broader socio-political climate. It will attempt to demonstrate that there were a number of parallels between the coverage of both tournaments, as well as significant differences between them. In particular, the chapter will focus on the jingoistic and xenophobic reporting in Euro '96, and its relation to the Euroscepticism of the then Conservative government, and the exaggerated and sensationalistic reporting of the disorder involving England fans during the initial part of France '98. The nationalistic and xenophobic coverage surrounding England's match with Argentina during the latter tournament will also be assessed.

Another feature common to both tournaments was the violence that occurred in various towns and cities in England once the English team had exited, with, on both occasions, large numbers of drunken youths involved in damaging property and clashing with the police.

The disorder that followed England's Euro '96 semi-final defeat against Germany was especially widespread, with disturbances occurring in Trafalgar Square, London, as well as in dozens of other locations around the country (O'Reilly, 1999). Following on from these events in 1996 the National Heritage Select Committee (1996: 1) released a report which explicitly criticised the tabloid press for their '... xenophobic, chauvinistic and jingoistic gutter journalism' exhibited during the tournament which, the MPs claimed, partly explained the anti-German violence that had occurred after England had lost to Germany. It is suggested here that the kind of criticism made by the Select Committee report is too simplistic in its assumption that the tabloid press is primarily responsible for the xenophobia undoubtedly evident during this period. Instead, it is argued in this chapter that the social and political context of Britain's relationship with the European Union (EU) in the 1990s, and especially during the years of Conservative government, reinforced the xenophobia sometimes apparent in the newspapers. Whilst it would be comforting to suggest that the sensationalist tabloid press were to blame for the violence witnessed in Trafalgar Square and elsewhere, such reassurance cannot easily be drawn.

Another similarity between the coverage of Euro '96 and France '98 was the newspapers', and especially the tabloids', employment of militaristic imagery in their coverage. As is detailed below, this use of overtly nationalistic and battlefield-obsessed metaphors provided almost the only framework through which sections of the press could analyse England's relations, sporting and otherwise, with other countries. Mangan (1996) analysed the links between sport and militarism, and showed that the language of warfare in Victorian and Edwardian Britain drew heavily on sporting metaphors. Values such as fair play, discipline and teamwork, associated with the playing field, were held to be essential characteristics for the British colonial soldier. It is argued below that the relationship between sporting and military discourses persists to this day, although the nature of the press coverage of Euro '96 and France '98 suggests that its direction has been reversed. In other words, whereas Mangan illustrated the way in which warfare was infused with sporting imagery in previous eras, popular cultural representations of sport in more recent times have relied heavily on militaristic rhetoric.

Another focus of this chapter is the reporting of the disorder that occurred around England's first match during the 1998 World Cup. As well as demonstrating an overreliance on military metaphors (describing the incidents as 'hooligan wars', for example), the coverage arguably demonstrated the characteristics of a 'moral panic' and an amplification and distortion of the actual events. It is therefore worth spending a short while discussing the role of the newspapers in conferring labels upon those they consider deviant, and the impact they can have in demonising certain social groups and creating a sense of moral public outrage regarding the activities of these groups. As Hall (1978: 23) stated, the emphasis that newspapers place on the reporting of 'bad' news, and then the sensationalised reporting of that news, can 'have the effect of changing, in the readers' minds, the size, scale and significance of the event or incident. There is some evidence to suggest that this tendency has been at work in the presentation of some social problems including football hooliganism. The battle for circulation may lead to newspapers, and particularly tabloids, to be driven to sensationalise and exaggerate stories, especially as the *Sun*, *Mirror* and the *Daily Star* are essentially competing directly with one another.

In the 'France '98' section below we will demonstrate how much of the coverage of the violence involving English supporters was prone to this type of exaggeration. We will also argue that one of the major weaknesses of this coverage was that it relied on simplistic reasoning when providing explanations for the disorders. On many occasions, the tabloids labelled those involved in disorder as 'louts', 'yobbos' and 'brain-dead scum' (to name but a few), although all were placed under the moniker of being 'football hooligans'. As Armstrong explained (1994: 320):

> 'Football hooliganism' lacks legal definition, structural coherence and precise demarcation of membership. It is ephemeral, renegotiated weekly, and constructs nomadic spaces for individuals and social groups to enter, perform and exit ... it is also a contested site in which political structures and institutions endeavour to impose simplified, prejudicial readings of complex and evolving practices, through the agencies of the police and various expert opinions.

Yet, as Hall (1978: 20) postulated, by the repeated use of derogatory terms and the application of the 'football hooligan' label, 'we stigmatise and degrade the actions of others. We implicitly flatter ourselves and our own "rational", moderate and well-controlled behaviour by comparison, and we legitimate any actions which we or the state might take in combating what we have so labelled.' During this process the label of 'football hooliganism' is deliberately applied to any incident related to football, however tenuously, and creates the impression that more hooliganism is taking place than is actually the case. This in turn creates a climate in which there is more moral opprobrium directed at the supposed deviants, a 'moral panic' (Cohen, 1981), and more pressure on politicians and others in authority to take action, in the form of legislation. The police then have renewed authority to undertake harsher methods to combat these 'outsider groups', which leads to further arrests, more media outrage and the increased polarisation of public opinion and distrust and suspicion between the two groups.

As Murphy *et al.* (1990) argued, football hooliganism has been reported in a particularly negative style since the 1960s, and has resulted in hooliganism attaining its current forms. Murphy *et al.* do not argue that sensationalist or exaggerated reporting of disorderly incidents actually *causes* hooliganism, but that the *forms* of hooligan manifestations have changed and reformed to its current 'gang' style partially as a result of the flavour of newspaper coverage. Also, football grounds were seen, through press reports, to be venues in which violence regularly occurred, and the publicity afforded to groups such as West Ham United's 'Inter-City Firm', and Leicester City's 'Baby Squad', elevated hooligans to 'folk-devil' status. As we shall discuss below, this process was evident during France '98, particularly in the case of a certain James Shayler, who became a high-profile 'hooligan icon' as a result of tabloid coverage.

The bulk of the discussion which follows is based upon a subjective reading of the newspaper reporting of Euro '96 and France '98. For the former, the *Daily Mail*, the *Sun*, the *Daily Mirror*, *The Times*, the *News of the World* and the *Guardian* newspapers were analysed from early May 1996 (one month before the championships started) until 7 July (one week after Germany lifted the trophy). For the latter tournament, the same papers plus the *Daily Star* and the *Express* were examined from the beginning of May 1998 until a week after the championships ended. Not all aspects of the coverage are considered here and what follows should be regarded as a tentative examination of some of the key themes rather than an exhaustive catalogue of the media coverage.

The next section of this chapter consists of the analysis of newspaper coverage of the two tournaments. It is split into two parts: first, the coverage of Euro '96 is discussed, and following that the reporting of France '98 is examined. Both parts detail the articles in chronological order, and the differences and similarities between the contents and tone of the coverage of both tournaments is noted. As we explain, these similarities (jingoism and occasional xenophobia; nostalgia for previous footballing glories; the use of military imagery; the exaggeration of the hooligan 'threat') outweigh the differences (there was less overt xenophobia exhibited by the press during France '98, and a bigger concentration on hooliganism, due to the outbreaks of disorder involving English supporters). In other words, although the newspapers changed their story *priorities* from Euro '96 to France '98, many of the basic ingredients that flavour the content of the articles were common to both eras.

Euro '96 – 'I know that was then, but it could be again ...'

Phase one: 'hippopotami led by hypocrites'

Phase one of our analysis of the press coverage of Euro '96 extends over the four weeks leading up to the first match.[74] During this time, much of the aggressive xenophobia which characterised the reporting of the latter stages of the tournament (see below) was absent. Instead a number of broad themes emerged: the potential for crowd disorder; nostalgic reminiscence over England's 1966 World Cup win; criticism of the England team's attitude, and of its drinking; and finally, on the eve of Euro '96, overt patriotism. Interestingly, these themes, as we shall outline later in this chapter, were replicated in the build-up to France '98. It is to the first of them that this chapter now turns.

'A masterplan for terror'

The readmittance of English clubs back into European competitions for the 1990/91 season marked the end of UEFA's ban on English teams competing on the European stage. The ban had come into effect after the disorder at the 1985 European Cup Final between Liverpool and Juventus at the Heysel stadium in Brussels, when 39 mostly Italian fans had died after disorder, and then panic, had caused a crush and a wall to collapse. This tragedy precipitated UEFA's ban, although supporters of English clubs, and followers of the national side, had been involved in many instances of violence in continental Europe before. Despite the reputation of English fans as the 'super hooligans of Europe' whom some gangs on the continent tried to emulate (Dunning, Murphy and Williams, 1990) the period immediately after the Heysel disaster witnessed a perceived decline in hooliganism (Redhead, 1991), and after the relatively good behaviour of England fans during the 1990 World Cup in Italy, English teams were allowed once more to compete in the three European cups. However, disorder involving England fans in Sweden for the 1992 European championships heightened concerns that Euro '96 would be the seat for major outbreaks of hooliganism. The police preparations were necessarily extensive (Garland and Rowe, 1995), but with 200 000 visiting supporters anticipated, and with the qualification of some nations whose supporters had a reputation for violence (especially a minority of fans from Italy, Germany, Turkey and Holland), the tabloid press prepared a number of exaggerated 'scare stories' on the topic.[75] The *News of the World* warned BABY-FACED FEUHRER TO BLITZ EURO '96 (19 May: 20–1), suggesting:

> Today we expose the German psychopath hell-bent on turning England's Euro '96 soccer championships into a bloodbath.
> The self-styled Feuhrer of thuggery, baby-faced Ronald Kirsch, has already drawn up his masterplan for terror and plans to invade with an army of yobs.

The article continued by unveiling the purported plans of German hooligans and the counterplans of England's 'far-right maniacs'. The piece concluded by urging readers to help their anti-hooligan campaigning, saying that 'Only with your help can we stamp out this horror'. *Daily Mirror* (5 June: 11) and the *Sun* (25 May: 17) subsequently ran similar stories, with the latter making the explicit link between football hooligans and the neo-nazi group Combat 18. The *Daily Mail*, not to be outdone, yet with little supporting evidence, claimed in HOOLIGAN ALERT (6 June: 80):

> 2,000 England fans will be at the [Scotland versus Holland] game, many intent on causing trouble with the Scots and Dutch supporters.

The *Sunday Mirror*, in an article about two Italian ticket agents operating in London, SOCCER TERROR TWINS IN EURO '96 TICKETS SCANDAL (2 June: 4–5) reported that:

> A massive security fiasco has left the Euro '96 soccer championship in serious danger of turning into a savage hooligan war.
> Two convicted neo-Nazi terrorists, wanted for questioning about a

horrific bomb massacre that killed 85 people, have become official ticket agents for the games ... [and] are free to supply tickets to fans, who could include fascist thugs, hell-bent on turning the most prestigious event in Britain for 30 years into a bloodbath.

The tabloids were not the only newspapers that dabbled in scare-mongering. On successive days (20 May: 4 and 21 May: 8) and then a week later (27 May: 5) *The Times* carried articles with headlines of NEO-FASCISTS AIM TO STAMP THEIR MARK ON EURO '96; NAZI LABEL OBSCURES TWO TRIBES WHO JUST WANT TO GO TO WAR and RIVAL GANGS PLAN FIGHTS BY FAX AND MOBILE PHONE. Each piece featured a graphic incorporating the Euro '96 logo next to the words 'Soccer Violence', thereby associating the two before any violence had manifested itself or, indeed, before the tournament had even started.

The common theme of these articles, that of violent foreign 'nazis' preparing to 'invade' England, was one that, as the championships unfolded, appeared to be very wide of the mark. For the most part, fans mixed freely and happily (Finn and Giulianotti, 1998), and something of a 'carnival' atmosphere was present at many games. The ticketing arrangements were such that segregation broke down inside most stadia, but there was little sign of trouble between fan groups. The invading nazis failed to materialise.

However, Euro '96 was by no means a trouble-free event as far as the English were concerned. Eyewitness accounts details significant disorder before and after England's fixture with Scotland (Brimson and Brimson, 1996). There was widespread violence after England lost the semi-final to Germany, with many towns and cities affected by disorder[76] as crowds of (often drunken) youths took to the streets. In Trafalgar Square, London, German-made cars were attacked and other property identified as German was targeted, and running battles were fought with the police for several hours. In Portslade near Brighton, it was reported that a Russian man was seriously assaulted by an English crowd who, not minded to distinguish between foreigners, mistook him for being German (Garland and Rowe, 1999).[77]

Yet, contrary to the way that the press reported the violence during France '98 (discussed below), the disorder after the England match against Germany was covered in a more 'sober' and factual fashion – banner headlines and sensationalism were largely absent. The *Sun* only ran a small piece on the violence (GANG STABS LAD, 28 June: 4) as did the *Daily Mirror* (NIGHT OF TERROR BLAMED ON YOBS, 28 June: 2). *The Times* gave the story a higher profile (ENGLAND FANS RIOT AFTER DEFEAT,

27 June: 1) but it was only the *Daily Mail*, with HOW THE THUGS PLANNED THE RIOT (28 June: 1) and OUT OF THE PUBS, INTO BATTLE (*ibid.*: 6–7) that featured the disorder at any great length.

'Old English values'

As Chapter 5 discussed, the notion that the English FA is still a central player on the international footballing stage, despite its lack of influence within FIFA[78] or any major tournament victories by England since the 1960s, pervades much of its thinking. This was reflected in the official slogan for Euro '96, 'Football's Coming Home', a phrase which suggested that the old mentality that 'We invented the game and taught it to a grateful world' was still alive within the football authorities. The slogan was also the main refrain of the Euro '96 unofficial anthem, *Three Lions*, a song taken to Number One in the charts during the tournament by comedians Frank Skinner and David Baddiel in conjunction with Liverpool group the Lightning Seeds. The phenomenal success of the single, and its adoption *wholesale* by the English supporters at Wembley, represented another example of the football/comedy/pop music cultural crossover that had begun with the England–New Order *World in Motion* single released at the time of Italia '90.

As is discussed in Chapter 5, the lyric to *Three Lions* was based around a nostalgia for England's 1966 World Cup win, something shared by the tabloid press during the build-up to Euro '96, and, as we mention later, to France '98. Before Euro '96 even got underway, the famous photo of 1966 England captain Bobby Moore holding the Jules Rimet trophy aloft was used repeatedly by the press, notably in full colour on the cover of *The Times Magazine* (1966 AND ALL THAT, 8 June: 1). This photo was 'doctored' by several newspapers so that faces of the Euro '96 team replaced those of players from 1966 (*Sunday Times Magazine*, ACTION REPLAY, 2 June: 1; 1996: THE PICTURE ALL ENGLAND FANS HOPE TO SEE, 2 June: 1; *Daily Mirror Euro '96 Special*, WE DID IT IN 66 WE'LL DO IT IN 96, 3 June: 1).

Six weeks before the start of the tournament several tabloid newspapers became involved in a competition to reclaim the ball used in the 1966 Final, which apparently had been appropriated by a German player at the end of the game and then taken to Germany. Over a number of days in April the story generated a plethora of anti-German articles, with the *Sun* (26 April: 1) labelling the owner of the ball and his son the GREEDIEST KRAUTS ON EARTH in response to their alleged cash demands for a photograph of the ball. The edition also featured a double-page spread full of anti-German sentiment (HANDS OFF MY BALL, HELMUT, *ibid.*: 4–5), something that was to become a regular feature of the press coverage of Euro '96. Nostalgic references to England's World Cup victory also recurred periodically throughout the five weeks of the competition, to the extent that when the England team had to wear its grey 'second strip' for the semi-final with Germany, sections of the press instigated a campaign to have it replaced with one similar to the red kit that the team wore in the 1966 Final.

The anti-German rhetoric exhibited by sections of the press took place in a political climate of Euroscepticism, and sometimes barely-concealed hostility towards the European Union from certain sections of the then governing Conservative Party. The implication that Britain's historical role has been superior to that of other European nations underlies much of the rhetoric of the Eurosceptics (Cohen, 1994). Xenophobic views were often aired by senior government ministers as well as tabloid headline writers.[79] In 1990, for example, the Trade and Industry Minister Nicholas Ridley was forced to resign after he commented: 'I'm not against giving up sovereignty in principle, but not to this lot [the Germans]. You might just as well give it to Adolf Hitler, frankly'.[80] At the Conservative Party conference in 1993, the Social Security Minister Peter Lilley remarked of the 'benefit tourists' he claimed were flocking to Britain from across Europe:

> Why do they come to scrounge off us? They certainly don't come for the climate. Just imagine the advice in a European phrase book for benefit tourists: 'Wo ist das hotel?' – Where is the housing department?; 'Ou est le Bureau de Change?' – Where do I cash my benefit cheque?; 'Mio bambino è in Italia' – Send child benefit to my child in Italy.[81]

Miles (1993: 98) recorded that a 1990 meeting between the Prime Minister, the Foreign Secretary and a number of academic experts considered the nature of the German character and the concomitant implications of reunification. The memorandum from the meeting identified the following, somewhat contradictory, characteristics of the German nation:

> their insensitivity to the feelings of others, their obsession with themselves, a strong inclination to self-pity, and a longing to be liked.

In the immediate period before Euro '96, relations between the British government and other EU nations worsened after the Union imposed a ban on the sale of British beef because of fears in Europe that Bovine Spongiform Encephalopathy (BSE) was linked to Creutzfeld–Jacob Disease, its human equivalent. This was seen by some tabloids as another threat from Brussels to the traditional British 'way of life', although it was probably the power and influence of the farming lobby that had primary influence on the British government's decision to develop a policy of non-cooperation with the European Union in response to the ban. The burgeoning political row was subsequently named in tabloid press and elsewhere as the 'beef war'.

Any sensible debate about the safety of British beef became infused with nationalist rhetoric as certain newspapers and retailers demonstrated their patriotism by asserting their commitment to the product. In this context, the *Sun* referred to THE CATTLE OF BRITAIN (22 May: 4–5), and, next to a photograph of Sir Winston Churchill, reported that:

> In a showdown on a scale rarely seen since the Battle of Britain, the beef fiasco has forced us to fight to save our traditions and freedoms.
> During our finest hour, in 1940, leader Sir Winston Churchill inspired the nation with his historic words 'Never in the field of human conflict was so much owed by so many to so few'.
> In 1996, we must draw on that bulldog spirit again – and show one of Sir Winnie's famous V-signs to the boors of Berlin, the killjoys of Cologne and the mutts of Munich.

The paper advocated a number of methods by which 'to hit back at the nations that voted against us' (20 THINGS TO STEER CLEAR OF, *Sun*, 22 May: 4), a piece littered with invective urging readers to burn the German flag and to play videos of the 1966 World Cup Final to German tourists. Next to the article was a piece by maverick Conservative MP Teresa Gorman THEY WON'T BE HAPPY UNTIL WE'VE SLAUGHTERED EVERY COW IN THE LAND (*Sun*, 22 May: 4) in which she stated 'We need to tell the bullies to go and get stuffed'.

The nature of the press coverage of the prohibition on British beef – of which only an outline has been given here – revealed a common simplification of images of the European Union. It is interesting to note – given the broader discussion in this chapter – the way in which xenophobic anti–German expression often dominates coverage of the activities of European Union political institutions. The extract from the *Sun* quoted above, refers to the ban on beef as though it had been purely a German initiative – rather than a policy developed at an EU level.

In the week leading up to England's first fixture, against Switzerland on 8 June, sections of the tabloid press became openly critical of the England team's behaviour as the true extent of its seemingly drunken excesses on a pre-tournament tour of China and Hong Kong came to light. Photographs of the team in the China Jump nightclub, with ripped shirts and beer bottles in hand, celebrating midfielder Paul Gascoigne's birthday, appeared in lurid detail in several of the papers (see, for example, the *Daily Mirror*, 3 June: 30; the *Sunday Mirror*, 2 June: 78; the *Daily Mail*, 3 June: 58), as did striker Teddy Sheringham, pictured strapped to a 'dentist's chair' in the club, having spirits poured down his throat (the *Daily Mail*, 3 June: 58). On the way home, the team were accused of causing £5000 worth of damage to the cabin of a Cathay Pacific aeroplane.

Amidst calls for the coach to be sacked and certain players dropped from the side, the *Daily Mirror* talked of ENGLAND RATBAGS (4 June: 1), ENGLAND SHAME (*ibid.*: 34–5), and claimed that the team were the 'laughing stock of the world' (*ibid.*: 36). The same paper continued in a similar vein the next day (JUMBO LIARS, 5 June: 28, SHAME OF ENGLAND, *ibid.*: 26), in a mode of coverage similar to that of other newspapers. *The Times* editorial (4 June: 19) called the party 'idiotic' and the alleged damage 'criminal' and 'dangerous', and commented:

> The impression is not so much of lions led by donkeys as of hippopotami led by hypocrites … the footballing authorities and their young men need to rediscover … old English values of discipline, modesty and common sense.

Despite this period of criticism, in the last few days prior to the first match the tabloids returned to giving the English team their full support, perhaps for fear of not appearing 'patriotic enough'. The *Daily Mirror* (8 June: 30–2) urged its readers to WAVE YOUR SCARF FOR ENGLAND and the *Sun* said ROAR FOR ENGLAND (5 June: 5), drawing on wartime speeches in its editorial on the day the tournament commenced (8 June: 6):

> England expects every fan to do his duty … Let's show Europe that the people who invented the game can still play it the best. Let's be proud of our country and our flag … This should be our finest hour.

In summary, the dominant themes that featured in our 'phase one' of press coverage were those of jingoism and Euroscepticism bordering upon xenophobia, coupled with a deal of scaremongering about the imminent invasion of foreigners (and very often 'nazis'). This 'little Englander' patriotism had been countered by a brief period of criticism and hostility towards the English players, something that which, along with anti-foreigner rhetoric, was to characterise phase two of the press coverage, detailed below.

Phase two: from David to Goliath

Phase two of the press coverage of Euro '96 is demarcated by England's opening match against Switzerland on 8 June through to the days immediately after the team's quarter-final victory over Spain on 22 June. During this period tabloid jingoism and xenophobia became increasingly overt as the England side progressed in the championships and large sections of the population became engrossed in the unfolding events on the pitch. As the 'savage hooligan war' failed to materialise, stories predicting such outcomes disappeared as it became apparent that the vast majority of the 'invading hordes' of fans were peaceable and determined to enjoy the 'carnival' atmosphere.

For the England team, Euro '96 began with a poor 1–1 draw with Switzerland, and its performance was roundly criticised. The *Sunday Mirror* (9 June: 76–7) proclaimed that THE CATHAY CLOWNS ARE A FIRST CLASS EURO DISASTER, whilst the *Daily Mail* called for Paul Gascoigne to be dropped from the side (GAZZA MUST GO,[82] 10 June: 64). Other tabloids returned to the alcohol theme: WE ARE SINKING IN A SEA OF BOOZE said the *Daily Mirror* (11 June: 35), and the *Sun* reported a trip to a nightclub by three England players as ENGLAND ACES BACK ON BOOZE (11 June: 1).

In retaliation, the England coach Terry Venables reportedly branded the team's critics 'traitors', prompting the following response from the *Daily Mirror* ('Comment', 12 June: 28):

> Try to imagine German superstar Jürgen Klinsmann in a nightclub at 2am during the opening week of a major tournament.
> It's unthinkable. In fact close to an act of disloyalty.
> Tel[83] knows there's a word for that. Traitor.

During the build-up to England's second match, versus Scotland on 15 June, the last of the hooligan scare stories appeared. This was to be the first match between the two countries since the annual fixture was called off by the football authorities in 1989 due to excessive crowd disorders. TARTAN ARMY PLOTS BLOODY EURO '96 BATTLE WITH AULD ENEMY reported *The Sunday Times* (9 June: 24), and *The Times* (10 June: 4) featured an article entitled HOW I BECAME A VICTIM OF A GERMAN THUG that described how the reporter, the 'victim', had, contrary to the initial impressions generated by the headline, only in fact received a 'minor cut' that was 'so small it did not need stitches'. Considering its earlier inflamed reporting of the prospects of hooliganism, and without any apparent sense of irony, the *Sun* (13 June: 64) threatened the Scots with WE WILL MCDUFF YOU UP.

The outcome of the match, a 2–0 win for England, marked the beginning of almost a fortnight of highly jingoistic and occasionally xenophobic coverage from the tabloids. The scorer of one of England's goals, Paul Gascoigne, was labelled lionheart by the *News of the World* (16 June: 72), and the paper announced:

> Robert the Bruce, Billy Connolly, Rod Stewart, Craig Brown – your boys took one Tel of a beating.

The *Sun* stated that it had taken '60 Seconds to Stuff 'Em' (17 June: 35), and continued:

> Dates are everything in Anglo-Scottish history – 1314, 1746 and now 16.39.[84]
> Forget Bannockburn and forget Culloden.
> In years to come students will be schooled in the precise moment Scottish forces were so heroically repelled by Lord Admiral David Seaman at Wembley on June 15.

This article, by mixing patriotism, celebration and football with military history, encapsulated the attitude of much of the tabloid coverage during this period. Again it was suggested that an invasion of England had been successfully thwarted. For a while it appeared that victory on the football field was a demonstration of English 'greatness' that ranked alongside battle victories of the past and, for some sections of the press, there was little difference between the two.

The example immediately above essentially encapsulated the flavour of tabloid reporting during this phase, and this theme continued in the build-up to England's next game against Holland, the final match of the group stage of the championships. The *Daily Mirror* instructed the team to GIVE THEM EDAM GOOD THRASHING (18 June: 1). In the same feature, the paper urged its readers to pull up their tulips, throw out their clogs and Edam cheese and, bizarrely, advised 'Don't go anywhere near a windmill'.

The result of the match, a 4–1 victory for England, was heralded as sensational, and broader parallels were drawn between sporting success and the general 'state of the nation'. Sections of the press were moved to suggest that national pride was enjoying a welcome renaissance. An editorial in *The Times*, for example, understood the effects of sporting achievement in the following terms (20 June: 1):

> In 90 minutes, and four goals, football has done what a thousand speeches by government ministers, and a hundred election promises by Tony Blair, have failed to do. England feels great about itself, almost invincible ...
> A David once anxious about its economy, its sporting prowess, its beef, has turned overnight into a Goliath ... Plunge your thermometer anywhere into England's psyche today and it emerges glowing red with patriotic fever.

Unsurprisingly, perhaps, the ghost of 1966 appeared once more. In ENGLAND TRAMPLE THROUGH THE TULIPS (19 June: 33), the *Sun* commented:

> Holland ... wilted like their famous tulips in the heat of an English onslaught that stirred all those marvellous memories of 1966 and all that.

'The nation that nicked our fish'

From England's victory over Holland until the defeat in the semi-final against the Germans, the press coverage of the home side's progress became increasingly aggressive and nationalistic. For some newspapers, support for the team became inseparable from xenophobic cliché and insult. Prior to England's next match, the quarter-final against Spain, the *Daily Mirror* warned YOU'RE DONE JUAN (20 June: 1) on a front cover that depicted the beheading of a Spanish matador by an English Beefeater. Inside the same issue, the 'paper outlined 10 NASTIES SPAIN'S GIVEN EUROPE (*ibid.*: 5), including syphilis, General Franco, 'carpet bombing' and, ludicrously, the short-lived English soap opera *Eldorado*. The same page also featured a number of anti-Spanish jokes (JOKERS SOCK IT TO THE SEÑORS) and a list of Spanish military defeats (WELL THEY DID WIN 425 YEARS AGO).

The *Sun's* front cover had a similar theme (GIVE 'EM A SPAINKING,

I.M. MARSH LIBRARY LIVERPOOL L17 6BD
TEL. 0151 231 5216/5299

20 June: 1), picturing a man dressed as Sir Francis Drake (the paper's 'mascot'), with the caption: 'Drake Says Sink the Señors'. Underneath a picture of English boxer Frank Bruno holding the flag of St George, it commented:

> Now the former world heavyweight champ wants to see Spain get the biggest spanking since Sir Francis Drake defeated their Armada in 1588.
> The battleground is Wembley – and all England is willing Terry Venables' warriors to sink the opposition.

The reliance on military imagery was again apparent, and was not untypical of other tabloids in the build-up to the match against Spain (see, for example, the *Daily Mirror*, GAZZA'S ARMADA (21 June: 1)). The game itself resulted in a win for England in a penalty shoot-out, after a tense 0–0 draw after normal and then extra time. The victory was greeted with WE KICK THEM IN THE CASTANETS from the *News of the World* (23 June: 4–5), in a piece which continued:

> It was the day the roar of England's lions saw off the Spanish bulls.
> The day we sent the paella-eaters packing.
> When the penalty drama at Wembley finished, it was – of course – our boys who got the result that matadored.
> For the nation that nicked our fish, there will be no plaice in the semi-finals.

The celebratory mood was explored by *The Sunday Times* (SEAMAN SAVES THE DAY FOR ENGLAND'S LIONS, 23 June: 1, 24), which detected:

> English patriotism, puffed up like a bulldog on steroids, was close to bursting last night ...
> ... Yesterday's result capped a buoyant week for English pride, which saw an end to Britain's beef war in Europe, rising house prices, good-to-firm going at Royal Ascot and the ball from the 1966 World Cup Final going on display at Waterloo Station.

It is worthwhile noting that the general groundswell of patriotism that was perceived to have gripped the population was not as widespread as the newspapers stated. As was touched upon in Chapter 5 and as Carrington (1998: 118) mentioned, whilst large sections of the white population supported the English side, many black people had 'either a large degree of ambivalence towards England or openly supported "anyone but England"', and felt uneasy about the nationalistic flag-waving of much of the Euro '96 coverage.

Phase three: 'but these are Germans' – the Euro '96 'soccer war'

England's progress through the quarter-final drew the team against the pre-tournament favourites, Germany, in the semi-final. This was to be the first meeting between the two in a major tournament since the World Cup semi-final in 1990, and is a fixture steeped in football rivalry.[85] In this instance, the match coincided with a degree of anti-German feeling generated by the so-called 'beef wars', as discussed earlier. Placed in the context of Britain celebrating the 50th anniversary of victory in the Second World War the year previously, the pairing of the two countries on the football field brought a predictable tabloid response. LET'S BLITZ FRITZ suggested the *Sun* (24 June: 4), whilst the cover of the *Daily Mirror* (24 June: 1) proclaimed ACHTUNG! SURRENDER next to pictures of English footballers Pearce and Gascoigne in World War Two-style tin hats.

The xenophobic and militaristic imagery did not end there. In MIRROR DECLARES FOOTBALL WAR ON GERMANY (24 June: 1, 6) the Editorial stated:

> I am writing to you from the Editor's Office at Canary Wharf, London.
> Last night the Daily Mirror's ambassador in Berlin handed the German Government a final note stating that, unless we heard from them by 11 o'clock that they were prepared at once to withdraw their football team from Wembley, a state of soccer war would exist between us.
> I have to tell you now that no such undertaking has been received, and that consequently we are at soccer war with Germany.
> ... May God bless you all. It is evil things we shall be fighting against – the brute force, the high tackle, the unfair penalty, the Teutonic tedium of their tactics, and the pretence of injury after a perfectly legitimate English tackle.
> Against these evils, I am certain that the inside right will prevail.

Not content with echoing wartime speeches, the *Daily Mirror* sent a message to the German Embassy requesting their team's 'immediate withdrawal from the tournament' (24 June: 2). However, the paper revealed that:

England's old enemy – defeated in two World Wars and one World Cup – formally announced that they would stand firm on the historical battleground in North London.

What followed were more offensive and xenophobic pieces. In THE MIRROR INVADES BERLIN (June 24: 2–3) the *Daily Mirror* reported:

> There is a strange smell in Berlin ... and it's not just their funny sausages. It's the smell of fear ...

The same article included pictures captioned 'Filthy Hun' and 'Zey Don't Like It Up Zem' (a catchphrase from the World War Two-based BBC comedy *Dad's Army*), and the war theme continued in a cartoon depicting a young child asking his father, 'What did you do in Euro '96, Daddy?' (*ibid*.: 6).

The overt xenophobia of the *Daily Mirror*'s coverage caused Sir Brian Nicholson, then President of the Confederation of British Industries, to lament 'this pungent atmosphere of romantic nationalism and churlish xenophobia' (Peterson, 1997: 41). In the days that followed the Press Complaints Commission received dozens of complaints about the tone and content of the *Daily Mirror*'s coverage, and the reaction from other sections of the media was also noticeable. The *Daily Mail* stated that ENGLAND DESERVES BETTER THAN THIS ORGY OF JINGO-ISM (25 June: 8), and in another article (THIS FIGHTING TALK PUTS US ALL TO SHAME SAYS SIR BOBBY [Charlton], 25 June: 18) reported:

> Asked if he would print racist headlines about West Indian crick-eters, Mr Morgan [the editor of the *Daily Mirror*] said: 'No we wouldn't, that would be deeply offensive – but these are Germans'.

It looked as though the *Daily Mirror* had seriously miscalculated the nature of its coverage, and the next day the paper toned-down its style. PEAS IN OUR TIME it declared on its front page (25 June: 1), refer-ring to a food hamper it had given to the German team as a 'goodwill gift'. In fact, the *Daily Mirror* dropped its 'war analogy' theme, as did the *Sun*, and there was no repeat of the overt xenophobia of previous issues. Although not explicitly referred to, the degree of opprobrium that the *Daily Mirror*'s coverage drew suggests that the 'football war on Germany' was the epitome of the kind of journalism condemned by the National Heritage Select Committee, mentioned in the introduc-tion to this chapter.

France '98 – the quest to 'win the Cup for Diana'

Phase one: little Napoleons

Phase one of our analysis of press coverage of France '98 covers the weeks leading up to England's first match of the tournament against Tunisia on 15 June.[86] In this period, the flavour of reporting, particularly from the tabloids, was in some ways similar to that of the same period before Euro '96, in that it featured a mixture of jingoism, nostalgia for 1966, and criticism of the England team's alcohol consumption. However, before we concentrate on this specific time period it is worth examining a small number of articles, from the *Express* and the *Daily Star*, which, although they are strictly speaking outside of the time period of our analysis, nevertheless neatly summarise many of the aspects of tabloid coverage of major football tournaments.

The piece in the *Express*, for example (7 December, 1997: 28), displayed the unerring ability of journalists to link football and battlefield triumph in a style seen countless times during Euro '96. In SMILE, YOU'RE IN FOR A WORLD CUP TREAT, a preview of the forthcoming tournament featuring a picture of the victorious 1966 England team, Hunter Davies commented:

> I wasn't there for 1066, which alas didn't go well for the home team. We all waited for Napoleon and later Hitler, hoping to duff them up, but they chickened out.
> But England against Romania, Colombia and Tunisia in the summer of 1998 . . . I just can't wait.

This casual toying with (rather feeble) war analogies hints at a kind of xenophobia that other tabloids were more open about. In March 1998, the *Daily Star* took it upon itself to campaign for a larger number of World Cup match tickets to be allocated to fans of England and Scotland (HAND 'EM OVER EU GREEDY LOT, 2 March: 6), and in its Editorial, FROGS NEED A GOOD KICKING (*ibid.*: 2) stated:

> French history is littered with acts of plunder, greed and cowardice. The way they've grabbed the lions share of World Cup tickets is typical of their slimy continental ways.
> So good on EU bosses for threatening savage fines if they don't hand some back.
> The EU mustn't back down.

As we proved at Agincourt and Waterloo, a good kicking on their Gallic derrieres is the only language the greedy frogs understand.

When a limited number of tickets were subsequently made available to the general public outside France, the *Daily Star* claimed victory (OUI WIN – FROGS CAVE IN ON WORLD CUP TICKETS, 5 March: 1) and claimed in its Editorial (OOH AAH, A WINNAH, *ibid.*: 2):

Now our campaign has paid off with a sensational victory against the greedy Gallic garlic guzzlers.
The little Napoleons at the French FA have buckled under our pressure.

The repeated use of xenophobic insult, evident in so much of the Euro '96 tabloid coverage and in the *Daily Star* examples immediately above, was, on the whole, absent from the reporting of France '98 until England's fixture with Argentina in the Second Round of the competition (see below). Also largely absent from pre-tournament coverage were the hooligan 'scare stories' that had such a high profile before Euro '96. Before the start of the 1998 World Cup, scaremongering was more or less restricted to crime and terrorist issues, with the *Mirror* detailing a PLOT TO BLOW UP WORLD CUP (13 May: 1) featuring Islamic 'fundamentalists', and the *Sunday Times* (24 May: 17) running COLOMBIA COCAINE CARTELS PLOT TO FLOOD WORLD CUP. A notable exception was 20 THUGS WHO ARE OUT TO WRECK THE WORLD CUP, a *Mirror*[87] 'investigation (12 January: 4–5) that pictured 20 of the 'British football yobs', a 'frightening number' of whom had links to 'vicious race hate' groups. The only evidence the paper could seemingly provide that those named would be 'wreckers' is that they were not subject to a restriction order that would stop them travelling to the World Cup.

Boozing, smoking and late nights

In the two weeks prior to England's opening fixture on 15 June, the main theme of the tabloid coverage was the drinking exploits of England's World Cup players. This theme, a replication of reporting before Euro '96, began with the news that Paul Gascoigne had been omitted from the squad for the championships, a decision based on a perceived lack of match fitness caused by some highly-publicised nights 'out on the town'. Initial press incredulity, as exemplified by HOD'S MAD ... OR HE'S GOT THE BALLS OF KING KONG (*Daily Star*, 2 June: 1), soon focused on Gascoigne's alleged excesses. BEERS OF A CLOWN – GAZZA

AT KARAOKE BOOZE-UP alleged the same paper (*ibid.*: 2–3), while the *Mirror* claimed GAZZA IS DONER FOR – BOOZING, SMOKING AND LATE NIGHTS BRING HIM DOWN (1 June: 4–5) and the *Sun* referred to Gascoigne as England's 'official beerleader' (3 June: 1).

However, when the *Sun* caught up with striker Teddy Sheringham in a Portuguese nightclub only a week before the start of the championships, the tabloids became as vocal and as critical as they were before the 'dentist's chair' incident before Euro '96 (described above). IT'S 6.45AM AS DRUNKEN SHERINGHAM, CIGARETTE IN MOUTH, GOES OFF FOR ROMP WITH BLONDE said the *Sun* on its front page (5 June: 1), and asked: HOW CAN TEDDY BE READY? BOOZING ACE SHOCKS FANS (*ibid.*: 2–3), describing his exploits:

> One [fan] described how the player, looking 'totally knackered', was so drunk he barely noticed as he stumbled into a table of drinks and sent it flying.
>
> Others looked on amazed as the striker puffed on a cigarette and disappeared into a toilet for half an hour with a sexy blonde, emerging red-faced and exhausted.

The *Mirror* claimed SIR BOBBY'S [Charlton's] OUTRAGE AT BOOZY SHERI (6 June: 2) and featured a succession of critical articles accusing England coach Glenn Hoddle of hypocrisy, in much the same way that Terry Venables had been branded a 'traitor' two years before (see, for example, HOD'S LAW – THOU SHALT BE CAST OUT IF YOU ARE GAZZA: THOU SHALT BE FORGIVEN IF YOU ARE SHERI (*ibid.*: 52). After a few days, as the furor began to subside, the *Sun* squeezed the last drop from the story with ENGLAND IN NEW BOOZE SENSATION (THEY HARDLY TOUCH A DROP) (8 June: 4–5).

In another parallel with the pattern of Euro '96 reportage, in the days leading up to the start of the tournament, newspaper reports reverted to being more positive in their tone as they invoked (once more) the 'spirit of '66' in order to back England. There are too many instances of these types of reports to list, but notable examples include 1966 AND ALL THAT, a large feature in the *Daily Mail* 'Weekend' section (6 June: 6–10),[88] and a wave of nostalgic reminiscences following the awarding of a knighthood to Geoff Hurst who scored a hat-trick in the 1966 final. The *Guardian* contributed HE THOUGHT IT WAS ALL OVER IN '66 BUT NOW IT'S A KNIGHTHOOD FOR GEOFF HURST (13 June: 1), and the *Mirror* ARISE SIR 1966 (13 June: 1–3) amongst three pages of nostalgia. The *Sun* urged the current squad to WIN IT FOR SIR GEOFF (13 June: 1), and later

I.M. MARSH LIBRARY LIVERPOOL L17 6BD
TEL. 0151 231 5216/5299

predicted the SPIRIT OF '66 WILL BE WITH US FOREVER (*ibid*.: 62), a self-fulfilling prophecy, as the tabloids, as is evidenced in this chapter, are reluctant to let it fade.

However, perhaps the most ludicrous story in this 'patriotic' period was DIANA'S WORLD CUP JACKPOT, a *Mirror* exclusive that revealed that the England squad would contribute World Cup win bonuses to the Princess of Wales's Memorial Fund (14 June: 1). The paper appeared to claim that this was one of the team's prime motivating factors in the tournament, and said of the players: THEY WILL PLAY THEIR HEARTS OUT TO WIN THE CUP FOR DIANA (*ibid*.: 4–5).

Whatever the true motivations of the England squad, some of those who travelled to France had agendas of their own, and it is to the disorder that surrounded England's first match, versus Tunisia, that this chapter now turns.

Phase two: 'He's a sick yobbo' says mum

It is estimated that as many as 20 000 England supporters made their way to the south of France, with most based in Marseilles, the venue for England's opening fixture on 15 June. Unfortunately, the weekend before the game witnessed widespread disorder as English fans clashed with Tunisians, local youths (many of North African descent) and the police, in a series of violent running battles concentrated in the old port area of the city. During the disturbances, two English fans were stabbed, a number of properties were damaged and the police utilised tear gas to quell the trouble.

The tabloid response was sensationalist as the disorders received widespread coverage. The *Daily Star* offered a double-page spread under the caption VINDALOONIES (15 June: 4–5) accompanied by graphic pictures of the rioting. The *Sun* featured a bloodied fan giving a V-sign under the headline A DISGRACE TO ENGLAND (15 June: 1), the theme of 'national disgrace' and 'shame' also picked up by the *Daily Mail* in SHAMED AGAIN BY THE LOUTS (15 June: 1). In the same edition, a report detailed what initially appeared to be a drink-fuelled violent assault on a young girl: SO ASHAMED AS THE DRUNKEN THUGS TURN THEIR HATRED ON A GIRL OF THREE (*ibid*.: 6–7):

> It was the sight of the little Tunisian girl screaming with terror as bottles flew inches past her head that sears into the memory and makes me utterly ashamed.
> I came to see a football match. What I have seen is a child attacked by English thugs ... 'Come on lads, let's get 'em', a yob in an

England T-shirt shouted. Faced with 80 charging hooligans, the Tunisians broke and ran for the safety of the side streets. The last I saw of the little girl was as she was being dragged away by her father, her face contorted by fear, pursued by a horde of drunken louts.

It was only by reading and examining the article that it becomes apparent that the girl was not, after all, targeted by a violent gang, but just (and admittedly very frighteningly and unfortunately) happened to be in the wrong place at the wrong time as violence erupted around her. The article admits that the 'attackers' did not catch up with her – we suspect they did not know they were even chasing her. The events had simply been salaciously distorted to make a better story.

The outcome of the match itself, a 2–0 win for England, was overshadowed by further violence, which this time also occurred away from the stadium, on a beach in front of a giant television screen, and was sparked by a reaction to England's first goal from Tunisian supporters who threw bottles and seats at England fans below. In the ensuing violence the police once again resorted to tear gas in an attempt to contain the disorder. Of particular interest in the reporting of these disturbances were two highly ambiguous stories that appeared to praise England's hooligan fans. The *Sun* exclaimed TWO NIL (16 June: 1) over pictures of triumphant England captain Alan Shearer and a defiant England 'hooligan', seemingly suggesting that 'two nil' meant two English victories, one on the pitch (England's win against Tunisia) and one off it (the 'victory' being that of England's fighting supporters). The *Daily Star* claimed FIRST BLOOD (16 June: 4–5) in an article about the disorder, suggesting that violent English fans had gained initial advantage in the series of fan battles that appeared to lie ahead.

In the same edition of the *Sun*, the defiant England 'hooligan' was named as James Shayler, who was about to become 'demonised' as *the* 'folk devil' of the World Cup. In the SAVAGE WHO STARTED IT (*ibid*.: 2–3), the *Sun* said:

The shaven-headed, tattooed thug who sparked the Marseilles riot that shamed England was last night named as soccer savage James Shayler.
Sick Shayler, a 32-year-old dad of three, was spotted hurling the first bottle from behind a crowd of fans.
The pot-bellied bully was also seen directing other boozed-up

hooligans and urging them to attack French riot cops and rival Tunisian supporters.

Just a few pages on, the *Sun* asked its readers to NAME ALL THE NUTTERS (*ibid.*: 6–7) pictured in the article that were involved in the 'Battle of Marseilles'. Those pictured were variously described as 'louts', 'yobs', 'hooligans', 'yobbos' and 'nuts' and later as 'drink-fuelled, shaven-headed, tattoo-wearing braindead soccer scum' (*ibid.*: 8).

The *Daily Star*, also in its 16 June issue (*ibid.*: 5) reported a police 'source' as saying that James Shayler was known to the police as 'the most violent sort of hooligan', whereas, in reality, he was not known to the police as a football hooligan at all. There was also little or no evidence that the violence was orchestrated,[89] despite the claims in I SAW IT HAPPEN (*ibid.*: 5):

> I hid in doorways with cowering locals as mobs charged around baying for blood ... And there's no doubt that this violence was orchestrated, despite all the protests of more naive supporters. I saw burly louts barking orders to drunken chanting hordes during the battles with cops, Arabs and French locals.

The *Mirror* (16 June: 1) asked Prime Minister Blair, on its front page: TOUGH ON CRIME PRIME MINISTER? THESE MORONIC, LOATHSOME YOBS ARE HUMILIATING OUR COUNTRY AND THEY'RE MAKING YOU LOOK WEAK. In the same issue, the whole of pages 2 and 3 were devoted to hooliganism, with the paper's chief political commentator calling for government intervention in WHY WE ALL FEEL BETRAYED (*ibid.*: 2):

> [Home Secretary Jack Straw] must have had the police intelligence on these men. Their names are well known. Their ugly faces are on record. Their movements are watched, particularly in the sensitive weeks and days before an event like the World Cup ... It was a failure of government ... When will the Home Secretary act?

The piece made the assumption that the violence was highly-organised and orchestrated by well-known hooligan 'faces', even though an article on the facing page, WORSE IS TO COME (*ibid.*: 3), claimed:

> Only three category C thugs – the most feared organisers of violence – were held in Marseilles.

In an alarming twist, the vast majority of troublemakers are not even known to police.

Also on 16 June, the *Mirror* continued the demonising of James Shayler in a two-page spread calling him THE PIG OF MARSEILLES – TATTOOED FATHER OF THREE SPEARHEADED RIOT THAT PUT ENGLAND IN DOCK (*ibid.*: 4–5), continuing:

> Shaven-headed James Shayler is exposed by the Mirror today as the porky thug who sparked World Cup violence that shamed England. The tattooed father of three was seen ordering fans to attack rival Tunisian supporters in Marseille.
> He is then believed to have launched the first missile with the gleeful words 'Come on lads, let's get them!'

Having created an 'icon' of hooliganism, the *Mirror* proceeded to call for the Government to take tough action in its Editorial BLAIR MUST CRUSH THESE SICK THUGS (*ibid.*: 6):

> ... Mr Blair and Mr Straw take a tough line on crime, yet they look weak when they fail to prevent a few known thugs from going to the World Cup
> ... If Tony Blair is to seriously revitalise this country he must take drastic and immediate action. He must show these thugs and the world that this country will no longer tolerate this kind of behaviour.

This article, by calling for the government to take 'drastic and immediate action', is perhaps an indication of the process of 'deviancy amplification' and 'moral panic' in effect. The tone of the piece, and indeed much of the *Mirror's* and the other tabloids coverage, was one of moral indignation that the 'thugs' that were 'shaming the nation' were not receiving the punishment they deserved. Many of the articles were an exaggerated version of events, with the *Daily Mail's* SO ASHAMED AS THE DRUNKEN THUGS TURN THEIR HATRED ON A GIRL OF THREE vividly illustrated. Yet while the tabloids created an amplified version of events underpinned by strong moral outrage, the explanations for the behaviour of these 'thugs' (or 'yobs', 'louts' or 'scum', depending on your favourite label) offered were simplistic, laying the blame on organised gangs governed by notorious ringleaders who are known to the police. As we shall argue in the conclusion to this chapter, these assumptions appear to have been inaccurate.

It is important to acknowledge here that the sensationalist reporting style was not restricted just to the tabloids. *The Times* (16 June: 1) devoted half of its cover page to hooligan stories, as well as all of page 2 (including MORE TROUBLE ON WAY, SAY POLICE) and all of page 3, which had, among other articles, SUSPECTED FOOTBALL HOOLIGAN IS 'A DECENT FAMILY MAN', yet another article about the beleaguered Shayler. The *Guardian* (16 June: 1) stated VIOLENCE TO WORSEN – POLICE on its front page, and inside, in a fatuous display of 'Colonel Blimpishness', Ruaridh Nicoll argued: SEND ENGLAND HOME (*ibid*.: 16):

> The only way football violence will ever be wiped out in England is for the nation to collective responsibility for what happened on Sunday night. Let the team be sent home, the nation in disgrace. Let the country take the body-blow to its pride and then see if this so-called 'hooliganism' survives.

The *Daily Mail* spread its coverage of the 'soccer war' over five pages, invoking the 'demon' of Shayler in its lead story (16 June: 1), describing him as THE SUBURBAN SOCCER THUG, and as a 'shaven-headed Middle England hooligan' in what could be construed as a crude attempt to place the 'demon' in every Middle Englander's own front room.

The *Mirror*, in its Editorial (17 June: 6) was still calling for tough action at government level, and in particular the prevention of violent offenders from travelling to France, irrespective of whether they have football-related convictions:

> Why the Government has not taken this action is beyond understanding.
> These yobs shame our nation. They bring down the world's contempt, not just on them, not even on just all English football fans, but on all of us.
> It is in the national interest for them to be stopped ... These vicious morons want war and that is what they must get.

In the same issue (*ibid*.: 6–7), the paper, in a feature OUR SONS SHAMED US, quotes James Shayler's mother as saying 'I can't believe [the] Pig of Marseilles is my boy' next to a picture of him throwing a rock. 'He's a sick yobbo' she apparently concluded. The *Sun* was busy creating folk devils of its own in 'NICE QUIET LAD' IS EVIL RIOT GENERAL (18 June: 9), this time featuring a Liam Yeomans, who was supposedly an 'evil soccer yob', a 'bull-necked brute' and a 'notorious thug' who was the 'general' behind the riots.

Interestingly, in the midst of all of this hyperbole, a *Times* article (18 June: 7) BLAIR CALLS FOR JAILED FANS TO BE SACKED detailed Prime Minister Blair's call for workers, particularly servicemen, to be sacked if convicted of hooligan offences at the World Cup. Whether this rather drastic plan of action was a direct result of the tabloids' calls for tough action from the Government is open to question, but the timing of the statement certainly provides food for thought.

Although there were other incidents of violence and disorder involving England supporters during the World Cup tournament, the number of sensationalist 'hooligan outrage' reports in the press decreased in the days following the trouble in Marseilles. The next phase of our discussion focuses on England's next two matches, marked by a more positive portrayal of England fans by the press as many papers turned their attention to the disturbances involving German supporters.

Phase three: beanz meanz cupz

In the relatively quiet news period following the violence in Marseilles, the tabloids either invoked 1966 – WE WON 66 WORLD CUP ON BEANZ (*Daily Star*, 19 June: 4–5, reacting to the England team's dietician's ban on the squad eating baked beans) – or called for tougher action against hooligans – NO CONVICTIONS PLEASE ... WE'RE BRITISH (*Sun*, 19 June: 11) and DON'T LET THESE HOOLIGANS GET AWAY WITH IT (*Sunday Mirror*, 21 June: 6). Indeed, the next big hooligan story to break involved German supporters, hundreds of whom had apparently been involved in extensive disturbances in Lens.

MIRTH AND MAYHEM – ENGLISH FANS HAVE FUN IN THE SUN WHILE GERMAN THUGS GO ON RAMPAGE said the *Mirror* (22 June: 6–7), contrasting the jovial and high-spirited behaviour of the English (hitherto ignored) with the violence of the Germans. In the first of many tabloid pieces linking the German violence with neo-nazis, the *Mirror* claimed that members of the British Royal Family were under threat (*ibid.*: 7):

British intelligence officers fear nazi-style louts may head for Lens this week for a showdown with England supporters before Friday's match against Colombia.
And there are fears for the safety of Prince Harry who will be at the match with his father.

The attention of the press was briefly diverted by England's next fixture, versus Romania in Toulouse on 22 June, which resulted in a 1–2 defeat. BECKS TO THE WALL said the *Sun* (23 June: 1), using the nickname of England midfielder David Beckham, who had been the subject of a press campaign to be included in the team's starting lineup. Interestingly, seeing as he came to be vilified later in the tournament, Beckham was referred to in the same article in the *Sun* as being the 'fans' hero'. Also worthy of note was the paper's positive portrayal of England fans' activities in Toulouse, including their drinking (THE RED WHITE AND BREWS, *ibid*.: 2–3).

The *Mirror* (24 June: 1) concentrated on the disturbances involving German supporters, suggesting, above a graphic picture of French policeman Daniel Nivel being savagely beaten, that the attack had been undertaken IN THE NAME OF FOOTBALL. The coverage continued inside (THE PICTURES THAT SHAME ALL GERMANY, *ibid*.: 4–5) including the use of more lurid pictures of the injured policeman lying in pools of blood. Although the paper repeatedly linked the violence with nazis, it contradicted itself by then admitting in NEO-NAZI ARMY FEEDS ON DESPAIR (*ibid*.: 4) that such activists were just 'among the hundreds of drunken fans who battled with police'.

The *Daily Mail* (25 June: 7), in CHARITY BOY WHO SHAMED HIS COUNTRY, managed to invoke its own 'folk demon', a Marcus Warnecke, whose story 'is a focus for a nation's horror over 'hundreds of soccer hooligans organised by neo-nazi fanatics'. The paper also claimed that the German fans were (*ibid*.: 7):

> Highly organised – and many of them linked to far-Right factions – the gang members contact each other via the Internet and mobile phones.

The *Guardian* (25 June: 1) carried a piece FRENCH WARN OF HOOLIGAN BATTLEFIELD AT ENGLAND GAME suggesting that the German fans may meet with their English counterparts in Lens, the venue for England's next match, for a violent confrontation. The same paper suggested that Lens was a TOWN BRACED FOR ENGLISH ONSLAUGHT (26 June: 1).

England's 2–0 victory in the match against Colombia on 26 June guaranteed the team's progress in the championships, and was greeted in the *Sun* (27 June: 1) with BECK ON TOP – WONDER GOAL BY DAVID AS ENGLAND GO THROUGH TO LAST SIXTEEN. Despite the predictions, the disorder that did occur surrounding the fixture did not involve battles between English and German fans, but, nevertheless, the *Sun* claimed that YOBS SHAME US ALL AGAIN (*ibid.*: 2), and referred to 'sickening violence', with 'louts' going on 'booze-filled rampages' in Lens and Lille, in acts of 'savagery' in which 'Hooligan ringleaders incited the ranks of thugs to take on the cops'. Once more, the 'conspiratorial' idea that the violence was orchestrated by hooligan leaders was championed with little supporting evidence. In a taste of things to come, the paper said WE GOTCHA, a direct reference to the infamous *Sun* headline GOTCHA that celebrated the sinking of the Argentinian ship General Belgrano during the 1982 Falklands War (*ibid.*: 56) as the England team had been drawn in the next round of the competition against Argentina.

The Times (27 June: 1) also covered the disorder with the headline ENGLAND WIN MARRED BY 450 ARRESTS, a clear exaggeration of the facts as, in total, only 286 English supporters were arrested in the whole of France '98 (NCIS, 1998).

In the next section, phase four of our analysis, we will look at the way that the tabloid press covered England's game against Argentina – coverage that was, in some aspects, reminiscent of the press's xenophobic stance during Euro '96.

Phase four: gotcha! perhaps not: posh spite kills the dream

The prospect of a World Cup second-round fixture with Argentina had a number of dimensions, both political and footballing, that guaranteed that the match would receive extensive coverage. Not only were memories of the 1982 conflict between the nations over the Falkland Islands still relatively fresh in the minds of some, but the fixture itself also had a bitter history. In particular two games, both held in World Cup finals, stood out – England's 1–0 win in the latter stages of the 1966 tournament which was marred by the sending off of the Argentinian captain Rattin, and Alf Ramsay's reference to the Argentine players as 'animals' – and the quarter-final in 1986 which Argentina won 2–1. The first Argentinian goal was the subject of much controversy as the ball had been punched into the England goal by Diego Maradona by what the player later called 'The Hand of God'.

The News of the World (28 June: 80) under the caption 'Why Our Brave Lads MUST Beat the Argies' said REVENGE – AFTER 12 YEARS DIRTY DIEGO FINALLY SAYS SORRY – BUT ENGLAND ACES REJECT IT, in reference to Maradona's apology for the 'Hand of God' incident. 'We Want Revenge' the paper exclaimed (*ibid.*: 74–5), with ex-England goalkeeper Peter Shilton, who had been involved in the controversial goal, exclaiming THE WAY HE [Maradona] REACTED STILL SICKENS ME.

The *Mirror* (29 June: 4) reminded its readers of the Falklands conflict with ARGENTINES SAY IT'S WAR – THEY WANT FALKLANDS REVENGE. If the tension surrounding the match was not already enough, the paper's editorial, FANNING THE FLAMES OF A SOCCER RIOT (*ibid.*: 6) raised the spectre of fan violence with another piece of scaremongering about the non-imposition of an alcohol ban in St Etienne, the match's venue:

> The World Cup game between England and Argentina could be a fantastic match on the pitch and a bloodbath off it.
> The brutality of the thugs and yobs who shamelessly pose as soccer fans has already left no doubt about why they are in France.
> It is not to watch football. Not to support England. They are there to cause trouble and to revel in violence.
> They must be met with action that is just as tough and ruthless as they are ... Yet the prefect of the Loire district is publicly making it open house for any hooligan and troublemaker who wants to start a riot.

The *Daily Star* continued to remind its readers of Maradona's controversial 1986 goal (29 June: 18–19) in a macho and bullish piece I WANTED TO STRANGLE CHEAT DIEGO by ex-England defender Terry Butcher, who is quoted as saying: 'I was in tears. It was lucky he lied to me [about the hand-ball] – that saved his life ...'.

The *Sun*, the 'Paper that Supports Our Boys' (30 June: 24–5), gave away a 'Hallowed World Cup Turf Mat' in its centre pages, a paper mat supposedly featuring 'hallowed Wembley turf' for England fans to kneel and pray upon. Underneath a 'Gotcha' caption, supporters were supposed to place their left knee over 'dirty Diego's' face, and their right knee over a picture of General Galtieri (the Argentine leader during the Falklands War).

The *Mirror* (30 June: 1) also picked up on the 'revenge' theme on its front cover, with the headline 8PM TONIGHT: PAYBACK TIME accompanied by a picture of the 'Hand of God' goal. Next to this piece was an article DON'T FIGHT FOR ME SAYS HERO SIMON about Falklands War veteran Simon Weston, thus contrarily reinforcing the militaristic and jingoistic undertones of the forthcoming match. On the same day the *Mirror* featured a crass cartoon strip (*ibid.*: 48) entitled MIRROR SPORT DREAMS UP PERFECT REVENGE. The 'story' in the cartoon involved England captain Alan Shearer scoring against Argentina with his hand, only for Glenn Hoddle to protest to the match officials in order to get the goal disallowed – therefore the 'Hand of Hod' had been used to create foot-balling justice as 'England want to win by fair means ... not like Argentina in '86'.

On 30 June, the day of the game, the *Daily Star* ran a picture of the 'Hand of God' goal on its front page with the headline FIST OF HOD, and once more recalled 1966 (30 June: 1):

> It's payback time tonight for the infamous Hand of God – when Diego Maradona broke English hearts with the sneakiest cheating in World Cup history.
> Twelve years on, the Argentinians can expect the Fist of Hod as coach Glenn Hoddle leads our lionhearts into battle in St Etienne ... England will play in all-white – just like Sir Alf Ramsey's side who beat the Argies 1–0 in 1966.

The match itself, which had been 2–2 at half-time, saw England player David Beckham controversially sent off in the second half. The game ended 2–2 after extra time, but England lost the resultant penalty shoot-out 4–3. The *Daily Star* reacted with OUTCHA! (1 July: 1), another reference to the Falklands conflict, while other tabloids blamed Beckham for the defeat (the *Mirror* – POSH SPITE KILLS OUR DREAM (1 July: 46–7) and the *Sun* – BECKHAM BRAINSTORM (1 July: 50–1).

The Times ran a small feature on the disorder in England after the match – 100 ARRESTS AFTER PUBS TURN OUT – and described it as being 'the most serious since the tournament began' (2 July: 5). The *Daily Star*, continuing with the vilification of David Beckham, contributed the woefully sexist SORRY LADS, NO TITS ON PAGE 3 TODAY ... ONLY BECKHAM (July 2: 1). The *Mirror*'s front page (2 July: 1) reminded its readership who its *real* enemies were with the headline COME ON EVERYONE CHEER UP – IT MIGHT HAVE BEEN WORSE, WE COULD HAVE LOST TO THE GERMANS AGAIN. In the same edition, the paper featured a piece A TALE OF TWO ENGLISHMEN ... THE BEST AND THE WORST – OWEN REPRESENTS ALL THAT IS GOOD IN THIS COUNTRY ... PASSION, BRAVERY AND MODESTY. SHAYLER IS ALL THAT'S LOUSY (*ibid.*: 7) in which journalist Tony Parsons compared the demonised 'hooligan' James Shayler with the 'Quiet, decent, inspirational Michael Owen, a true hero'. The fact that Owen had appeared to dive in order to win England a penalty in the match against Argentina, thereby 'cheating' in a similar fashion to 'dirty Diego' all those years before, seemed to have escaped his attention.

I.M. MARSH LIBRARY LIVERPOOL L17 6BD
TEL. 0151 231 5216/5299

Conclusion – the press, hooliganism and popular nationalism

In critically discussing the tone and content of the press coverage of both Euro '96 and France '98 we have shown that there were several themes that were common to both, including xenophobia; military metaphors; nostalgia for 1966; and sensationalist reporting of the hooligan 'threat'. The xenophobia that was so pervasive in reports and features during Euro '96 manifested itself again during France '98, only this time instead of 'greedy krauts' we had 'cheating dagos'. Readers were repeatedly reminded that both opponents had been vanquished on the battlefield, and that both fixtures had their equivalents in the 1966 World Cup.

This overt xenophobia in a footballing context was evident for a smaller time period than it was during 1996, and was mainly concentrated around the Argentina game. This may be due to the fact that the press had taken heed of the criticisms of the National Heritage Select Committee made immediately after Euro '96, and decided not to repeat ACHTUNG! SURRENDER in another context. It may also be that following the election of a more 'Eurofriendly' Labour party in May 1997, the overriding macro political climate was less conducive to anti-foreigner rhetoric of the type that was typical of the press's attitude in 1996. As Peterson (1997: 29) commented of that era:

> By 1996 it was hard to argue that the domestic debate about Britain's place in Europe had not deteriorated to a level of ill-informed dogma. A virulently anti-European press – much of it under non-British ownership – found EU-bashing to be a comfortable and even popular theme.

This attitude was exemplified by *Sun* columnist Garry Bushell in the days following the defeat of the England team in Euro '96 in a piece pride of lions which read like a 'call to arms' (*Sun*, 28 June 1996: 9):

> As we count the cost of Europe with the losses to our fishing fleet, our beef farmers, and even our gold reserves ... the English will come to realise what we have lost and will seek to reclaim it. It won't be achieved without effort and sacrifice.

The type of Eurosceptic, bordering on xenophobic utterances from senior politicians in the previous Conservative government like those emanating from Nicholas Ridley and Peter Lilley mentioned above were suddenly anachronistic to the 'forward-thinking' new Labour Government, on the surface at least, keener to play a more involved role within the EU. Yet, even in the supposedly more pro-Europe atmosphere in 1998, the *Sun* was still persisting with the notion that Europe was posing a threat to British cultural values. In OUTRAGE AS EURO NUTTERS BAN OUR BRANDY BUTTERS, the *Sun* claimed (22 June 1998: 21) that the EU was attempting to outlaw brandy butter, and in its Editorial (NOSES OUT (*ibid.*: 8)) stated:

> The meddling busybodies of Europe are at it again.
> That great British Christmas treat, brandy butter, is to be outlawed by order of the EU ... *What the heck has it got to do with them?* ... What we put on our Christmas puddings is our business.

Two days later the same paper asked IS THIS THE MOST DANGEROUS MAN IN BRITAIN? (24 June 1998: 1) about Prime Minister Tony Blair after he had indicated a more positive attitude towards the single European currency. The *Sun* then instigated a telephone poll to gauge its readerships attitude to the euro, and subsequently declared (27 June 1998: 8) that 120,000 READERS' VOTES AGAINST THE EURO KEEP POURING IN. This represented 97 per cent of those who voted, and was, according to the paper, '... the second largest response ever to a 'You the Jury' phone poll – the largest being in 1991 when '177,660 of you rang in over a week to say child murderers should be executed' (*ibid.*: 8).

The Euroscepticism displayed by the *Sun* in its mainstream news coverage during France '98 is therefore an indicator that the tabloids' attitudes to Europe had changed little in the two years since Euro '96. It may, therefore, be the case that regardless of the more positive attitude towards the EU from the newly-elected Labour government, the reductions in the levels of overt and aggressive xenophobia displayed in the tabloids during their coverage of France '98 may simply be due to the fact the England side did not play the Spanish or the Germans, or indeed any EU member states' team in the World Cup, as it had in Euro '96, and therefore the press simply lacked the opportunity to display its Europhobia during the tournament.[90]

In any case, it is clear that much of the reportage of both Euro '96 and France '98 relied upon an offensive 'Little Englandism' and portrayed (whether intended as 'humour' or not) xenophobic caricatures of England's opponents. When, as the National Heritage Select Committee alleged during Euro '96, such coverage impacts on public disorder in British cities it is important to acknowledge that merely scapegoating the press is unhelpful – the roots of this aggressive and jingoistic English national identity extend much further than that. For example, after the disorder involving English supporters in Marseilles during France '98, English MP Alan Clark spoke of the violence as being 'a kind of compliment to the English martial spirit', and stated that it was 'perfectly natural' for the English to be 'obstreperous'. He believed that it was right for fans to throw back a bottle that had been thrown at them (HOOLIGAN MP, *Mirror*, 18 June 1998: 7). These sentiments were very similar to those of an England follower caught up in the disturbances:

> We do it because we're England, because this is what we do ... These French would be Krauts if it wasn't for the English. We're here to represent England, you don't get respect otherwise. (*Guardian*, ANGLOPHILE CITY BRACED FOR INVADING HORDES, 16 June 1998: 3)

The sensationalist way in which much of the disorder was reported, coupled with newspaper demands for tough action against the hooligans from the police and government, were reminiscent of other press attempts at the generation of a 'moral panic' (Cohen, 1981). The simplistic press assumption that those involved were part of highly organised gangs appeared to be contradicted by the arrest figures for England supporters during France '98 that reveal that over 80 per cent of those arrested were not known to police at all.[91] Whether the provocative reporting resulted in an 'amplification spiral' that then became a factor in further disorder is open to conjecture.[92] It may be that the 'amplification' of the hooliganism stories was simply regarded as a 'good angle' for what otherwise might have been fairly routine newspaper copy of football disorder. Notwithstanding this, the tabloids' complicity in maintaining the myth of 'highly organised hooligan gangs', and its creation of 'demonised leaders' like James Shayler can only have helped to reassure the police and government that their preconceptions of who would be involved in the trouble were correct. As Murphy *et al.* (1990: 125) suggest:

> having, by their crass treatment of the phenomenon [hooliganism] contributed to the generation of a smoke screen of misunderstanding, the tabloids stand back in apparently unselfconscious innocence and berate politicians and football officials for their

failure to eradicate the problem. The editorial policies responsible for such treatment seem to be a consequence of political opportunism, the increasingly fierce battle for circulation, a scant regard for any explanation that ventures beyond the simplistic, the narrow or the monocausal, and a lack of either the time or the taste for reflection, save the regulation dose of nostalgia.

The tabloids' sensationalist reporting of the disorder during France '98 was as simplistic and as crass as the xenophobia exhibited during Euro '96. The hypocrisy of those who, on the one hand indulge in nostalgic and jingoistic celebrations of past military victories and who display an aggressive attitude towards Europe, while on the other hand they condemn those who 'fight for England' abroad, almost goes without saying. Yet the values championed by many of the tabloids as being admirable characteristics for players to have are also claimed by those fans who feel they are 'on duty' for England when abroad (Brimson, 1999). The *Sun* seemingly lauded the way that Liz Pearce described her husband, the England player Stuart Pearce, as a 'good soldier, a great person to have fighting for us' and that 'If he ever went to war, and every soldier had the same passion for his country as Stuart, we could never lose' (*Sun*, STU OR DIE, 25 June 1996: 2). Yet these values are not a million miles from those also championed by a 'friend' of James Shayler's, who was quoted as saying of Shayler (*The Times*, SUSPECTED FOOTBALL HOOLIGAN IS 'A DECENT FAMILY MAN', 16 June 1998: 3):

> He's walking proud, proud to be English ... If you had 400 Tunisians walking after you, you wouldn't walk away. I think he's a proud man.

7
Conclusion: Racisms and the Cultures of Football

Introduction

In many respects the discussion contained in the preceding chapters reveals a series of contradictory tendencies in respect to racism and anti-racism in British football. Consideration of some aspects of the game, for example the continuing serious underrepresentations of British Asians at professional levels, reveal racist stereotypes about diet, religion or physical limitations that are more usually associated with the crude propaganda of extremist far-right parties. On the other hand, the success of black players, both collectively in terms of the numbers playing the game professionally and individually in terms of high-profile stars – some of whom have become managers once their playing careers have finished – continues to be widely invoked as a role model from which other aspects of contemporary society might learn. The victory of the 'multiracial' French team in the 1998 World Cup was greeted as evidence of the vitality of a plural society by that country's President, and similar claims have been made about the apparent successful integration of black players into the British game. Contradictions can also be identified in the media coverage of the game. While the sections of the media readily and sensationally feature alleged racist clashes between high-profile players – and castigate those who are claimed to have used racist language against opponents – the press itself, as amply demonstrated in the previous chapter of this book, has been responsible for xenophobic portrayals of foreign teams faced by domestic clubs and the English national side. Even while sections of the media, and the tabloid press in particular, have crudely stereotyped teams from elsewhere in Europe, the increasing number of foreign players appearing in the domestic game

176

has been an important and celebrated part of the recent rehabilitation of football.

Similarly, in the arena of football fandom contrary tendencies can be identified. Although the folkloric image of the moronic football thug may have been eclipsed during recent years, problems of hooliganism – closely, if simplistically, conflated with the issue of racism – are rarely far from the policing and political agenda. During the mid-1980s British football was at its nadir – bedeviled by problems of hooliganism with English clubs banished from European competition and a government advocating an identity-card scheme that would have denied the 'casual supporter' the chance to attend matches. Yet it was during this period that a number of grassroots campaigns began to give voice to the interests of fans who wished to articulate a popular anti-racist and relatively progressive vision for the game. It was while football fans were collectively public enemy number one, in the minds of some powerful élites, that small groups of supporters were beginning to develop campaigns that would greatly influence mainstream debate surrounding the game in the years that followed. Indeed it could be argued that such grassroots activity culminated in the establishment of the Football Task Force in 1997, which, it was claimed, would give voice to the interests of the ordinary supporter in the face of the 'football industry'. The salience of racism and anti-racism within the game was evidenced by the fact that these were first subjects addressed by the Task Force.

How can these diverse trends be explained? First, they reflect the scope and diversity of football, ranging from the prestigious and most highly-paid professional sport in Britain[93] – for male if not female athletes – to amateur schools, pub and club teams in which many thousands participate. In addition to those who play the game are the legions of fans who 'consume' the game live in stadia and via television in public houses and private living rooms, and indirectly through the pages of newspapers and in every conceivable form of high and low culture. When the heterogeneity of participants and manifestations of contemporary football is considered it may not be surprising that such diverse forms of racism and anti-racism can be discerned.

Alongside the sheer breadth and scope of football, the nature of racism itself must be considered if a convincing analysis of its position in the game is to be achieved. In Chapter 1 theories of racism and anti-racism were discussed and it was argued that a relatively broad approach to the former was favourable since it drew attention to the relationship between racism and the diverse social context in which it develops. This broad approach is also favoured since it conceives of racism as a concept that changes over time, and draws upon cultural as well as biological or genetic referents. What is more, by rejecting approaches to racism that privilege a particular ideological content to the concept, the understanding of racism adopted here allows for internal contradiction and inconsistency. In essence, it was argued in the introduction that racism is best understood as a socially-constructed concept, subject to change and variance over time and place: in short it is essentially contestable. Given this it is clearly not the case that racism and anti-racism are elements in a 'zero-sum game' whereby an increase in one necessarily entails a decrease in the other – as though they were columns on either side of a balance sheet. This does not necessarily mean that racism cannot be reduced or marginalised by combined processes of education, prohibition or popular antipathy; however, it does follow that racism is a problem that cannot be resolved once and for all, as though it were a parasite within, but distinct from, an otherwise healthy organism. Instead, anti-racist strategies need to be capable of responding to the changing terrain of racism, able to present fresh challenges to distinct manifestations as they unfold.

In the remainder of this chapter we will provide an overview of some of the central themes that have been raised by this book, and suggest that each of them provides support for our central contention that the problem of racism within British football needs to be reconsidered. Additionally, we question the common conception of football as a force for social progress. Although we recognise that much commendable anti-racist work has been done in relation to the game, it is argued that it is simplistic to claim that the relative success of black players means that football represents a role model for others to emulate. Finally, the chapter considers the importance of the culture of professional football and how this might inhibit efforts to rid the game of racism. While the concept of institutional racism has been subject to considerable scrutiny in recent years, particularly in relation to the police and criminal justice system, it is suggested here that it provides a useful starting point for consideration of the case of football. In particular it provides a framework for understanding what might be called 'elusive' racism.

Racism, hooliganism and 'antisocial behaviour'

That concern regarding racism in British football has been closely linked to efforts to rid the game of hooliganism has already been noted at various points throughout this book. Prior to its amendment by the 1999 Football (Offences and Disorder) Act, many complained that the 1991 Football (Offences) Act provided insufficient power to tackle individuals engaging in racist abuse within stadia, since it only prohibited such chanting 'in concert' with others. While this may have been a significant loophole in the legislation, and one that was properly closed by the 1999 Act, criticism of the 1991 legislation was misplaced in the sense that it was never primarily intended to banish racism from the game. Rather, it is clear from the other provisions of the Act – such as making running on to the pitch illegal and increasing powers to move against ticket touting – and the parliamentary debate that accompanied it, that the prohibition of disorderly behaviour was the main concern. Introducing the Football (Offences) Bill for its third reading in the Commons in April 1991, the Home Office Minister Peter Lloyd made it clear that the need to tackle racism was part of a broader concern with hooliganism:

> We needed to think clearly about the context in which the proposed offence [of racialist or indecent chanting] would be committed. At a designated football match, attended probably by thousands of people, the crowd may sing, shout, groan, gasp or sound like the House of Commons on a particularly good evening, in an atmosphere of considerable tension and excitement – again, like the House on occasions that we can all remember. The volume of collective sounds will be considerable. In that noisy and volatile atmosphere, racialist or indecent chanting is not only socially objectionable but becomes, potentially at least, a risk to public order.
>
> Against that background, it would be a mistake to criminalise a single racialist or indecent remark that might not be widely audible in the ground; to do so would set the threshold for criminal behaviour too low. We wish to prevent group chanting, which is repeated and loud and may spark trouble, and if it occurs, to prosecute and punish the offenders.[94]

Racism was included primarily because it was understood as part of the broader problem of hooliganism. While this association between

I.M. MARSH LIBRARY LIVERPOOL L17 6BD
TEL. 0151 231 5216/5299

racism and crowd misbehaviour may be justifiable to some extent, and it seems clear that far-right groups have sought to propagate racism through the 'street politics' of hooliganism, it is apparent that the two problems are far from coterminous. As was mentioned previously, it also appears that in the late 1990s football hooliganism is of relatively minor importance to far-right groups, although it may have been more significant in earlier periods.

The growth in support for initiatives designed to rid the game of racist supporters has developed in close parallel to attempts to banish more general forms of 'antisocial behaviour' from football stadia. This is most notable when warnings against racist chanting or abuse are given in tandem with cautions against the use of 'obscene or foul language', as the phrase often runs. In this respect the discourse against racism in the game is closely allied to efforts to 'sanitise' football in order to render it more attractive to family and television audiences. Whether attempts to discourage the machismo associated with the football stadium are valid is a legitimate matter of debate, as some bemoan the passing of 'traditional' fan culture that was founded on abuse of opposing teams and their supporters and others have argued that such apparently benign efforts are bound up in more general processes of social control (Brick, 2000). Allirajah (1997/98: 8), for example, has argued that 'it is precisely by making racist chanting unacceptable, that the criminalisation of all forms of "unacceptable" behaviour at matches has been made possible'. Even those who favour the prohibition of racist behaviour from within stadia admit that the commercial and cultural success of the game in recent years has been a motor for the 'cleansing' of football. The Chair of the Commission for Racial Equality, Sir Herman Ouseley, for example, recognised the role played by 'the game's new found financial health. For the unprecedented wealth that now flows into football from TV and sponsorship, depends on it being a commercially attractive product with a clean, non-controversial image' (Ouseley, 1998).

The commercial interests that motivate football clubs, advertisers and television companies to act against racist chanting, the display of neo-fascist banners and the like present both opportunities and limits on those seeking to advance an anti-racist agenda. The high profile of contemporary football clubs and players has contributed to an environment in which anti-racism can be advanced, especially when paralleled with a more general rise of similar issues up the political agenda in the light of the Macpherson Inquiry into the death of Stephen Lawrence (Macpherson, 1999). However, it seems that much of the effort expended to prevent these manifestations of racism is rarely extended to confront less-publicly-visible dimensions of the problem. Commercial interests induce clubs to provide free entrance to schoolchildren from districts with relatively high minority ethnic populations, and so make some return from merchandise and refreshments or tickets that would otherwise have remained unsold. In such circumstances the promotion of anti-racism or multiculturalism within the game coincides with the financial interests of clubs in a manner that seems only to benefit both. Football clubs who regularly sell all seats to their home fixtures, though, are likely to face financial losses from giving away tickets – although the marketing of reserve games as 'family'-oriented matches, might be examples of how commercial interests can be developed in ways that broaden attendance.

In some circumstances, then, it seems that commercial pressures can run parallel to anti-racist projects in that they might provide impetus to tackle forms of racism that directly tarnish the image of the club in the public and media eye and can engender community outreach work designed to attract a wider fan-base. The political, social and cultural foundations of anti-racism are likely to remain of secondary importance though. The financial performance and public image of a club may be regarded as healthy as long as games are sold out and there is no evidence of racism, neo-fascist groups or hooliganism within the stadium. Such a goal might reasonably be shared by those committed to anti-racist activity, but it betrays a narrow understanding of the problem. It is conceivable that a situation might develop in which all of those attending games are white, even in areas with high minority ethnic populations, and that an absence of racist chanting might be sufficient to satisfy the 'anti-racist' demand of clubs concerned with their commercial profile. Perceptions of racism coupled with prohibitively expensive ticket prices might effectively exclude black or Asian supporters from attending games that are actually – from this narrow perception of racism – paradigms of wholesome family entertainment. The conflation of racism with hooliganism and 'antisocial' behaviour does not necessarily advance a more inclusive and progressive vision of anti-racism. The ultimate objectives of the diverse parties to much of the current anti-racist activity within the game may not coincide.

In the short term, though, it does appear that the association of racism in football with the problem of hooliganism might provide some strategic advantages – not least because it establishes an easily-recognised 'folk demon' against which groups who might otherwise be relatively uninterested in tackling racism will feel able to operate (Back *et al.*, 1995). Furthermore, the use of policing and legal powers to banish racist behaviour from within grounds must be central to efforts to attract those minority ethnic groups who continue to be vastly underrepresented among supporters attending live games, in part at least because they perceive football grounds to be hostile racist environments (Holland, 1992). If the football authorities' public commitments to tackle racism in football are to be any more than superficial, it is vital that club regulations and the law are used to ensure that those engaging in racist abuse or chanting, spraying graffiti or distributing racist literature are expelled from stadia and prosecuted where possible. While many clubs seem to have taken steps to facilitate such action it is less often that such provisions are actively enforced. There may be a range of reasons that explain the failure of clubs, stewards and the police to act against racist behaviour, ranging from a lack of personnel and resources[95] to ignorance of the law or an unwillingness to implement it (Maynard and Read, 1997).

Even if fully enforced, legal provisions are necessary but insufficient measures against racism within the game. It was argued earlier that the prohibitive aspect of anti-racism focuses upon the behaviour or expression of individuals, and is relatively unconcerned with belief and attitude. In addition to uncoupling racism from antisocial and hooligan behaviour, since racism is a distinct problem that needs no broader justification for action, it is important that it is conceived in much wider terms than has often been the case. The few football clubs in Britain that have devised equal opportunities policies and sought to tackle racism and discrimination within the club more generally provide rare examples of attempts to broaden the scope of anti-racism within the game and to focus attention on the boardroom and the directors' boxes. The extent to which the culture of the game will mitigate against such anti-racist initiatives will be considered later in this conclusion, but it might be that the relative ease with which coalitions are built against racist and 'antisocial' fans is less apparent when questions are asked about exclusion from other aspects of the game.

The discussion of anti-racism in Chapter 3 of this book contrasted strategies that are conceived primarily in opposition to racism with those that seek to build a more positive political, social or cultural strategy founded upon notions of diversity and pluralism. Following this dichotomy it seems that much of the activity within the context of football has understood anti-racism in narrow terms of opposition to particular types of racism that have tended to coincide with wider concerns to rid the game of those considered to be antisocial and detrimental to the broader commercial interests of the game. The next section of this conclusion will consider dimensions of racism within football that have remained relatively unaffected, even by some of the most high-profile examples of anti-racist activity.

Racism and the cultures of football

In contrast to the easily-identifiable racism emanating from the archetypal skinhead hooligan are more elusive racialised forms within football. While some of these are related to structural and institutional factors that have parallels in other aspects of society, others are more particular to the culture of football and the celebrity of élite players. Whereas the issues discussed in the preceding section were described as narrow forms of racism around which a consensus for limited action could be relatively easily agreed, those scrutinised here are broad in scope and may be considered more ambiguous, at least to the extent that they sometimes stem from features of the game that are more widely valued and considered centrally important. Personal qualities such as teamwork and group loyalty that are seen as essential to the game may prove detrimental to anti-racist initiatives. Before considering the manner in which the culture of football might serve to limit the scope of anti-racism, the ambiguity of some aspects of fandom will be outlined.

Consideration in an earlier chapter of the long history of black players in British football indicated the bestowing of nicknames has often reflected a racialised understanding of the fortunes of those footballers concerned. Many decades after their playing careers finished it might be relatively widely understood that the application of nicknames such as 'Darkie' and 'Dusky' to Arthur Wharton and Walter Tull reflected a racialised view of the world that was consistent with the ideology of English society at the turn of the nineteenth and twentieth centuries. During the last four or five decades the language applied to 'racial' and ethnic groups has been the subject of intense political debate and the labels preferred by individuals are held to reveal their broader perspectives and to act as a basis for action. One of the classic examples of this is the use of the word 'nigger', once the preserve of Southern racists in the United States; the term has been occasionally reclaimed, sometimes as 'nigga', by youth subcultures that revolve around assertions of black pride and identity, and themselves reflect racialised understandings of violent masculinity (Back, 1996). While similar processes of reclamation have occurred in relation to other marginalised groups, another good example being the word 'queer' which has been partly stripped of its derogatory content by a celebratory gay-rights movement, labels and vocabulary have been subject to intense political agitation in the context of ethnic relations. An apposite example of this has been the way in which the Macpherson inquiry into the racist murder of Stephen Lawrence in London in 1993 spent some time considering a police officer's use of the term 'coloured' to refer to black people (Macpherson, 1999). Although it may be of proper concern that the officer appeared unaware that the word 'coloured' was considered offensive to many black people – and indicative of the officer's relative ignorance – it seems important to recognise that the term itself was, until relatively recently, considered a relatively neutral expression that stood in polite contrast to other more offensive nouns. Whatever the circumstances surrounding that particular police officer, it is important to recognise that the use of language is relative and not absolute, not least because its social significance changes over time.

Nicknames such as 'Darkie' would be regarded as offensive by many today and widely held to be unacceptable, and yet analysis of racialised beliefs would be particularly limited if we could not recognise that those using such phrases decades ago were often doing so in a superficially affectionate and benign manner. Any stereotype, however apparently positive, can be understood as ultimately negative since the elevation of a selected attribute inevitably involves the denigration of another (Cole, 1996a). It was shown in Chapter 3 that Wharton, as the first professional black player, was subject to racist abuse on occasion but was also the recipient of popular acclaim and celebration. In the context of late nineteenth-century British society the epithet 'Darkie' might be considered relatively innocuous. Implicitly, nonetheless, it ultimately reinforced Wharton's 'otherness' and proclaimed his inferiority as a black person, even though in the eyes of many of those who referred to him by the nickname he was a popular hero.

The ambiguity of Wharton's nickname needs to be recognised, particularly as similarly contradictory aspects of fandom can be identified in the contemporary game – and these pose a conceptual challenge to anti-racists who usually might be inclined to simplistic condemnation. The difficult terrain, which celebrated black players face, is illustrated by the case of the Liverpool and England striker

Emile Heskey. In the few seasons in which he established himself at his first club, Leicester City, the young black striker become a favourite with the supporters who greatly value his remarkable combination of strength, speed and agility. Heskey's feats on the pitch were regularly greeted with appreciative chants of 'Bruno, Bruno', in reference to the English former heavyweight boxing champion Frank Bruno. On the few occasions on which he has spoken on the subject, Heskey has denied that he has much experience of racism within the domestic game, and it is clear that this nickname was intended to flatter and celebrate. Beyond this superficial level, though, the suggested parallel between the footballer and the boxer reveals racialised stereotypes that are worthy of future scrutiny. At a fairly straightforward level there are superficial similarities between the two men: both are large and physically dominating, and relatively inarticulate, at least in public. However, very many professional footballers and heavyweight boxers share such characteristics. In these terms their blackness does not mark them out either, since many of their competitors in their respective sports are also black. The link between Heskey and Bruno, then, is not straightforward.

The unthinking association of one high-profile black sportsman with another is significant not only because it denies their individual identity but also because, in this case, the star referred to embodies predominant conceptions of the model black person in British society. Bruno's sporting and public persona (since retirement from boxing he has become a minor media celebrity and mainstay of the pantomime season) comprises a series of features that coincide with, rather than challenge, common stereotypes of black men. His success is founded on a physical power matched by a jovial personality and apparent inarticulacy, features reminiscent of older stereotypes of the eye-rolling black minstrel. This latter quality is epitomised by his catchphrase, 'know what I mean, Harry?', which invites the older white commentator Harry Carpenter to translate Bruno's experience to the wider world. The dichotomy between the physical and the mental is personified in the respective forms of the black boxer and the white commentator.

Coupled with these stereotypical qualities is Bruno's image as a patriotic British citizen, loyal to flag and country. During the mid-1980s, when Bruno's sporting career was in its ascendancy, the association of black and British was relatively rare, and more often the two were regarded as antithetical rather than complementary.[96] Against such a background Bruno was celebrated in the right-wing press as a model black citizen who represented English virtues of self-deprecation and humility, and reflected the primacy of brawn over brain. Gilroy (1993: 87) bemoans that failure of much cultural analysis to consider the popular reaction to Bruno:

> If the radicals and the anti-racists either ignored or ridiculed Frank, those who did notice him – on the right and in the tabloid press – elected to celebrate his performance, seeing in it a deep cultural affiliation to the British national community. It was his predictable failure that cogently expressed all that community's sterling masculine qualities. Failure became heroic rather than disappointing.

The power of Frank Bruno's celebrity as a metaphor for the ideal-type assimilated minority ethnic community is matched, Gilroy argues, by the contrary discourse surrounding the Rushdie affair, which began around the time that the boxer lost his championship bout against Mike Tyson. While the physical Bruno was held to be closely allied to British tradition, the cerebral Rushdie came to be regarded as significantly alien:

> Frank's physical accomplishment ... conveys a clear message that *some* representatives of the ethnic minorities in this country *are* capable and willing to make the cultural and social adaptations demanded of them in the wake of *The Satanic Verses*. For a while, Frank's muscular black English masculinity became a counterpart to the esoteric and scholastic image of Rushdie – the middle class intellectual *immigrant* – so remote from the world of ordinary folk that he was able to misjudge it so tragically. (Gilroy, 1993: 88, emphasis in original)

That Emile Heskey be celebrated by Leicester City supporters by association with a high-profile black sportsman who is wholly assimilated with white culture might be considered significant, it certainly betrays a deep ambivalence about the status of black celebrities. Crucially Heskey, like Bruno, is non-threatening to the mainstream white community and appears unassuming, modest and loyal. Prior to his transfer to Liverpool his apparent allegiance to the relatively small Leicester City, in the face of persistent rumours that he was set to depart for more lucrative pastures, cemented his image as a 'down to earth' player prepared to bide his time. Hall (1992: 255) has noted:

The play of identity and difference which constructs racism is powered not only by the positioning of blacks as the inferior species but also, and at the same time, by an inexpressible envy and desire.

In the context of racialised chanting and the popular acclaim revealed through nicknames, perhaps football provides a cultural space in which 'envy and desire' can be articulated and expressed, albeit in a crude form.

The experience of the former Nottingham Forest player Jason Lee further reveals the complex and contrary position that black players occupy on occasion. Lee's dreadlocks were subject to ridicule on the BBC comedy show *Fantasy Football* that was prominent for a few years in the mid-1990s and starred David Baddiel and Frank Skinner whose song *Three Lions* has been mentioned elsewhere in this book. The show 'joked' about Lee's hairstyle with a chant 'he's got a pineapple on his head', which was quickly taken up by opposition supporters and has since been directed at other black players with dreadlocks. While the song was not overtly hostile to the player, and Baddiel and Skinner emphatically denied any racist overtone, Lee subsequently claimed that it had undermined his confidence and adversely affected his game. Ignorance, whether deliberate or otherwise, of the cultural significance of dreadlocks to many black people is a fairly common complaint. Carrington (1998: 108) highlighted the cultural resonance of dreadlocks and so the impact of the 'jokes' directed at Lee and others:

> dreadlocks have long since come to signify the most politically assertive form of black resistance – the enunciation of 'dread' or 'Rasta' acting as a form of acknowledgement and respect between black peoples ... [the sketches about Lee] constituted a public challenge to one of the most powerfully symbolic forms of black cultural resistance to white supremacy.

The defence that such taunts amount to nothing more than the abuse that all footballers must face – or is equivalent to name-calling directed at those who are balding or perceived as overweight ignore the specificity of racism. As was pointed out in a previous chapter, ridicule of those with ginger hair or one of a myriad of other features that might be seen as notable from time to time rarely escalates to physical abuse, harassment or murder. There is an exclusionary logic to racialised abuse that cannot be equated to many other forms of banter or 'jokes'. The above examples also illustrate the capacity of contemporary culture to articulate racialised themes in a coded manner that lacks overt racist language or references.

That successful black players are understood in racialised terms so that their physical prowess is explained in terms of 'natural' properties and they are bestowed with nicknames associated with their 'racial' status, indicates that the development of a broad anti-racist agenda will have to confront many of the cultural properties of the game. The ambivalent celebration of black footballers, so that they are reminded of their fundamentally inferior status even as they are lionised, is something common to other minority groups in relation to mainstream culture. The tolerance of black, Asian, Irish or gay people, or 'eccentrics' such as New Age Travellers or eco-warriors, is conditional, dependent on their explicit or implicit acceptance of their own marginality and that they do not pose a threat to the majority. In this, black footballers are little different to other minority groups.

And yet, of course, the fame and riches that élite black players receive, and the centrality of football in general to much popular culture, is such that high-profile black footballers, like all élite footballers, are in a radically different position. The provisional nature of their acceptance is overlaid by a similar, if non-racialised conditionality that effects all players. The heroic status of black players that means they are allowed to transcend the 'racialised barriers' (Small, 1994) that circumscribe the lives of other black people, does perhaps depend upon them being 'ideal-type' minorities who are assimilated into the mainstream. More than this, though, it also depends upon them being successful players who perform wonders for their team, and it is on this basis that the status of *all* footballers is conditional. It is sometimes remarked upon with confusion that football fans can racially abuse black players on opposing teams, while praising black members of their own side. Pointing out such inconsistencies does much to expose the contradictory and flawed nature of racism, and yet, somehow, this perplexed reaction seems to overlook the cultural context of football that determines that fans' support for a player usually depends upon two factors only: membership of the right team, and being 'on form'. If that is taken into account then it may be that it is logical in terms of the internal culture of the game to abuse opponents on the basis of some arbitrary characteristic, while paying no attention to the same criteria possessed by players on one's own team.

To this extent the exclusionary intent and group identity of football culture closely resembles that associated with racism. Back, Crabbe and Solomos (1998: 79) describe the complex and contradictory nature of aspects of football fandom by highlighting the 'instability of … supporters' expressive tradition' that is contingent upon particular players, the respective performance of both teams, local club and fan rivalries, and a myriad of other contextual factors.

Acknowledgement that there might be a 'logic of racism' (Cashmore, 1987) in such circumstances might appear antithetical to anti-racism, but to recognise that racism provides a 'practically adequate' (Miles, 1989), albeit flawed and abhorrent, way of understanding the world does not mean that it should be left unchallenged. Indeed it might be argued that it is only by understanding the meaning of racism to those who perpetuate it that a viable project to undermine it can be developed.

The cultures of football fandom reflect and perpetuate racialised expressions that pose challenges for anti-racists, not least because it is likely to be harder to build a consensus for action. Discussion of the 'Jason Lee incident', which should perhaps be known as the 'Baddiel and Skinner incident', often suggested that the player ought to be able to take a joke or – if he was really bothered – could always change his hairstyle (Carrington, 1998), revealing a common-sense response that effectively denies any racist content. Racism proves elusive in such circumstances. In the context of football, racism has come to be associated solely with the stereotypical football hooligan, an outsider against whom 'decent football fans' can set a collective face.

One implication of attempts to broaden conceptions of racism in a manner that would render anti-racist projects more effective is that they are likely to face challenges to their credibility. Given that much of the game now espouses anti-racist credentials this may be regarded by some anti-racists as a dilemma. Discourses of anti-racism that recognise the tensions and complexities of racialised social formations are likely to prove more enduring than those that rely upon simplistic and misleading associations with hooliganism or conceive of racism only in terms of far-right political extremists.

Cultural features integral to the game can also pose problems for anti-racism, in particular a phenomenon we have labelled 'elusive racism'. This terms refers the combination of team loyalty, professional identity and conservatism that leads many players, coaches and club officials to recognise that racism is a problem for the game while emphatically denying that it is one that impinges upon their club.

One tension surrounding current developments in the game is that most professional clubs have felt able to lend their support, however superficially, to high-profile anti-racist campaigns that recognise the general nature of the problem within the game. At the same time, though, the need to maintain a positive public profile encourages them to deny that racism is a feature of their club – or if it is, then it is one caused by extremist hooligan outsiders who are not 'real football fans'. Collectively this leads to a situation whereby there is a broad consensus that racism exists within the sport, and yet an equally widespread insistence that the difficulties are primarily elsewhere – somebody else's concern. Racism, in these circumstances, becomes an elusive problem that is both everywhere and nowhere. Most clubs accept that it exists, and yet most clubs insist it is not within their experience.

A common feature of the biographies of black footballers that have played at the highest levels in Britain during the last few decades has been the ambivalence of their response to the racism that they have often faced. One recurring theme is that often they did not seek to confront racism emanating from their fellow players, managers or coaches but instead resolved to confound their critics by redoubling their own effort at the game. The frequent celebration of sport as one of few arenas in which black people are treated on the basis of merit alone, sits uneasily with the testimony of many black players who recount the additional efforts and talents required of them in contrast to their white colleagues (Cashmore, 1982: 175–7). To confront racism directly might be to risk being identified as a 'trouble maker' and so court further isolation – the need to maintain team loyalty regarded as paramount. While calculations of possible risks and benefits that might arise from challenging specific incidents of racist abuse and harassment will be made in many diverse circumstances, the cultural context of football poses a particular framework that may be relatively unusual. The value placed upon a certain conception of masculinity, that revolves around physical and mental toughness – 'bottle' – and is predicated upon group loyalty and camaraderie – 'taking the joke' – may mean that the black footballer who wishes to challenge racism risks isolation and aspersions being cast on his 'character'.

The experience of a black player who directly confronted the racism he faced from fellow players and others in the game provides ample illustration of the professional consequences that may arise from direct personal challenges to racism. A player who had appeared for Portsmouth, Birmingham City and other league clubs, interviewed by the authors, faced considerable racist abuse, sometimes conveyed as 'humour', an experience that he found increasingly difficult to tolerate. He recalled the consequences of his challenge to the racism he faced, his experiences provide ample illustration of the point made here, and so are quoted at some length:

> I was playing for Birmingham at Halifax and I had been sent off. The opposing team's coach came in our dressing room and called me a variety of names associated with the colour of my skin. But being still quite angry, I decided that a discussion about racism wasn't on the agenda, so I punched him. I recounted this story to my club manager and I was told that I ought to be able to take it. My argument that the man could dis my ability or lack of it, or my London accent, but not on the basis of the colour of my skin fell on deaf ears.
>
> ... Subsequently, I went down to Torquay United on trial and the assistant manager there, when it got to the end of training, liked to have a game of five-a-side. He said 'we'll have the white boys over here, and the coons over there'. I asked him to repeat himself, which he did and threw in a few other expletives. I actually said 'do you know what my name is? If you can't use it, then don't talk to me'. He persisted and in the end I just told him in no uncertain terms he would be met with a very unfavourable reaction. I ended up on the train home the next day.

That those who experience racist harassment and abuse also suffer broader external consequences from its aftermath is not in itself unusual. What is notable, though, is the fact that the culture of football, a game that has sought to make much of its anti-racist credentials in recent years, effectively discourages professional players from challenging the racism they face. Against such a context it is perhaps not surprising that black players have often felt more comfortable internalising their response to racism and seeking to translate it into a motivational spur.

Something of the culture of the game is revealed in that even the relatively progressive anti-racist programmes in place at a handful of clubs tend to acknowledge the separate sphere of the dressing room or team training session. Although a few football clubs have introduced equal-opportunities structures designed to facilitate anti-racism throughout the organisation, these seem to consciously avoid anything that might be construed to 'interfere' with the sanctity of

I.M. MARSH LIBRARY LIVERPOOL L17 6BD
TEL. 0151 231 5216/5299

the manager's freedom to select players. The autonomy of a manager to sign players and select teams is so firmly entrenched that it seems eccentric to suggest that their actions might be subject to some kind of external review. In a sport where managers face the kind of job insecurity rarely tolerated in other fields, their freedom to act with independence might seem inviolable. Given the evidence of racialised stereotyping and ignorance about black and Asian peoples emanating from football managers that has been provided in this book, and in many others, it might be argued that this is a sphere in which the logic of anti-racism is sorely needed. Anti-racist projects that confront the associations between the physical properties of players and their racialised 'natural abilities', for example, might encourage managers and coaches to recognise that black footballers have a more fully-rounded role to play. Equally undermining similarly racialised notions that Asian footballers lack stature or have the 'wrong' diet to succeed in the game, might also expand the pool from which clubs seek new talent.

Football and social progress

Football has come to be regarded as something of a success story in contemporary British race relations. Élite forms of the sport have been enjoying a profound and potentially fundamental transformation, fuelled largely by a media revolution which saw, in November 1999, Sky TV table a bid of £1 billion for the rights to Premiership football for three years. At the same time the phenomenon of racist chanting within grounds has subsided and black players serve as heroes to black, white and Asian girls and boys across the land. The positive role that the game can play within the provision of education and as a facility to the community at large is repeatedly stressed. Football seems to be more truly the *national* game, in terms of audiences, participants and wider constituent groups, than at any time before, and the concerns that have been documented here about encouraging minority ethnic audiences have been extended to women and disabled fans (Williams and Woodhouse, 1991; Williams and Perkins, 1997). That the British game, and the English in particular, was facing a profoundly bleak future a decade and a half ago only further highlights the astonishing fortune of football at the current time. Finally this book will consider the extent to which the apparent achievements of the diverse groups associated with football who have been concerned to promote anti-racism might herald more profound changes in British society. By implication this discussion impinges upon the notion that football can be harnessed as a progressive force for social progress. Even to seriously entertain such a notion would have seemed remarkable in the mid-1980s.

We argue in the following paragraphs that the gains made by anti-racists, significant though they have often been, are likely to be of limited benefit to society more generally. Given that this might appear a controversial statement it is important to stress that it in no way implies criticism of the motivation or approach of many of those involved in campaigns and strategies across the country. As has been argued throughout this text, many of their achievements have been remarkable in the context of a sport usually noted for its insularity and conservatism and, while many agencies have sought the credit for the general progress of anti-racism in the game, it should be acknowledged that much of the success is due to the grassroots involvement of countless committed individuals. The limited scope with which anti-racism within football can be transferred to society more generally relates to the nature of the problem, rather than the efficacy of activists. Since diverse racisms can be identified in complex social formations the potential for anti-racism confronting the problem in a unitary manner is limited. One strength of anti-racism that has been advanced by groups of football supporters is that it has been articulated in the context and culture of the sport, rather than being transplanted from elsewhere. Consequently it seems unlikely that such strategies can be wholly reapplied in other spheres, although it might have some application in different contexts, as campaigns such as 'Hit Racism for Six' that seeks to address English cricket might indicate.

A further limit to the potential of the anti-racist work in football has been frequently remarked upon in respect of the apparent discrimination black people face in other spheres. In the specific case of British sport, Cashmore (1982) noted nearly twenty years ago that the achievements of black athletes are often at the expense of educational progress, since teachers and others may encourage their performance on track and field much more than with book and pen. Historically, Vasili (1998) has shown that the excellence of black footballers coincided with, rather than confronted, racialised discourse established in imperial Britain. Their athleticism and physical talent were construed as evidence of 'natural' propensities, reinforcing racialised conceptions that placed greater value on the mental capacity conversely associated with whites. Just as black success in music and entertainment tend to reflect rather than undermine racist biological and cultural determinism, so too evidence of sporting prowess might not transfer to other spheres. Such assumptions might explain (the relative absence of British Asians from the professional game, since the specific discourses surrounding these communities tends to present them as physically unsuited to the game and to prioritise their educational and professional ambition. The possibility that élite black footballers might act as significant role models to inspire black kids to similar success may be problematic not least because the chances of making it as a professional are so severely limited. Images of black people succeeding in a wide variety of spheres might provide more appropriate and realisable aspirations for black children.

It is also claimed that black footballers' positions as idols to white youths presents an opportunity for anti-racism. That the celebration of black footballers can itself often reflect racialised discourse has already been noted, but even in circumstances where this is not the case it may be that the wider social promotion of anti-racism might not be so great. The complexity of identity is such that the acceptance of black people in the context of football does not necessarily transfer beyond that relatively narrow arena. The high status afforded to élite black football stars remains conditional and is temporally and spatially specific. That young white males idolise certain black players does not mean they are recognise any inconsistency in maintaining racist beliefs and practices in other circumstances away from football.

Another dimension by which football is held to provide an appropriate example to society more generally derives from its evident 'multiculturalism' whereby diverse 'racial groups' conjoin in a united team. Such celebration effectively reinforces notions of racial difference and partially reproduces the politics of tolerance that holds that British society ought to value its apparent capacity to 'absorb' groups of alien outsiders (Holmes, 1991). The implication that integrated teams of black and white footballers provide illustration of a successful model of 'race relations' can be criticised on a number of levels. It subtly reinforces the notion of racial difference since, instead of refuting the biological or cultural basis of 'race', it represents these as transcended. Furthermore, the accommodation is relatively fragile and is strictly focused upon results: the transitory and migratory careers of élite footballers –their ability to transfer should relations sour for any reason – is not something reflected elsewhere.

Finally, then, a central conundrum needs to be addressed by those involved in football in whatever capacity who wish to develop an anti-racist agenda. It is justifiable that the game has received considerable acclaim for the efforts that have been made to eliminate some explicit forms of racism. Although it might be argued that the motivation for these developments has been, to some extent at least, associated with broader moves to sanitise the game and develop a commercially acceptable public image, there has been a coincidence of interests with antiracist agendas. So effective in these efforts has football been that it is widely regarded as a role model to be emulated in other fields.

The difficulty remains, however, that many other forms of racism, less visible to the public gaze, continue relatively undisturbed. Campaigning groups and some journalists might raise questions about the chronic underrepresentation of minority ethnic groups within the institutions of the game, but few individual clubs seem inclined to recognise this problem and racism continues to be addressed only in its narrow forms. Racism continues to be associated with the actions of unruly and undesirable supporters, it is rarely regarded as a problem of the dressing room or the executive box, and almost never associated with the boardroom. In an era in which many sections of British society are reflecting on the notion of institutional racism there seems little sign that football clubs or the football authorities are interested in considering the extent of unwitting racism that may arise from the policies, practices and cultures of the game. It is to these questions that those engaged in antiracist work must now turn.

Notes

1 Introduction

1. For an opposing view of the changing composition of crowds, see Malcolm, Jones and Waddington (2000).
2. The interviews were either semi-structured or unstructured and conducted by one or both of the authors. Some survey work, of fanzine editors and of football club safety officers undertaken in the period 1995–96 also informs this work. The authors would like to acknowledge with thanks the work of Mark Carver, who participated in the formative part of this research.
3. From an interview conducted for this book, May 1998.
4. Excerpt from an interview conducted for this volume, January 1998.
5. Interview undertaken for this book, November 1997.
6. From an interview for this work, August 1997.
7. Conservative leader William Hague, in a speech to the Centre for Policy Studies in 1999 spoke of an 'emerging English consciousness' that was a 'ticking time bomb' under the constitution of the United Kingdom. Interestingly, he viewed the manifestation of the widespread painting of the St George Cross on the faces of England football supporters as evidence of this new nationalism (Shrimsley, 1999).

2 Football, 'Race' and the Forging of British Identity

8. Collins, who had the 'affectionate' nickname of 'Darkie', took Rochdale to the League Cup Final in 1962, losing 4–0 on aggregate to Norwich City.
9. Interview with Jeff Simons, November 1997.
10. Interview with Brendon Batson, February 1998.
11. Interview with Cyrille Regis, February 1998.
12. *Ibid.*
13. The *Guardian*, 26 January 1979.
14. Dave Bennett of Manchester City and Garth Crooks and Chris Houghton of Tottenham.
15. Interview with Tom Matthews, October 1997.
16. The *Observer*, 28 September 1997, Sport: 4.
17. Interview with Brendon Batson, February 1998.
18. The *Guardian* (1979) 'Orient Cry Foul over Anti-Nazi Movement', 13 February: 3.

3 Standing Together? Charting the Development of Football's Anti-Racism

19. Interview conducted with CRE Campaigns Unit, December 1994.
20. Organisations supporting the CRE/PFA-led campaign included the Scottish FA and Scottish Football League and the Association of Chief Police Officers (Scotland).
21. A total of 14 bodies.
22. Funding bodies for KIO include the FA Premier League, the CRE, the Football Trust, PFA and the FA.
23. In January 1999 Norwich City banned two supporters from attending Carrow Road for five years after they were found guilty of racist chanting.
24. From an interview with Councillor Jaspal, a Labour representative, conducted by the authors.
25. In 1998 Leeds United and Sheffield Wednesday were also criticised for allowing Bernard Manning to perform at functions inside their stadia (Kempson, 1998).
26. Noteworthy examples include the antiracist work undertaken at Millwall, Wycombe Wanderers, Exeter City, Preston North End and Everton.
27. Interview conducted with CRE Campaigns Unit, December 1994.
28. The only context where it was decided that the equal-opportunities policy did not apply was in the purchasing of players, where it was deemed impractical.
29. Northampton Town are known as the 'Cobblers', an acknowledgment of the local prominence of the shoe industry.
30. Space restrictions mean it is impossible to do justice to the remarkable story of Walter Tull. See Vasili (1996) for a full account of a footballer described as 'Britain's first multicultural icon' (*Guardian*, 1998).
31. The memorial was officially unveiled at a ceremony in July 1999.
32. Interview conducted by the authors with Brian Lomax, Director, Northampton Town FC.
33. Interview with a former manager of a club based in a multi-ethnic Midlands city, conducted by the authors.
34. Interview with secretary of a club based in a multi-ethnic Midlands city, conducted by the authors.
35. Interview conducted by the authors with the secretary of a London-based Premier League club.
36. From an interview conducted with Arts and Leisure Department, London Borough of Waltham Forest, 3 March 1995.
37. *Ibid.*
38. 'The Boys ...' contains the lyric 'Oh son I see in memory to far off days when being just a lad like you I joined the IRA'.
39. Millwall Football Club has also been active in combating antiracism through the work of an Anti-Racism Committee formed in 1994 (AGARI, 1996).
40. These agencies included the police, Kick It Out, local authorities, supporters' groups and the Martin Shaw King Trust.
41. Kick It Out has worked with a number of fan initiatives, including those at Fulham, Exeter, Rotherham and Southampton.

42. Other football fan groups to originate from Anti-Fascist Action include Celtic Anti-Fascists and Man. United Anti-Fascists (Anti-Fascist Action, 1994).
43. Other fanzines produced by antiracist fan groups include *You Wot!* (Gulls Against Racism – Torquay United), *Red Attitude* (Man Utd Anti-Fascists – Manchester United) and *Doon by Gorgie* (SCARF – Hearts). *Filbo Fever* is now called *When You're Smiling*.
44. Space limitations mean that the significant impact of fanzines cannot be fully discussed here. For a more in-depth discussion of the role of fanzines see, for example, Jary, Horne and Bucke (1991).
45. From an interview conducted with Football in the Community Officer, Leyton Orient, January 1995.

4   Policing Racism in Football

46. Combat 18 are an avowedly violent neo-nazi group formed by BNP supporters who became disaffected with the party's public commitment to democratic politics. The groups name is taken from the alphabetical position of Adolf Hitler's initials, A = 1 and H = 8. In practice, it has been suggested, the distance between the BNP and C18 is much closer than the former publicly acknowledge (*Dispatches*, 1994), although the future of C18 is open to speculation following the life imprisonment of leader Charlie Seargent (The *Observer*, 1998a).
47. Williams *et al.* (1989: 150).
48. Cited in *Searchlight*, July 1985: vii.
49. A newspaper report in April 1998 claimed that senior C18 leaders were utilised as informants by the British security services in order to glean information about the activities of loyalist extremists. The report alleged that links with MI5 meant that C18 enjoyed a degree of immunity from the police in respect of some of its other activities (The *Observer*, 1998b).
50. See *Sunday Times*, 19 February 1995: 7.
51. 'No Surrender to the IRA' is also chanted by supporters of English club teams on occasion. One of the authors of this study witnessed this slogan directed by supporters of Oxford United against Swansea City in season 1994/95, presumably those involved associated the Welsh fans with a Celtic identity shared with the Irish.
52. The *Guardian*, 17 February 1995: 2.
53. For example, Home Office (1993).
54. See Beck and Willis (1995).
55. Interview with authors, October 1995.
56. See, for example, South (1988); Johnstone (1992); George and Button (1996); Murray (1996).
57. Home Office (1993).
58. For example, *Dispatches* (1994).
59. *Ibid.*
60. Some indication of the number of people playing football is found in the FA Premier Fan League Survey 1996–97 which suggested that 79.6 per cent of men who attend matches had played (or did play) junior 11-a-side foot-

ball and that 62.8 per cent had played (or did play) 11-a-side football when aged over 15 years. Perhaps unsurprisingly, the figures were much lower for women, at 7.8 per cent and 5.6 per cent respectively.

61. Although Malcolm, Jones and Waddington (2000) suggest that the extent of this transformation in the demographic make-up of football crowds is seriously exaggerated.

5 A Design for Life: Deconstructing the Game's National Identities

62. In Scotland, 74.3 per cent of the electorate voted for devolution, and in Wales, 50.3 per cent (1998a, b).

63. Lipton (1999) notes that at the end of the 1998/99 season there were 172 overseas players attached to Premiership clubs, an increase of 111 from the figure in 1995. Of these, the largest contributing nations were Norway (22 players), France (21), Holland (16) and Italy (14).

64. The edition on 7 June 1999 featured teams comprised solely of players or commentators synonymous with the 1966 World Cup win.

65. Cited in the *Guardian*, 31 December 1993.

66. Interview conducted with Arsenal fan, October 1997.

67. Havelange defeated Englishman Stanley Rous, the incumbent FIFA president, in the 1974 election.

68. The head of the PFA, Gordon Taylor, invoked the 'national interest' as an argument against the relaxation of rules for non-EEA players (Parkes, 1999).

69. These include: proving that every avenue had been explored in trying to find a suitable EEA player first; that the proposed signing had played in at least 75 per cent of competitive games for his country in the last two years; demonstrating the player's worth by paying him a suitable salary.

70. Roberts conducted the Rangers crowd in the singing of sectarian songs, whilst Gascoigne mimed playing the flute, something linked to loyalism and Orange parades.

71. For example, Cardiff reached the semi-final of the European Cup Winners' Cup in 1967/68 (losing to Hamburg), and the quarter-finals twice (1964/65 and 1970/71), while Newport County reached the quarter-finals of the same competition in 1980/81.

72. The *Sun* (27 May 1999) noted of Manchester United's support at the 1999 European Cup Final in Barcelona that there were banners from '... Sri Lanka, Singapore, Malta, Holland, Norway, Sweden and Hawaii. There were groups from Glasgow, Leighton Buzzard, Hastings, Swansea, Northampton, Bury and Salford – not to mention the Hesketh Arms, Southport'.

73. Peter Kenyon, Manchester United's deputy-chief executive, described his club as 'the football *brand* on everyone's lips' (*Guardian*, 19 June 1999: 23: emphasis added by authors).

6 Mad Dogs: England, the Media and English Supporters during Euro '96 and France '98

74. Unless explicitly stated, all the newspaper extracts referred to in this Euro '96 section are from 1996.
75. See, for example, Cotton (1996).
76. O'Reilly (1999: 32–3) lists the towns affected by violence as: Bradford, Norwich, Brighton, Kidderminster, Reading, Milton Keynes, Luton, Bradford, Dunstable, Boreham Wood, Potters Bar, Cheshunt, Whetsone, Mansfield, Haywards Heath, Portsmouth, Bournemouth, Exeter, Basingstoke, Birmingham, and he explains his list is 'not exhaustive'.
77. 1148 people were arrested during Euro '96. Total attendance from all 31 games was 1 285 191. The most common offences were 'drink-related' (constituting 22.8 per cent of all arrests), and 'ticket touting' (15.1 per cent) (NCIS, 1996).
78. Tomlinson's (1999: 23) analysis of FIFA's executive and standing committee members shows that in the mid-1990s England contributed just two representatives.
79. For further discussion of racism and xenophobia in the British press, see Murray (1989) and Searle (1989).
80. The *Spectator*, 14 July 1990: 8.
81. Cited in the *Guardian*, 31 December 1993.
82. 'Gazza' refers to the England midfielder Paul Gascoigne.
83. 'Tel' was the press nickname for the England coach Terry Venables.
84. '16.39' refers to the exact time in the game when England's goalkeeper, David Seaman, saved a Scottish penalty.
85. This rivalry stems from three matches in particular: the 1966 World Cup Final (England 4, West Germany 2), the 1970 World Cup quarter-final (West Germany 3, England 2) and the 1990 World Cup semi-final (West Germany won 4–2 on penalties).
86. Unless explicitly stated, all the newspaper extracts referred to in this France '98 section are from 1998.
87. By France '98 the *Daily Mirror* had shortened its name to the *Mirror*.
88. This edition of the *Daily Mail* also included a free 1966 World Cup video for every reader offer.
89. See O'Reilly (1999).
90. Interestingly, as we mentioned above, other common themes included tabloid outrage at the players' alcohol consumption before the tournament began, and the branding of the team coach as a 'traitor' or 'disloyal' (Wagg, 1991, noted a similar phenomenon before Italia '90).
91. Only 35 out of the total of 286 England fans arrested during France '98 were classed by NCIS as category C supporters – considered as organised hooligans. A further 16 (5.6 per cent) were recorded as 'known category B' fans, classified as those liable to become involved in disturbances should they occur, and one (just 0.3 per cent) was category A, considered non-violent supporters. These totals suggest 234 of the 286 England fans arrested in France, some 81.8 per cent, were not known to the police (source: NCIS, 1998).
92. See, for example, Cohen (1981) or Ingram (1978) for discussions on the

media's role in amplifying disorder and 'demonising' certain social groups.

7 Conclusion: Racisms and the Cultures of Football

93. One recent attempt to rank the 300 most powerful individuals in Britain ranked players David Beckham and Michael Owen at 69 and 264 respectively, managers Sir Alex Ferguson and Kevin Keegan at 104 and 261, and Manchester United chairman Martin Edwards at 215 (the *Observer*, Life, 24 October 1999: 39–67.

94. *Hansard*, 19 April 1991, col. 732–3.

95. One league club visited by the authors lacked the facilities to hold more than one detained person at a time, placing a basic physical limit on the capacity of arresting fans breaching the law. The legal power of stewards to detain fans or to demand names and addresses is uncertain – if they are unable to identify offenders the ability of clubs to subsequently ban fans is significantly reduced.

96. Other black sports stars have also come to be regarded as popular symbols of patriotism. Prior to Bruno this role was fulfilled by the decathlete Daley Thompson, who draped himself in the Union Jack at the 1984 Olympic Games; later the sprinter Linford Christie was afforded similar respect. Cashmore (1982: 135) notes that Thomspon actively denied his identity as a black man preferring to self-categorise himself as white, on first meeting Cashmore he declared: 'I don't know what you want to talk to me for, I'm not black'.

Bibliography

Adams, D. (1998) 'On the Ball?', *Police Review*, vol. 106, no. 5477, pp. 16–17.

Adams, T. (1998) *Addicted*, London: HarperCollins.

Advisory Group Against Racism and Intimidation (AGARI) (1996) *Alive and Still Kicking: A Report by the Advisory Group Against Racism and Intimidation*, London: Commission for Racial Equality

Ahmed, K. (1997) 'The Gold Coast Showman: Tale of a Lost Star', *Guardian*, 26 November, p. 3.

Allirajah, D. (1997/98) 'Getting a Good Kicking', in *Offence: Express Yourself*, London: Libero! Football Supporters Network, pp. 8–9.

Anti-Fascist Action (1994) *Fighting Talk: Football Special*, London: Anti-Fascist Action

Anti-Racism and Intimidation Group (ARIG) (1996) *Action Plans for the 1995/96 Season Incorporating the 'Let's Kick Racism Out of Football' Campaign*: London Anti-Racism and Intimidation Group.

Arbena, J. (1988) *Sport and Society in Latin America*, Westport, CT: Greenwood Press.

Arc Theatre Ensemble (1996) *Review of 1995/96*, Barking: Arc Theatre Ensemble.

Armstrong, G. (1994) 'False Leeds: The Construction of Hooligan Confrontations', in R. Giulianotti and J. Williams (eds), *Games Without Frontiers: Football, Identity, Modernity*, Aldershot: Gower, pp. 299–326.

Armstrong, G. (1998) *Football Hooligans: Knowing the Score*, Oxford: Berg.

Armstrong, J., Blackman, O., Young, S., Daniels, B. and Disley, J. (1998) 'The Pig of Marseille', the *Mirror*, 16 June, pp. 4–5.

Askwith, R. (1998) 'He was a War Hero and a Football Star, the First Black Officer in the British Army and the First Player to Suffer Racist Abuse. Ever Heard of Him?', *Guardian*, 25 March, p. 6.

Back, L., Crabbe, T. and Solomos, J. (1998) 'Racism in Football: Patterns of Continuity and Change', in A. Brown (ed.), *Fanatics! Power, Identity and Fandom in Football*, London: Routledge, pp. 71–87.

Back, L. (1996) *New Ethnicities and Urban Culture*, London: UCL Press.

Back, L. (1998) 'Kicking Racism Into Touch', the *Streatham Mercury*, 19 February, p. 1.

Back, L. and Crabbe, T. (1997) 'Cultures of Racism in Football', paper presented at the *Challenging Racism in Football* conference conducted by the Scarman Centre for the Study of Public Order, University of Leicester, 4 September.

Bains, J. and Johal, S. (1998) *Corner Flags and Corner Shops: The Asian Football Experience*, London: Victor Gollancz.

Bains, J. with Patel, R. (1996) *Asians Can't Play Football*, Birmingham: Asian Social Development Agency.

Bairner, A. (1994) 'Football and the Idea of Scotland', in G. Jarvie and G. Walker (eds), *Scottish Sport in the Making of the Nation*, Leicester: Leicester University Press, pp. 9–26.

Ball, P. (1996) 'Osasuna the Better?', *When Saturday Comes*, no. 117, November, pp. 26–7.

Ball, W. and Solomos, J. (eds) (1990) *Race and Local Politics*, London: Macmillan – now Palgrave.

Banton, M. (1985) *Promoting Racial Harmony*, Cambridge, Cambridge University Press.

BBC2 (1999) *Home Ground – Pride and Prejudice: Sectarianism*, 27 July.

Beck, A. and Willis, A. (1995) *Crime and Security: Managing the Risk to Safe Shopping*, Leicester: Perpetuity Press.

Beck, P.J. (1999) *Scoring for Britain: International Football and International Politics 1900–1939*, London: Frank Cass.

Billig, M. (1978) *Fascists: A Social Psychological View of the National Front*, London: Harcourt Brace Jovanovich.

Billig, M. (1995) *Banal Nationalism* , London: Sage.

Birmingham Evening Mail (1990) 'Front's New Sinister Bid: Fresh Peril for British Soccer', 26 January, p. 1.

Bishop, S., Brown, A., Crabbe, T., Ennis, G., Galbraith, R. and Thomas, P. (1994) *United Colours of Football*, Liverpool: Football Supporters' Association.

Boon, G., Phillips, A. and Hann, M. (2000) '20 Richest Clubs in the World', *FourFourTwo*, January, pp. 67–74.

Boyle, R. (1994) '"We Are Celtic Supporters ...": Questions of Football and Identity in Modern Scotland', in R. Giulianotti and J. Williams (eds), *Games Without Frontiers: Football, Identity, Modernity*, Aldershot: Gower.

Bradley, J. (1998) '"We Shall Not be Moved"! Mere Sport, Mere Songs: A Tale of Scottish Football', in A. Brown (ed.), *Fanatics! Power, Identity and Fandom in Football*, London: Routledge, pp. 203–18.

Brailsford, D. (1991) *Sport, Time and Society – the British at Play*, London: Routledge.

Brain, L. (1993) 'Foxes Crack Down on Race Thugs', the *Leicester Mercury*, 4 August, p. 1.

Brick, C. (2000) 'Taking Offence: Modern Moralities and the Perception of the Football Fan', in J. Garland, D. Malcolm and M. Rowe (eds), *The Future of Football: Challenges for the 21st Century*, London: Frank Cass.

Brick, C. and Allirajah, D. (1997) 'Racism and the Football Fan: Perceptions of the Problem', in Partnerships to Keep Racism Out of Football Conference 4 November 1997, Reading: Public Impact Communications, p. 10.

Brimson, D. and Brimson, E. (1997) *England, My England: The Trouble with the National Football Team*, London: Headline.

Brimson, E. (1999) *Tear Gas and Ticket Touts: With the England Fans at the World Cup*, London: Headline.

Brown, A. (ed.) (1998) *Fanatics! Power, Identity and Fandom in Football*, London: Routledge.

Brown, M. (1997) 'Minority Issue', *When Saturday Comes*, no. 129, November, pp. 20–1.

Butler, B. (1991) *The Official History of the Football Association*, London: Queen Anne Press.

Carrington, B. (1998) '"Football's Coming Home", but Whose Home? And Do We Want It?: Nation, Football and the Politics of Exclusion', in A. Brown (ed.), *Fanatics! Power, Identity and Fandom in Football*, London: Routledge, pp. 101–23.

Carver, M., Garland, J. and Rowe, M. (1995) *Racism, Xenophobia and Football: A Preliminary Investigation*, Leicester: Scarman Centre.

Cashmore, E. (1982) *Black Sportsmen*, London: Routledge & Kegan Paul.

Cashmore, E. (1987) *The Logic of Racism*, London: Allen & Unwin.

Celtic Football Club (1996a) *Celtic's Social Charter: Information Pack*, Glasgow: Celtic Football Club.

Celtic Football Club (1996b) *Celtic's Social Charter*, Glasgow: Celtic Football Club.

Cesarini, D. (1996) 'The Changing Character of Citizenship and Nationality in Britain' in D. Cesarini and M. Fulbrook (eds), *Citizenship, Nationality and Migration in Europe*, London, Routledge, pp. 57–73.

Charlton Athletic Race Equality Partnership (CARE) (1996) *Tackling Racial Barriers to Watching Football*, Leatherhead: Parker Tanner.

Charlton Athletic Race Equality Partnership (CARE) (1998) *Annual Report 1997–98*, London: CARE.

Clarke, J. and Critcher, C. (1986) '1966 and All That: England's World Cup Victory', in A. Tomlinson and G. Whannel (eds), *Off the Ball: The Football World Cup*, London: Pluto, pp. 112–26.

Clayton, A. (1987) 'Sport and African Soldiers: The Military Diffusion of Western Sport throughout Sub-Saharan Africa', in W.J. Baker and J.A. Mangan (eds), *Sport in Africa – Essays in Social History*, New York: Africana Publishing Company, pp. 114–37.

Cohen, P. and Bains, H.S. (1988) *Multi-Racist Britain*, London: Macmillan Educational.

Cohen, R. (1994) *Frontiers of Identity: The British and the Others*, London: Longman.

Cohen, R. (1995) 'Fuzzy Frontiers of Identity: The British Case', *Social Identities*, vol. 1, no. 1, pp. 35–62.

Cohen, S. (1981) *Folk Devils and Moral Panics*, London: Paladin.

Cole, M. (1996a) '"Race" and Racism', in M. Payne (ed.), *The Dictionary of Cultural and Critical Theory*. Oxford: Basil Blackwell, pp. 449–53.

Cole, M. (1996b) '"Race", Racism and Nomenclature: A Conceptual Analysis', in U. Merkel and W. Tokarski (eds), *Racism and Xenophobia in European Football*, Aachen: Meyer & Meyer, pp. 11–22.

Cosgrove, S. (1986) 'And the Bonnie Scotland Will Be There: Football in Scottish Culture', in A. Tomlinson and G. Whannel (eds), *Off the Ball: The Football World Cup*, London: Pluto, pp. 99–111.

Cotton, P. (1996) 'Pre-emptive Strike', *Police Review*, 104 (5381), 9 August.

Crabbe, T. (1994) 'Gunning for Promotion', *When Saturday Comes*, no. 92, October, p. 17.

CRE Communications Team (1994) *Kick It!*, London: Commission for Racial Equality.

Critcher, C. (undated) *Football Since the War: A Study in Social Change and Popular Culture*, Birmingham: University of Birmingham Centre for Contemporary Cultural Studies Stencilled Occasional Paper series.

Crockett, T. (1996) 'Up for the Cup', *When Saturday Comes*, no. 113, July, pp. 10–11.

Cross, J. (2000) 'French in Race War', the *Mirror*, 18 March, p. 64.

Datar, R. (1996) 'Black and White TV', *Guardian*, 5 July, p. 11.

Davage, M. (1995) *Glorious Canaries Past and Present, 1902–1994*, Norwich: Norwich City Football Club.

Davies, P. (1990) *All Played Out: The Full Story of Italia '90*, London: Mandarin.

Davis, T. (1998) 'Same Old Stories?', *When Saturday Comes*, no. 138, August, pp. 18–19.

Dimeo, P. (1995) 'Ducking the Issue', *When Saturday Comes*, no. 106, December, pp. 23–24.

Dimeo, P. and Finn, G.P.T. (1998) 'Scottish Racism, Scottish Identities: The Case of Partick Thistle', in A. Brown (ed.), *Fanatics! Power, Identity and Fandom in Football*, London: Routledge, pp. 124–38.

Dispatches (1994) 'Terror on the Doorstep', 26 October, London: Channel Four Television.

Dispatches (1994) 'Accident Waiting to Happen', 19 October, London: Channel Four Television.

Donnelly, K. (1997) 'Army Surplus?', *When Saturday Comes*, no. 122, April, pp. 12–13.

Duke, V. and Crolley, L. (1996) *Football, Nationality and the State*, Harlow: Addison Wesley Longman.

Dunning, E. (1979) *Soccer: The Social Origins of the Sport and its Development as a Spectacle and Profession*, London: Sports Council and Social Science Research Council.

Dunning, E. and Sheard, K. (1979) *Barbarians, Gentlemen and Players – a Sociological Study of the Development of Rugby Football*, Oxford: Martin Robertson.

Dunning, E., Murphy, P., Newburn, T. and Waddington, I. (1987) 'Violent Disorder in Twentieth Century Britain', in G. Gaskell and R. Benewick (eds), *The Crowd in Contemporary Britain*, London: Sage, pp. 19–75.

Dunning, E., Murphy, P. and Williams, J. (1988) *The Roots of Football Hooliganism – an Historical and Sociological Study*, London: Routledge & Kegan Paul.

Eimer, D. (1994) 'The Hard Left', the *Guardian*, 25 November, p. 4.

Fanon, F. (1967) *The Wretched of the Earth*, Harmondsworth: Penguin.

Fielding, N. (1981) *The National Front*, London: Routledge & Kegan Paul.

Finn, G.P.T. and Giulianotti, R. (1998) 'Scottish Fans, Not English Hooligans! Scots, Scottishness and Scottish Football', in A. Brown (ed.), *Fanatics! Power, Identity and Fandom in Football*, London: Routledge, pp. 189–202.

Flemimg, S. and Tomlinson, A. (1996) 'Europe and the Old England', in U. Merkel and W. Tokarski (eds), *Racism and Xenophobia in European Football*, Aachen, Germany: Meyer & Meyer Verlag, pp. 79–100.

Flew, A. (1987) *Power to the Parents*, London: Sherwood.

Football Association (1997) *World Cup England 2006*, London: The Football Association.

Football League, Football Association, Premier League, Football Licensing Authority, and the Football Safety Officer's Association (1995) *Stewarding and Safety Management and Football Grounds*.

Football Task Force (1998) *Eliminating Racism from Football*, London: Football Task Force.

I.M. MARSH LIBRARY LIVERPOOL L17 6BD

TEL. 0151 231 5216/5299

Football Unites Racism Divides (1999) *Court Case Illustrates 'Epidemic' of Racism in Amateur Football*, 13 September, press release.

Foxes Against Racism (1993) *Filbo Fever!*, Leicester: Foxes Against Racism fanzine, no. 2.

Fryer, P. (1984) *Staying Power – the History of Black People in Britain*, London: Pluto.

Garland, J. and Rowe, M. (1995) 'Pitch Battles', *Police Review*, vol. 103, no. 5340, 20 October, pp. 22–4.

Garland, J. and Rowe, M. (1996) 'Challenging Racism and Xenophobia', in U. Merkel and W. Tokarski (eds), *Racism and Xenophobia in European Football*, Aachen: Meyer & Meyer Verlag, pp. 101–23.

Garland, J. and Rowe, M. (1996) *War Minus the Shooting? Jingoism, the English Press and Euro '96*, Leicester: Scarman Centre Research paper no. 7.

Garland, J. and Rowe, M. (1998a) 'Scottish Devolution', *Politics Review*, vol. 7 no. 3, p. 32.

Garland, J. and Rowe, M. (1998b) 'Welsh Devolution', *Politics Review*, vol. 7 no. 4, p. 32.

Garland, J. and Rowe, M. (1999) 'The "English Disease": Cured or in Remission? An Analysis of Police Responses to Football Hooliganism in the 1990s', *Crime Prevention and Community Safety: An International Journal*, vol. 1, no. 4, pp. 35–47.

Garland, J. and Rowe, M. (1999) 'Selling the Game Short: An Examination of the Role of Anti-racism in British Football', *Sociology of Sport Journal*, vol. 16, no. 1, pp. 35–53.

Garland, J. and Rowe, M. (1999) 'War Minus the Shooting: Jingoism, the English Press and Euro '96', *Journal of Sport and Social Issues*, vol. 23, no. 1. pp. 80–95.

Garland, J. Malcolm, D. and Rowe, M. (eds) (2000) *The Future of Football: Challenges in the Twenty-First Century*, London: Frank Cass.

George, B. and Button, M. (1996) 'The Case for Regulation', *The International Journal of Risk, Security and Crime Prevention*, vol. 1, no. 1, pp. 53–7.

Gilroy, P. (1987) *There Ain't No Black in the Union Jack: The Politics of Race and Nation*, London: Hutchison.

Gilroy, P. (1993) 'Frank Bruno or Salman Rushdie?', in *Small Acts: Thoughts on the Politics of Black Cultures*, London: Serpents Tail, pp. 86–94.

Gilroy, P. (1993) *Small Acts*, London: Serpents Tail.

Gilroy, P. (1999) 'The End of Anti-Racism' in M. Bulmer and J. Solomos (eds), *Racism*, Oxford: Oxford University Press, pp. 242–9.

Giulianotti, R. (1991) 'Scotland's Tartan Army in Italy: A Case for the Carnivalesque', *Sociological Review*, vol. 39 no. 3, pp. 503–27.

Giulianotti, R. (1997) 'Enlightening the North: Aberdeen Fanzines and Local Football Identity', in G. Armstrong and R. Giulianotti (eds), *Entering the Field: New Perspectives on World Football*, Oxford: Berg.

Glanville, B. (1999) 'Sir Alf, Shy Hero of Wonderful '66', *The Sunday Times*, 2 May, pp. 8–9.

Gordon, P. and Rosenberg, D. (1989) *Daily Racism: The Press and Black People in Britain*, London: The Runnymede Trust.

Guardian (1979) 'Orient Cry Foul Over Anti-Nazi Movement', *Guardian*, 13 February, p. 3.

Guardian (1979) *'Race Fears on Black v. White Soccer Match'*, 26 January, p. 23.

Hall, S. (1978) 'The Treatment of Football Hooliganism in the Press', in R. Ingham *et al.* (eds), *Football Hooliganism*, London: Inter-Action Imprint.

Hall, S. (1992) 'New Ethnicities', in J. Donald and A. Rattansi (eds), *'Race', Culture and Difference*, London: Sage, pp. 252–9.

Hall, S. *et al.* (1978) *Policing the Crisis: Mugging, the State and Law and Order*, London: Macmillan – now Palgrave.

Hamilton, A. (1982) *Black Pearls of Soccer*, London: Harrap.

Harding, J. (1991) *For the Good of the Game – the Official History of the Professional Footballers' Association*, London: Robson Books.

Harris, N. (1971) *The Charlton Brothers*, London: Stanley Paul.

Haynes, K. (ed.) (1999) *Come On Cymru! Football in Wales*, Wilmslow: Sigma Leisure.

Hewitt, D. (1992) 'Supporters Campaign Against Racism and Fascism', in *Tackling Back: Report of a Conference Organised by Sterling District Council*, Sterling: Sterling District Council.

Highfield Rangers (1993) *Highfield Rangers: An Oral History*, Leicester: Leicester City Council Living History Unit.

Hill, D. (1989) *Out of His Skin: The John Barnes Phenomenon*, London: Faber & Faber.

Hill, D. (1996) 'Patriot Games', *When Saturday Comes*, no. 112, June, pp. 14–17.

Hobsbawm, E. (1990) *Nations and Nationalism Since 1780: Programme, Myth, Reality*, Cambridge, Cambridge University Press.

Hobsbawm, E. and Ranger, T. (eds) (1983) *The Invention of Tradition*, Cambridge: Cambridge University Press.

Holland, B. (1993) 'Colour Field', *When Saturday Comes*, no. 72, February, pp. 16–17.

Holland, B. (1995) 'Kicking Racism Out of Football: An Assessment of Racial Harassment in and around Football Grounds', *New Community*, vol. 21, no. 4, October, pp. 567–86.

Holt, R. (1989) *Sport and the British: A Modern History*, Oxford: Oxford University Press.

Home Office (1998) 'UK Shares World Beating Expertise in Policing Football', Press Release 076/98, 27 February, London: Home Office.

Home Affairs Select Committee (1992) *Policing Football Hooliganism. Second Report*, London: Home Office.

Horne, J. (1996) 'Kicking Racism Out of Soccer in England and Scotland' *Journal of Sport and Social Issues*, no. 1, February, pp. 45–68.

Horton, E. (1997) *Moving the Goalposts: Football's Exploitation*, London: Mainstream Publishing.

Houlihan, B. (1997) 'Sport, National Identity and Public Policy', *Nations and Nationalism*, vol. 3, no. 1, pp. 113–37.

Hounslow Council (1997) *Anti-racist Initiative on Council Owned Football Pitches*, London: Hounslow Council.

Howard, S. (1999) 'Ninety Seconds of Pure Genius: Subs Sink Germans', *Sun*, 27 May, p. 59.

Human Rights Watch (1997) *Racist Violence in the United Kingdom*, Washington: Human Rights Watch.

Humphries, S. (1981) *Hooligans or Rebels? – an Oral History of Working-Class Childhood and Youth 1889–1939*, Oxford: Blackwell.

Ingram, R. (1978) *Football Hooliganism*, London: Inter-Action Inprint.

Jary, D., Horne, J. and Bucke, T. (1991) 'Football "Fanzines" and Football Culture: A Case of Successful "Cultural Contestation"', *Sociological Review*, vol. 39, no. 3, pp. 581–97.

Jenkins, B. and Sofos, S.A. (eds) (1996) *Nation and Identity in Contemporary Europe*, London: Routledge.

Jenkins, R. (1990) 'Salvation for the Fittest: A West African Sportsman in Britain', *International Journal of the History of Sport*, vol. 7, no. 1, pp. 23–60.

Johnstone, L. (1992) *The Rebirth of Private Policing*, London: Routledge.

Kempson, R. (1998) 'Clubs Face Wrath of Anti-Racism Campaign', *The Times*, 5 December, p. 34.

Kick It Out (1998) *Annual Report 1997–98*, London: Kick It Out.

Kick It Out (1998) *Kick It Out*, London: Kick It Out.

Kirk-Greene, A. (1987) 'Imperial Administration and the Athletic Imperative: The Case of the District Officer in Africa', in W.J. Baker and J.A. Mangan (eds), *Sport in Africa – Essays in Social History*, New York: Africana Publishing Company, pp. 81–113.

Kliman, L. (1997) 'Chants and Cant', the *Guardian*, 10 December, p. 7.

Korr, C.P. (1978) 'West Ham United Football Club and the Beginnings of Professional Football in East London, 1895–1914', *Journal of Contemporary History*, vol. 13, pp. 211–32.

Kuper, S. (1994) *Football Against the Enemy*, London: Orion.

Lacey, N. (1992) 'From Individual to Group', in B. Heppie and E. Szyszczak (eds), *Discrimination: The Limits of Law*, London: Mansell.

Lansdown, H. and Spillius, A. (eds) (1990) *Saturday's Boys: The Football Experience*, London: Collins Willow.

Law, I. (1996) *Racism, Ethnicity and Social Policy*, London: Prentice Hall.

Le Bon, G. (1895) *The Crowd: A Study of the Popular Mind*, London: T. Fisher Unwin.

Le Monde (1997) 'Comment la Coupe De Monde Joue La Securite', http://www.lemonde.fr/football.securite.model.htm, 19 September.

Leadbetter, R. (1996) 'Carry On Singing', *Evening Times*, 8 March, pp. 4–5.

Lee, J. (1998) 'Game for a Laugh at Wembley', *Observer*, 11 January, p. 7.

Leeds Trades Union Council and Leeds Anti-Fascist Action (1987) *Terror On Our Terraces: The National Front, Football Violence and Leeds United*, Leeds: Leeds Trades Union Council and Leeds Anti-Fascist Action.

Lewis, S. and Haynes, K. (1999) 'Flowers in the Dustbin', in K. Haynes (ed.), *Come On Cymru! Football in Wales*, Wilmslow: Sigma Leisure, pp. 131–38.

Lipton, M. (1999) 'Don't Kill Off the Breeding Ground', *Daily Mail*, 23 June, pp. 74–5.

Little, K. (1947) *Negroes in Britain*, London: Kegan Paul.

Lloyd, C. (1994) 'Universalism and Difference: The Crisis of Anti-Racism in Britain and France', in A. Rattansi and S. Westwood (eds), *Racism, Modernity and Identity*, Cambridge: Polity Press.

Lomax, B. (2000) 'Democracy and Fandom: Developing a Supporters' Trust at Northampton Town FC', in J. Garland, D. Malcolm and M. Rowe (eds), *The*

Future of Football: Challenges in the Twenty-First Century, London: Frank Cass, pp. 79–90.

London Programme (1998) 'Leagues Apart', 6 June, London: London Weekend Television.

Longmore, A. (1988) *Viv Anderson*, London: Heinemann Kingswood.

Lunn, K. (1996) 'Reconsidering "Britishness": The Construction and Significance of National Identity in Twentieth Century Britain', in B. Jenkins and S.A. Sofos (eds), *Nations and Identity in Contemporary Europe*, London: Routledge, pp. 83–100.

MacGregor, A. (1998) 'Tartan Barney', *When Saturday Comes*, no. 138, August, p. 21.

Macpherson, Sir W. (1999) *The Stephen Lawrence Inquiry: Report of an Inquiry by Sir William Macpherson of Cluny*, London: Home Office, CM 4262-1.

Malcolm, D. (1997) 'Stacking in Cricket: A Figurational Sociological Reappraisal of Centrality', *Sociology of Sport Journal*, vol. 14, pp. 263–82.

Malcolm, D., Jones, I. and Waddington, I. (2000) 'The People's Game? Football Spectatorship and Demographic Change', in J. Garland, D. Malcolm and M. Rowe (eds), *The Future of Football: Challenges for the Twenty-First Century*, London: Frank Cass.

Malik, K. (1996) *The Meaning of Race: Race, History and Culture in Western Society*, London: Macmillan – now Palgrave.

Mangan, J. A. (1996) 'Duty Unto Death: English Masculinity and Militarism in the Age of the New Imperialism', in J.A. Mangan (ed.), *Tribal Identities – Nationalism, Europe, Sport*, London: Frank Cass, pp. 10–38.

Mason T. (1986) 'Some Englishmen and Scotsman Abroad: The Spread of World Football', in A. Tomlinson and G. Whannel (eds), *Off the Ball – the Football World Cup*, London: Pluto Press, pp. 67–82.

Mason, T. (1980) *Association Football and English Society, 1863–1915*, Sussex: The Harvester Press.

Maynard, W, and Read, T. (1997) *Policing Racially Motivated Incidents*, Police Research Group, Crime Detection and Prevention Series Paper no. 84, London: Home Office.

McArdle, D. and Lewis, D. (1997) *'Kick Racism Out of Football': A Report on the Implementation of the Commission for Racial Equality's Strategies*, London: Centre for Research in Industrial and Criminal Law.

Middleton, N. (1993) *Football: Policing the Supporter*, London: HMSO.

Miles, R. (1984) 'Marxism versus the Sociology of Race Relations'?, *Ethnic and Racial Studies*, vol. 7, no. 2, pp. 217–37.

Miles, R. (1989) *Racism*, London: Routledge.

Miles, R. (1993) *Racism After 'Race Relations'*, London: Routledge.

Miles, R. (1994) 'Explaining Racism in Contemporary Europe', in A. Rattansi and S. Westwood (eds), *Racism, Modernity and Identity*, Cambridge: Polity Press.

Miller, D. (1970) 'Alan Ball', in R. Hayter (ed.), *Soccer Stars of Today*, London: Pelham.

Moorhouse, H. (1991) 'On the Periphery: Scotland, Scottish Football and the New Europe', in J. Williams and S. Wagg (eds), *British Football and Social Change: Getting into Europe*, Leicester: Leicester University Press.

Moorhouse, H. (1994) 'From Zines Like These? Fanzines, Tradition and Identity in Scottish Football', in G. Jarvie and G. Walker (eds), *Scottish Sport in the Making of the Nation*, Leicester: Leicester University Press, pp. 172–94.

Moorhouse, H.F. (1996) 'One State, Several Countries: Soccer and Nationality in a "United" Kingdom', in J.A. Mangan (ed.), *Tribal Identities – Nationalism, Europe, Sport*, London: Frank Cass.

Moran, R. (2000) 'Racism in Football: A Victim's Perspective', in J. Garland, D. Malcolm and M. Rowe (eds), *The Future of Football: Challenges in the Twenty-First Century*, London: Frank Cass, pp. 190–200.

Morgan, R. and Newburn, T. (1997) *The Future of Policing*, Oxford: Clarendon Press.

'MP's call to ban comic' (1997) *Wolverhampton Express and Star*, 22 January, p. 5.

Murray, C. (1996) 'The Case Against Regulation', *The International Journal of Risk, Security and Crime Prevention*, vol. 1, no. 1, pp. 56–62.

Murphy, P., Dunning, E. and Williams, J. (1990) *Football On Trial*, London: Routledge.

Murray, B. (1988) *Glasgow Giants: A Hundred Years of the Old Firm*, Edinburgh: Mainstream.

Murray, B. (1998) *The Old Firm in the New Age: Celtic and Rangers Since the Souness Revolution*, Edinburgh: Mainstream.

Murray, N. (1989) 'Anti-racists and Other Demons', in Institute of Race Relations (ed.), *Racism and the Press in Thatcher's Britain*, London: IRR, pp. 1–19.

Murray, N. (1989) *Racism and the Press in Thatcher's Britain*, London: Institute for Race Relations.

National Criminal Intelligence Service (NCIS) (1996) *N.C.C. Euro '96, Total Arrest by Offence*, private correspondence.

National Criminal Intelligence Service (NCIS) (1998) *Football Intelligence Unit Arrest Sheet World Cup '98*, NCIS, private correspondence.

National Heritage Committee (1996) *Press Coverage of the Euro '96 Football Competition*, London: HMSO.

North, S. and Hodson, P. (1997) *Build a Bonfire: How Football Fans United to Save Brighton and Hove Albion*, Edinburgh: Mainstream.

Nottage, J. (1993) *Paul Gascoigne: The Inside Story*, London: HarperCollins.

O'Reilly, S. (1999) 'World Cup 2006? An Examination of the Policing of Risk in the Context of Major Sporting Events', *Risk Management: An International Journal*, vol. 1, no. 2, pp. 21–33.

Oliver, G. (1999) 'Song Sung Blue', *When Saturday Comes*, no. 149, July, p. 11.

Orakwue, S. (1998) *Pitch Invaders: The Modern Black Football Revolution*, London: Victor Gollancz.

Ouseley, H. (1998) 'Only a Game?', *Citizen*, summer, London: Charter 88, pp. 4–5.

Parkes, I. (1999) 'Taylor Fears for the English Game', *Sporting Life* website http://www.sporting-life.com/soccer/news/, 4 July.

Patel, Y. (1998) 'CARE-ing about Racism and Discrimination', *Streatham Mercury*, 19 February, p. 34.

Pearson, D. (1995) 'Racism', *Gwladys Sings the Blues*, issue 4, pp. 16–17.

Pearson, G. (1984) *Hooligan: A History of Respectable Fears*, Basingstoke: Macmillan – now Palgrave.

Pearson, H. (1996) 'You've Got Your Troubles', *When Saturday Comes*, no. 118, December, pp. 22–3.

Perkin, H. (1989) 'Teaching the Nations How to Play: Sport and Society in the British Empire and Commonwealth', *International Journal of the History of Sport*, vol. 6, no. 2, pp. 145–55.

Perryman, M. (1998) 'Same Old Stories', *When Saturday Comes*, no. 138, August, pp. 18–19.

Peterson, J. (1997) 'Britain, Europe and the World', in P. Dunleavy, A. Gamble, I. Holliday and G. Peele (eds), *Developments in British Politics*, vol. 5, Basingstoke: Macmillan – now Palgrave.

Pinto, T., Drew, D. and Minhas, N. (1997) *Sheffield Divided or United? A Study of 'Race' and Football*, Sheffield: Sheffield Hallam University.

Police Foundation and Policy Studies Institute (1996) *The Role and Responsibilities of the Police – the Report of an Independent Inquiry*, London: Police Foundation and Policy Studies Institute. Popplewell, Mr Justice (1986) *Final Report – Committee of Inquiry in Crowd Safety and Control at Sports Grounds*, London: HMSO.

Pryke, C. (1998) 'Racist Leeds Fans "Should Be Banned"', *Leicester Mercury*, 9 February, p. 3.

Ramdin, R. (1987) *The Making of the Black Working Class in Britain*, Aldershot: Gower.

Rattansi, A. (1992) 'Changing the Subject? Racism, Culture and Education', in J. Donald and A. Rattansi (eds), *'Race', Culture and Difference*, London: Sage/Open University.

Rattansi, A. (1994) 'Western Racisms, Ethnicities and Identities in a "Postmodern" Frame', in A. Rattansi and S. Westwood (eds), *Racism, Modernity and Identity*, Cambridge: Polity Press.

Reading Council for Racial Equality (1998) *Partnerships to Keep Racism Out of Football: Conference Proceedings*, Reading: Public Impact Communications.

Redhead, S. (1991) 'An Era of the End, or the End of an Era: Football and Youth Culture in Britain', in J. Williams and S. Wagg (eds), *British Football and Social Change: Getting into Europe*, Leicester: Leicester University Press, pp. 145–59.

Redhead, S. (1997) *Post Fandom and the Millennial Blues: The Transformation of Soccer Culture*, London: Routledge, p. 30.

Reicher, S. (1987) 'Crowd Behaviour as Social Action', in J.C. Turner, M.A. Hogg, J. Oakes, S. Reicher and M.S. Wetherall (eds), *Rediscovering the Social Group – a Self-Categorization Theory*, Oxford: Blackwell.

Reid, T. (1999) 'English Cricket Fans Have Team to Support', *The Times*, 5 June, p. 7.

Reng, R. (1999) 'Abroad Sweep', *When Saturday Comes*, no. 149, July, pp. 22–3.

Rex, J. (1970) *Race Relations in Sociological Theory*, London: Weidenfeld & Nicolson.

Rex, J. (1986) *Race and Ethnicity* , Milton Keynes: Open University Press.

Rex, J. (1995) 'Ethnic Identities and the Nation State: The Political Sociology of Multicultural Societies', *Social Identities*, vol. 1, no. 1, pp. 21–34.

Rich, P. (1990) *Race and Empire in British Politics*, Cambridge: Cambridge University Press.

Rivlin, M. (1995) 'Albert Memorial', *When Saturday Comes*, no. 105, November, pp. 10–11.

Root, J. and Austin, H. (1980) 'Novelty Apart', *Root*, March, pp. 24, 31, 79.

Rowe, M. (1998) *The Racialisation of Disorder in Twentieth Century Britain*, Aldershot: Ashgate.

Saggar, S. (1992) *Race and Public Policy*, Aldershot: Avebury.

Searchlight (1985) 'Oxford Nazis Told "Never Again"', London: Searchlight Publications, April, p. 8.

Searchlight (1987a) 'Chelsea NF Thugs Plot European Violence', London: Searchlight Publications, September, p. 13.

Searchlight (1987b) 'Soccer Terror Network Exposed', London: Searchlight Publications, December, p. 9.

Searchlight (1995) 'At War With Society – the Exclusive Story of a Searchlight Mole Inside Britain's Far Right', London: Searchlight Magazine Limited.

Searle, C. (1989) *Your Daily Dose: Racism and the Sun*, London: Campaign for Press and Broadcasting Freedom.

Show Racism the Red Card (1998) *Annual Report 1997–98*, Newcastle: Show Racism the Red Card.

Shrimsley, R. (1999) 'Devolution has Created "Timebomb", says Hague', in the *Electronic Telegraph*, issue 1512, 16 July.

Sir Norman Chester Centre for Football Research (1997) *Factsheet 6: Racism and Football*, http://www.le.ac.uk/snccfr/research/fsheets/fofs6.html.

Sir Norman Chester Centre for Football Research (1998) *FA Premier League National Fan Survey 1996/97: Summary*, Leicester: Sir Norman Chester Centre for Football Research.

Sir Norman Chester Centre for Football Research (2000) *FA Premier League Fan Survey 1998–99*, Leicester: Sir Norman Chester Centre for Football Research.

Sir Norman Chester Centre for Football Research (undated) *Black Footballers in Britain*, Football Unites Racism Divides, http://www.furd.org/archive/nccfr/fofs4.html.

Small, S. (1994) *Racialised Barriers: The Black Experience in the United States and England in the 1980s*, London: Routledge.

Solomos, J. (1988) *Black Youth, Racism and the State: The Politics of Ideology and Policy*, Cambridge: Cambridge University Press.

Solomos, J. (1993), *Race and Racism in Britain*, 2nd edn, London: Macmillan – now Palgrave.

Solomos, J. and Back, L. (1996) *Racism and Society*, London: Macmillan – now Palgrave.

South, N. (1988) *Policing for Profit*, London: Sage.

Sugden, J. and Tomlinson, A. (1998) *FIFA and the Contest for World Football: Who Rules the Peoples' Game?*, Cambridge: Polity Press.

Taylor, R. (1992) *Football and its Fans: Supporters and Their Relations with the Game, 1885–1985*, Leicester: Leicester University Press.

Taylor, R. (1997) 'A Death Foretold?', *When Saturday Comes*, no. 125, July, pp. 38–9.

The *Observer* (1998a) 'War of the Nazis', 25 January, The Review, pp. 3–4.

The *Observer* (1998b) 'Police Kept Neo-Nazi on Payroll', 5 April, p. 5.

Thomas, P. (1993) 'Leeds by Example', *When Saturday Comes*, no. 72, February, pp. 18–19.

Thomas, P. (1995) 'Kicking Racism Out of Football', *Race and Class*, vol. 36, no. 4, April–June, pp. 95–100.

Thynne, J. (1997) 'Red, White and Black', *News Shopper*, 25 June.

Tomlinson, A. (1986) 'Going Global: The FIFA Story', in A. Tomlinson and G. Whannel (eds), *Off the Ball: The Football World Cup*, London: Pluto, pp. 83–98.

Tomlinson, A. (1999) 'Out of Their League', *When Saturday Comes*, no. 144, February, pp. 22–3.

Varley, N. (1997) 'Task Force Aims to Build on Charlton's Good Example' in the *Guardian*, 31 September.

Vasili, P. (1993) 'Colonialism and Football: The First Nigerian Tour to Britain', *Race and Class*, vol. 36, no. 4, pp. 55–70.

Vasili, P. (1996) 'Walter Daniel Tull, 1888–1918: Soldier, Footballer, Black', *Race and Class*, vol. 38, no. 2, pp. 51–69.

Vasili, P. (1998) *The First Black Footballer: Arthur Wharton, 1865–1930 – An Absence of Memory*, London: Frank Cass.

Verma, G.K. and Darby, D.S. (1994) *Winners and Losers: Ethnic Minorities in Sport and Recreation*, London: Falmer Press.

Wagg, S. (1984) *The Football World – a Contemporary Social History*, Brighton: The Harvester Press.

Wagg, S. (1991) 'Playing the Past: The Media and the England Football Team', in J. Williams and S. Wagg (eds), *British Football and Social Change: Getting into Europe*, Leicester: Leicester University Press, pp. 220–38.

Wagg, S. (1995) 'The Missionary Position: Football in the Societies of Britain and Ireland', in S. Wagg (ed.), *Giving the Game Away: Football, Politics and Culture on Five Continents*, Leicester: Leicester University Press.

Wagg, S. (1998) 'Technically Speaking', *When Saturday Comes*, no. 142, December, pp. 34–5.

Walsh, N. (1977) *Dixie Dean – the Life Story of a Goal Scoring Legend*, London: Macdonald & Jane's.

Walvin, J. (1986) *Football and the Decline of Britain*, Basingstoke: Macmillan – now Palgrave.

Ward, C. (1989) *Steaming In: Journal of a Football Fan*, London: Simon & Schuster.

Watson, N. (1997) *Football in the Community: Who Needs It?*, paper presented to the Challenging Racism in Football conference, Leicester, 4 September.

Whelan, T. (1998) 'Introduction', in P. Vasili *The First Black Footballer: Arthur Wharton, 1865–1930 – An Absence of Memory*, London: Frank Cass, pp. xxiii–xxviii.

When Saturday Comes (1993) 'Inside Right', *When Saturday Comes*, no. 81, November, p. 12.

White, J. (1997) 'The £12m Lad Done Good', *Guardian*, 'The Week', 4 October, p. 3.

Williams J. and Perkins S. (1997) *Leaving the Trackside: A National Survey of Disabled Football Spectators*, Leicester: Leicester University, Sir Norman Chester Centre for Football Research.

Williams, J. (1992) *Lick My Boots: Racism and British Football*, Leicester: Sir Norman Chester Centre for Football Research

Williams, J. and Woodhouse, J. (1991) 'Can Play, Will Play? Women and Football in Britain', in J. Williams and S. Wagg (eds), *British Football and Social Change: Getting into Europe*, Leicester: Leicester University Press, pp. 85–108.

Williams, J., Dunning, E. and Murphy, P. (1989) *Hooligans Abroad: The Behaviour and Control of English Fans in Continental Europe*, 2nd edn, London: Routledge.

Wrench, J. and Solomos, J. (1993) *Racism and Migration in Western Europe*, Oxford: Berg.

Wright, I. (1996) *Mr Wright: The Explosive Autobiography of Ian Wright*, London: HarperCollins.

Index

I.M. MARSH LIBRARY LIVERPOOL L17 6BD
TEL. 0151 231 5216/5299

LIVERPOOL
JOHN MOORES UNIVERSITY

I.M. MARSH LRC
Tel: 0151 231 5216